(Continued)

Diversity and Developmentally Appropriate Practices

······

Challenges for Early Childhood Education

Editors

Bruce L. Mallory and Rebecca S. New

TEACHERS
COLLEGE
PRESS

Teachers College, Columbia University
New York and London

Published by Teachers College Press, 1234 Amsterdam Avenue, New York, N.Y. 10027

Library of Congress Cataloging-in-Publication Data
Diversity and developmentally appropriate practices : challenges for
  early childhood education / editors, Bruce L. Mallory and Rebecca S.
  New.
        p. cm. — (Early childhood education series)
    Papers based on the NAEYC 1991 annual conference, held in Denver.
    Includes bibliographical references and index.
    ISBN 0-8077-3300-8 (alk. paper). — ISBN 0-8077-3299-0 (pbk. :
  alk. paper)
      1. Early childhood education—United States. 2. Minorities—
  Education (Early childhood)—United States. 3. Handicapped
  children—Education (Early childhood)—United States. 4. Child
  development—United States. I. Mallory, Bruce L. II. New, Rebecca
  Staples. III. Series.
  LB1139.25.D58 1994
  372.21—dc20   93-11912

ISBN 0-8077-3300-8
ISBN 0-8077-3299-0 (pbk.)

Printed on acid-free paper
Manufactured in the United States of America

99 98 97 96 95 94   8 7 6 5 4 3 2 1

Contents

• • • • • •

Introduction

The Ethic of Inclusion

● ● ● ● ● ●

REBECCA S. NEW AND BRUCE L. MALLORY

It is hard to think of any word in the English language that is more socially constructed and context bound than the term "appropriate." The word invites diverse interpretations as to what behaviors and attitudes may be sanctioned in a particular setting with a particular group of people. When applied to subjective constructs of behavior, or political processes of resource distribution, or ideological beliefs about social relations, the term's ambiguities become unavoidable. Thus, when the field of early childhood education reaches a point of apparent consensus, allowing its leading professional organization to publish a detailed description of what is judged to be "developmentally appropriate practice," it is not surprising that the consensus turns out to be ephemeral.

In 1987, following a lengthy and thoughtful process that involved the solicitation of input and feedback from literally thousands of early childhood practitioners, the National Association for the Education of Young Children (NAEYC) published guidelines reflecting the profession's "consensus definition of developmentally appropriate practice" (DAP) in programs serving children from birth through age 8 (Bredekamp, 1987). The NAEYC effort was motivated primarily by the need to respond to the increasingly pervasive pressure for early childhood programs to conform to an academic model of instruction typical of programs designed for older children. Throughout the document, there is also evidence of the intent to advocate for the field's long-standing core values of respect for and nurturing of young children as among the necessary means to achieve the democratic goals of a just and compassionate society.

In spite of the good intentions of these aims, the document has come under increasing scrutiny. In fact, one of its features that has contributed to its popularity may also have invited controversy. The published guidelines state—in behaviorally specific terms—a thesis about what constitutes appropriate early childhood practices as well as an antithetical listing of practices deemed inappropriate. By framing the choice for teachers as a dichotomous variable rather than a continuous one (Johnson & Johnson, 1992), it was, perhaps, inevitable that the dialectic would not remain stable for long.

Our purposes are neither to quibble with the original intent of the NAEYC guidelines nor to detract from what they have thus far accomplished. In a field that is still coming of age, the guidelines' very existence has served to convey a much needed sense of solidarity in the early childhood profession. At a time when both policymakers and the public are finally acknowledging the status of children's early development as an indicator of our society's well being, the guidelines for determining what is and what is not "developmentally appropriate practice" have met a critical need. That many refer to the widely distributed document as "the Bible" is an indication of how strongly they feel the need for such a directive, and the degree to which many believe in the truth and power of its contents.

Rather, our primary aim in this volume is to provide a forum for the presentation of new challenges to both the conception and the determinants of appropriate practices in early childhood education. The rationale for this exchange of ideas, as articulated in the chapters to follow, is based on the belief that the current conceptualization is overly narrow in its general interpretation of the role of the teacher, and specifically with respect to acknowledging variations associated with cultural and developmental diversity.

CONTEXTS OF THE CRITIQUE

The idea for this volume was conceived in 1991 at NAEYC's annual conference in Denver, in response to the intensity and substance of debate that followed a symposium critiquing the theoretical framework and the didactic tone of the guidelines (Mallory, 1991; New, 1991). The discussion has continued and joins other critical perspectives concerned with the appropriateness (dare we use the term?) of the form, function, and content of NAEYC's guidelines. Some engaged in this stimulating discourse have challenged the overly heavy reliance on Piagetian theory (O'Loughlin, 1991), while others question the value of using individual development as a guiding post for early education (Bloch, 1991; Fernie & Kantor, 1992). Still others have called for an entire reconceptualization of the field (Kessler & Swadener, 1992; Swadener & Kessler, 1991).

The interest that has been generated at the national level by the thoughtful and dynamic exchanges taking place in publications (e.g., Bredekamp, 1991; Kessler, 1991), formal symposia (at national as well as regional conferences), and informal discussions was surely a motivating factor behind the decision to compile this volume. A more proximal source of motivation for taking on this task has been our own experiences as teacher educators in an early childhood and early childhood special education graduate program at the University of New Hampshire. In this role, we have witnessed the susceptibility of both beginning and veteran teachers to packaged curricula and prescribed pedagogical approaches. We have also participated in their struggles to reconcile the complexities of working with children of varying needs, interests, and abilities in light of the nomothetic assumptions underlying traditional early educational practices. Their experiences as teachers have not only called into question the assumptions of prevailing paradigms, but have served as powerful reminders of the problems inherent in helping practitioners to acquire and inquire simultaneously. Even as we have distributed copies of the NAEYC guidelines on developmentally appropriate practice, we have cautioned teachers against remaining dependent on others' prescriptions to inform their practice, particularly when their circumstances might allow them to co-construct new models of pedagogy to accommodate the challenges presented by the diversity of children in their classrooms.

The stance to be taken in this volume is one of questioning both the process and the goals associated with the articulation of such guidelines. Indeed, as noted in chapter 4, "The issue is not whether practice should be developmentally appropriate: Clearly it should." The concerns addressed by our contributors are centered around the questions of *who* should make such a determination, and on the basis of *what* knowledge, values, and goals. Our intent, then, is to expand the definition of developmentally appropriate *practices* to include alternative theoretical and practical perspectives necessary for addressing the needs of young children with cultural and developmental differences; and to present new views on the role of teachers and other adults in determining more inclusive early educational goals and practices.

DIVERSITY AS A SHARED ATTRIBUTE

As others have noted, there are a number of conceptual and methodological points of debate in the NAEYC guidelines. We have chosen to focus on the exclusion of children representing cultural and developmental differences for a number of reasons, not the least of which is that their particular circumstances and needs have not been focused on sufficiently. There is little question that the guidelines were intended to refer to all children—and indeed, subsequent related NAEYC publications have devoted complete sections to the discussion of issues related to aspects of diversity (e.g., Bredekamp & Rosegrant, 1992). Yet the lauda-tory aim to be all encompassing fails to acknowledge the extent to which these recommendations draw upon a particular set of social, theoretical, and pedagogical norms rooted in more exclusive than inclusive paradigms. That initially some children were inadequately represented is consistent with other, albeit more significant, forms of exclusion that have resulted from our society's history of discriminatory practices aimed at children belonging to ethnic and racial minorities as well as those with intellectual, physical, or behavioral impairments. The pervasiveness of this history of exclusion mandates more than even the most thoughtful "mentioning" of these concerns (see Lubeck, chapter 1 of this volume).

A History of Exclusive Practices

There is a well-documented historic precedent for both the physical and psychological exclusion of children of ethnic and racial minority groups from early childhood settings. In spite of several decades of judicial man-dates for the integration of public school settings, the concentration of ethnic and racial groups in self-contained neighborhoods has continued to result in de facto segregated early childhood programs in those com-munities. This segregation has been exacerbated by the presence of means-tested social programs that have the effect of grouping children of low socioeconomic status, who often also belong to similar ethnic or racial groups (e.g., Head Start and "Title XX" daycare programs). Their more affluent peers, who tend to be Caucasian, are more often enrolled in private preschools and kindergartens. This phenomenon of perhaps well-intended segregation may also represent the first stages of educa-tional tracking, which has its own set of disjunctive aims and outcomes (Oakes, 1985).

Similarly, there is a long history of the physical exclusion of young children with disabilities from early childhood settings. While such exclu-sion is no longer legal in publicly funded programs, it remains a problem in private centers, which continue to serve a large portion of the preschool population. Reasons given for this continued pattern of exclu-sion are many, including the physical inaccessibility of some program facilities; the lack of teacher preparation deemed necessary to meet the complex needs of children with disabilities; the resistance against inte-grated programs by parents who fear that the education of their own nor-mally developing children would be compromised; the lack of financial resources for equipment, renovations, and special therapies; and the availability of self-contained programs in some communities. Continued patterns of exclusion are also apparent in programs associated with earlier models of mainstreaming in which children who are "different" remain socially and psychologically separate from their peers even when placed in common schools or classrooms. The intractability of these patterns reflects the limitations of both the concepts and the resultant policies associated with mainstreaming. These limitations are apparent when practices focus primarily on children's physical proximity (how close are they to one another?), temporal measures (how often are they together?), and structural matters (where are they, and with whom?); and little or no attention is given to the possibility that these children's needs, abilities, and ways of living might be included from the *outset* in the determination of program goals and practices.

Thus, while we have made great strides in designing policies and programs that create more integrated settings, "separate but equal" services for children of diverse cultures as well as for those with disabilities have been maintained in many communities. The implementation of several decades' worth of policies and programs has not been sufficient to overcome traditional practices and basic social attitudes regarding the *inclusion* of culturally and developmentally diverse children. It would seem to be the case that any guidelines purporting to describe developmentally appropriate practices for all children would therefore need to make explicit attempts to reverse this long-established national trend.

The ethical and legal imperatives to provide for the full consideration of *all children*—regardless of acquired or attributed characteristics—in the planning and implementation of early educational experiences are sufficient to warrant the consideration of these two broadly construed populations in a single volume. Indeed, a conscientious effort, which is reflected in the early childhood literature, has been made to address the concerns of practitioners regarding these dimensions of diversity in the classroom (e.g., Derman-Sparks & the A.B.C. Task Force, 1989). There is a second and equally fundamental reason for the dual interpretations of diversity in this volume. Forms of exclusion are also found in the theoretical and empirical models that have affected the design of social policies and early education programs. In effect, exclusionary practices have conspired with exclusionary thinking.

The Dominant Discourse

The field of child development remains heavily influenced by the intellectual and social traditions of Western industrialized societies, which include, among other things, individualistic and meritocratic emphases with Eurocentric interpretations of optimal development. Thus, children with disabilities as well as those from culturally diverse populations have tradionally been left out of Western models of development as well as the accompanying research. As a result, early childhood programs are characterized by assessment practices, curriculum models, educational goals, and norms for child and adult roles that reflect those traditions and their accompanying theoretical paradigms. Indeed, the persistence of these traditions is rooted in the myth that schooling in our society— beginning at the earliest stages—is for the purpose of creating a more blended and homogeneous culture, which serves the purpose of maintaining a stable, cohesive citizenry and workforce. Such a goal is in ironic juxtaposition to that of a democratic society which has historically measured its worth in terms of its respect for diversity.

Yet this second rationale for focusing on children with cultural and developmental differences—that they have been omitted from our research models and theoretical paradigms—is based on more than the desire to set the record straight. Our admittedly more ambitious aim is to stimulate new thinking about child development theory and research in general; and theory, research, *and practice* in the particular areas of early childhood education and early childhood special education. The lives of young children who represent diverse cultural or developmental experiences can serve as stark mirrors to hold up against our extant theoretical frameworks. When a child is unable to speak or to speak the predominant language, unable to move because of motor impairment or because she is swaddled until age two, unable to play with friends because of an uncontrollable temper or because his skin is darker than that of his peers, we are challenged to reconsider the presumed causes and consequences of these differences before we can even begin to consider appropriate responses. The simultaneous consideration of children with developmental and cultural differences may serve as a provocative guide in the critical examination of prevailing paradigms of child development and early education.

The benefits of looking beyond so-called normative examples of development have been articulated before, especially by those engaged in cross-cultural studies of human development. At the least, a more inclusive approach to the study of development, as manifest in comparative research, challenges unitary depictions of developmental processes. For example, it is now well known, though less well acknowledged, that environmental influences on motor development are expressed differently in diverse contexts, whether those contexts are culturally or individually determined. The incorporation of such variations in a theory of development would serve to expand our understandings of the range of typical behavior. It has also been established that what is considered deviant in one context may be viewed as normal in another. More thoughtful consideration of such dimensions of human behavior in our approach to research and theory building would present much needed opportunities for better understanding the role of the environment, and for "unpackaging" independent variables (Whiting, 1976) such as gender, chronological age, type of disability, or social class.

Even as child development theorists call for more inclusive models that address matters of diversity, most continue to neglect differences associated with disability. A recent discussion on diversity in a child development publication defined the construct as representing

> a host of differences among people, including differences in their sex and gender, ethnicity, cultural, subcultural experiences, socioeconomic status and associated living conditions, and in the composition and structure of families. (Eisenberg, 1992, p. 10)

In this discussion, the closest thing to an acknowledgement of differences in developmental sequelae as a function of disability was in the added comment, "Broadly speaking, it [diversity] also includes differences among people in their special circumstances—for example, in regard to exposure to various stressors" (p. 10). To fail to include direct mention of developmental differences (such as those associated with cerebral palsy, Down syndrome, or autism) as forms of diversity, even when "broadly speaking," is likely more than an oversight. Such an omission is symptomatic of the more critical failure to incorporate the study of individuals with variant developmental processes and outcomes into our understanding of human development. This omission is no less serious than the failure to acknowledge the interplay between a child's sociocultural context and her developmental processes and outcomes.

To summarize thus far, our reasons for examining both cultural and developmental differences reflect our overarching aims of inclusion— such that *all* children, including those who may be seen as different, will be included a priori in the articulation and implementation of developmentally appropriate early childhood practices. As well, the theories and pedagogical models which inform such practices will be based on a view of human development that incorporates aspects of diversity into its definitions of what is normal and desirable.

THE WHOLE CHILD—A NEW FRAME ON AN OLD IDEA

In most American early education programs, curricular and pedagogical decisions are responsive to concerns regarding *what a child should be able to do*. That is, there is a normative perspective, informed by child development theory and supported by teacher and parental ideologies, that focuses on the attainment of numerous and specific milestones or benchmarks by individual children. Thus, infants are expected to begin crawling sometime during the second half of the 1st year of life, 3-year-olds should be able to demonstrate at least a rudimentary grasp of the expressive components of a language, and 5-year-olds will surely know how to hold a pencil. The accomplishment of those criteria signifies normal development, while failure to reach the predetermined criteria signifies "at risk" status or pathology, either in the child or in the environment. By adopting such *culturally specific* indicators of normal development, the lenses through which we view children's behavior and development highlight deficiencies rather than competencies. Such a narrow view also hinders our ability to consider alternative pathways to development.

By contrast, a view of the child that embraces an attitude of inquiry rather than prescription encourages a broader, less linear view of development and, by implication, results in more inclusive strategies of care and education. Such a view characterizes the approach taken by early childhood educators in the community of Reggio Emilia, Italy (New, 1990). Within this community setting—whose public infant and preprimary programs have received world-wide acclaim—the child is understood as having not only needs but competencies and rights as well (Edwards, Forman, & Gandini, 1993). Implicit in this view is the recognition of the child's embeddedness in a family, a community, a culture, and a society. It is thus the responsibility of the teachers, in active collaboration with parents and other members of the community, to acknowledge and respect those rights, to identify and understand those competencies, and respond collectively to those needs. In order to fulfill this role, teachers in Reggio Emilia become researchers in their own classrooms, regularly making and sharing observations and interpretations that lead to new hypotheses about learning and development rather than reifying existing conceptions (see chapters 3 and 6, this volume, for further elaboration of this role of the teacher). This perspective supports a more continuous and optimistic view of development in which each child is seen to contain multiple potentials, and to be capable of expressing those potentials through their "hundred languages" (Malaguzzi, 1993).

By beginning with the question *Who is this child, and what can she do?* teachers are more likely to be able to accommodate diverse expressions of development, whether resulting from individual differences or environmental factors associated with cultural diversity, than if they take the normative perspective that characterizes most American models. Indeed, the challenge of truly understanding young children necessitates the ongoing examination of both these sources of variation because they mutually influence one another. In considering the individual child, teachers can learn a great deal about the child's abilities, pleasures, and frustrations—all of which are functions of his or her particular experiences and ontogenetic processes. Teachers' lenses are microscopic here, enabling a close examination of what Bruner (1976) has called the "interior culture" of the child—those subtle differences and nuances that each child brings to the classroom. Shifting and widening the focus to the sociocultural context, teachers are then in a position to gather information about the family, the community, and other features of the environment that support and interpret that child's development. Combined, teachers begin to understand the meaningfulness and complexity implied by the term *the whole child*.

This attitude of inquiry on the teacher's part into both the individual and shared sources of diversity among children represents a dramatic departure from the traditional interpretation of the teacher as mere dispenser of knowledge. The potential impact of this view of children may be to lead to more inclusive theories of child development and practices in early education. A change of this scope in our theoretical orientation would support major revisions in current interpretations of the aims and processes of education, such that they would be responsive to the "special needs" and abilities of *all* children, not just those currently identified as culturally or developmentally diverse.

ORGANIZATION OF THE BOOK

The 13 chapters that follow represent the multiple analyses that can occur when questions about diversity, inclusion, and appropriate early educational practices are raised. From the beginning, we wanted to include contributions from individuals who are interested in the broad range of political, theoretical, social, and practical concerns related to early childhood. Across these various conceptualizations of the problem, a number of common themes have emerged:

- the view that the *concept* of developmentally appropriate practice is a necessary but insufficient framework for guiding inclusive early education practices
- a critique of the traditional child development theoretical and empirical knowledge base as ethnocentrically narrow
- a concern regarding the degree of congruence between the values, beliefs, and goals embedded in typical early education programs

and those of the children and families for whom the programs are designed

- a desire to construct new means of assessment, instruction, and program design that are responsive to the most significant (as opposed to the most salient) characteristics of young children.

Expressed within each of these themes is the belief in the power and responsibility of teachers to inform and improve their own practice.

The book is divided into four parts, each with its own brief introduction to the chapters included therein. We begin in Part I by focusing on the sociopolitical and historical contexts in which early childhood programs have evolved in the United States. Chapters 1 and 2 situate the contemporary discourse about diversity and inclusiveness within cultural norms and ideological systems that have affected both theory and practice in early education.

In Part II, critical perspectives on theory are offered. Chapters 3–6 emphasize the inadequacies of current child development theory, suggest ways to expand the knowledge base through the use of alternative empirical approaches, and argue for a new conceptualization of the role of teacher as reflective practitioner and researcher. These chapters demonstrate the value of selectively drawing from the traditional child development framework while using newer forms of interpretation drawn from cross-cultural, behavioral, and post-Piagetian conceptualizations of development.

Part III focuses on the difficult negotiations that must occur between home settings and early childhood programs for children with developmental or cultural differences. Chapters 7 and 8 illustrate the potential discontinuities between home and school as experienced by African-American and Native-American children, respectively. Broader questions about the "dominant professional culture" are addressed in chapter 9. The effect of these three contributions is to raise questions about the processes and sources of cultural transmission and the sometimes conflicting roles of parents and teachers as definers of what is "appropriate."

Chapters 10–13 in the final part of the book address early educational practices, both in their problematic and promising manifestations. The authors identify shortcomings of current interpretations of "best practice" and describe alternative strategies with respect to developmental differences, issues of assessment, and language development. Here, the role of direct instruction, parents' and teachers' views and judgments of children's behavior, and multiple understandings of early learning are emphasized as critical factors in the achievement of more effective and inclusive practice.

As we had anticipated at the outset of this project, the authors of these chapters raise far more questions than answers regarding the aims and means of defining and implementing appropriate educational practices. What is also evident throughout the book is an ethic of inclusion which embraces the physical, psychological, and social aspects of diversity in our society. *To be included is not merely to be present, but to participate, to influence, and to be influenced by the communities in which one lives, works, and learns.*

This ethic has powerful implications for *what* we define as appropriate in early childhood education, and *how* those definitions are asserted and negotiated within the complexities of our professional disciplines and in the classrooms in which children learn. To respond to these challenges, we must incorporate the ethic of inclusion not only in our work with young children, but with teachers, parents, and others whose actions and decisions affect the lives of the youngest members of our society.

ACKNOWLEDGMENTS

The publication of this volume was made possible by many people who contributed crucial ideas, worked long hours under very tight timelines, and were patient with the distractions that occurred as the project proceeded. We wish to acknowledge first the leadership and commitment of Sue Bredekamp of the National Association for the Education of Young Children, who from the beginning sought broad input into the formulation of the original guidelines for developmentally appropriate practice, and who continues to value a climate of open debate as the early childhood community strives to articulate its understanding of effective education for young children. Susan Liddicoat of Teachers College Press had the foresight to recognize a timely and critical topic, and encouraged us to pursue this effort. Her constant support, patience, and good advice were invaluable. At the University of New Hampshire, Micki Canfield and Debbie Brooks handled the majority of the production and communication tasks associated with the book, and we are grateful for their good spirit and outstanding skills. Throughout the past year, our graduate students tolerated our foibles and gave us helpful feedback about the ideas we were trying to express. Finally, we offer our profound thanks to the 23 authors who participated in this adventure. Their insights, diligence, and commitment to young children imbue each page of the volume.

Our children, Case and Francesca Prince and Anna and Graham Mallory, sustained us with their love, understanding, and delightful presence. This book is dedicated to them.

REFERENCES

Bloch, M. (1991). Critical science and the history of child development's influence on early education research. *Early Education and Development, 2* (2), 95–108.

Bredekamp, S., (Ed.). (1987). *Developmentally appropriate practice in early childhood programs serving children from birth through age 8.* Washington, DC: National Association for the Education of Young Children.

Bredekamp, S. (1991). Redeveloping early childhood education: A response to Kessler. *Early Childhood Research Quarterly, 6* (2),199–210.

Bredekamp, S., & Rosegrant, T. (Eds.). (1992). *Reaching potentials: Appropriate curriculum and assessment for young children* (Vol. I). Washington, D.C.: National Association for the Education of Young Children.

Bruner, J. S. (1976). *On knowing: Essays for the left hand.* Cambridge, MA: Harvard University Press.

Derman-Sparks, L., & the A.B.C. Task Force (1989). *Anti-bias curriculum: Tools for empowering young children.* Washington, DC: National Association for the Education of Young Children.

Edwards, C., Forman, G., & Gandini, L. (Eds.). (1993). *The hundred languages of children: The Reggio Emilia approach to early childhood education.* Norwood, NJ: Ablex.

Eisenberg, N. (1992). Social development: Current trends and future possibilities. *SRCD Newsletter,* Fall Issue. Society for Research in Child Development. Chicago: University of Chicago Press.

Fernie, D., & Kantor, R. (1992, September). *Early childhood classrooms as "developmental communities": An orienting image for child-centered practice.* Paper presented at the Conference on Reconceptualizing Early Childhood Education, Chicago.

Johnson, J. J., & Johnson, K. M. (1992). Clarifying the developmental perspective in response to Carta, Schwartz, Atwater, & McCollum. *Topics in Early Childhood Special Education, 12* (4), 439–457.

Kessler, S. A. (1991). Alternative perspectives on early childhood education. *Early Childhood Research Quarterly, 6* (2), 183–198.

Kessler, S. A., & Swadener, B. B. (Eds.) (1992). *Reconceptualizing early childhood education curriculum: Beginning the dialogue.* New York: Teachers College Press.

Mallaguzzi, L. (1993). History, ideas, and basic philosophy. In C. Edwards, L. Gandini, & G. Forman (Eds.), *The hundred languages of children: The Reggio Emilia approach to early childhood education.* Norwood, NJ: Ablex.

Mallory, B. L. (1991). *Developmental diversity: Improving developmentally appropriate practice through professional preparation.* Paper presented at the National Association for the Education of Young Children conference, Denver, CO.

New, R. S. (1990). Excellent early education: A town in Italy has it. *Young Children, 45* (6), 4–10.

New, R. S. (1991). *Culture and child development: Implications for early child-hood teacher and administrator education.* Paper presented at the National Association for the Education of Young Children conference, Denver, CO.

Oakes, J. (1985). *Keeping track: How schools structure inequality.* New Haven, CT: Yale University Press.

O'Loughlin, M. (1991, October). *Rethinking early childhood education: A socio-cultural perspective.* Paper presented at Conference on Reconceptualizing Research in Early Childhood Education, Madison, WI.

Swadener, B. B., & Kessler, S. (Eds.). (1991). [Special Issue]. *Early Education and Development, 2* (2).

Whiting, B. (1976). Unpackaging the packaged variable. In K. Riegal and J. Meacham (Eds.), *The changing individual in a changing world.* Chicago: Aldine.

PART I

Sociopolitical and Historical Contexts

● ● ● ● ● ●

The aim of the two chapters in Part I is to examine some of the broad issues related to the social, political, and historical contexts in which early childhood programs have evolved in the United States. Such an examination is important in order to understand the contemporary discourse about developmentally appropriate practice, including the underlying values and theoretical assumptions that determine policies and program designs. Why is it, for example, that early childhood programs intended to compensate for educational and economic disadvantage sometimes rely on "separate but equal" means to democratic ends? How are political, empirical, theoretical, and pedagogical belief systems interrelated, and what is the relative weight of each when it comes time to decide what is appropriate?

In chapter 1, Lubeck discusses the politics embedded in official definitions of "developmentally appropriate practice." She explores the relationship of culture, class, and curriculum as they are revealed in early childhood education. In the process, she finds that current embodiments of "best practice" do not look significantly different from previous ones. Such inertia is problematic, especially when the children being served in early education programs are from increasingly diverse backgrounds. The status quo becomes more entrenched as the field of practice increasingly takes on a "professional" identity that works against the full involvement of lay parents, especially those belonging to ethnic minorities. Lubeck's critical perspective challenges us to acknowledge ideological differences that have perhaps been glossed over in the quest for consensus that has characterized the field of early childhood education in recent years. Lubeck then goes beyond the level of critique by suggesting additional guidelines capable of "dismantling the power relations and rhetorical strategies" that characterize the current definitions of "DAP."

In the second chapter, Mallory provides an historical review of the evolution of social policies in the United States that have influenced services for young children with developmental differences. He explicates the linkages between policy, theory, research, and practice in the fields of early education and, later, early childhood special education. Core social values related to equal opportunity and participatory decision-making are analyzed with respect to compensatory education for disenfranchised children and special education for disabled children. The values and practices underlying these movements have recently been joined together in programs that integrate typical and atypical young children. However, this integration has created a new set of theoretical problems when the question is raised of which pedagogies can and should be applied to diverse children within the same classrooms. Mallory argues that perhaps the teaching practices and developmental assumptions that have been applied differentially to diverse groups of children are more complementary than competing. Inclusive practices demand inclusive theory. The convergent model proposed here is intended to achieve that end.

1

•••••

The Politics of Developmentally Appropriate Practice
Exploring Issues of Culture, Class, and Curriculum

SALLY LUBECK

They told me the small pastries we made were called 'Butterflies.' My Mamá called them 'Buñuelos.' They said my mother was wrong. She said they were called 'Buñuelos' in México.

They told me it was the 'Rio Grande.' My Mamá told me it was the 'Rio Bravo.' They said she was wrong. In México it is the Rio Bravo, she said.

They told me Columbus discovered America. My Papá said, how could you discover something when civilizations were already here? They said my father was wrong.

They told me that the Aztecs and Incas were savages that ate people. Mis Papas told me that they were astronomers and mathematicians and farmers and writers and warriors, and they took baths, too.

They told me my parents were wrong, their stories irrelevant. They told me to stop asking questions. They told me to stop putting the accent on my name. They told me to stop doing my math the way my father showed me. They told me that I should be more like the other boys and girls. They told me that my parents were wrong.

They never stopped to think that maybe they were wrong.

Mónica Byrne-Jiménez (1992, p. 18)

The dictionary defines politics, first and foremost, as the science of government. In the United States and other liberal democracies, a political system exists for administering, legislating, and adjudicating. Bunce (1990) describes five characteristics that help define a democratic political system: rule of law, extensive civil liberties guaranteed by law, representative government, a Weberian bureaucracy, and some dispersion of economic resources (p. 399). Politics, in this sense, is seen to support but be removed from daily experience.

17

Perhaps more in the public eye is the push and pull of politics, as elected officials struggle both to undermine their opponents and to have their own agendas and promises understood and believed. Recent educational research has been involved with politics in this second, more active and conflictual, sense, concerned with politics "involving relations of order and power among people" (Gee, 1990, p. 27). Scholarship on the politics of the curriculum, for example, what Apple (1992) has most recently called "the politics of official knowledge" and "the politics of cultural incorporation," defines the political as a continuing contest over meaning, over what and especially whose knowledge will be sanctioned. As Apple writes, "what counts as legitimate knowledge is the result of complex power relations and struggles among identifiable class, race, gender, and religious groups" (p. 4). Peshkin (1992) also recognizes the profoundly political nature of educational practice by seeing schools as arenas for competing views about what to teach, what to emphasize, what level of challenge to provide, and how to evaluate. In his succinct phrase, curriculum is a "many fitting thing."

Too often, however, the contest over meaning has been waged between *unequal* partners, subverted, or entirely silenced. In her 1992 master's thesis on the role of culture and language in the education of Latino children, Mónica Byrne-Jiménez begins each section with memories from her childhood as a Latina in the United States (see above). Her confusion and self-doubt, so much a reaction to the demands of two worlds, have changed to indignation. Monica has become a survivor and a force for change. Yet many will be less fortunate. Data indicate that disproportionate numbers of children from certain ethnic, racial, and linguistic groups, notably those from African-American, Latino, and Native-American backgrounds, fare poorly in American schools. They are disproportionately represented in special education classes and differentially placed in low tracks and streams (e.g., Goodlad, 1981; Oakes, 1985), and they are far more likely to drop out of school (e.g., U.S. Bureau of the Census, 1989).

Beginning in the 1960s, early childhood education was proposed as a way to ameliorate the poor scholastic performance of many children from traditionally disadvantaged groups. Before that time, low scores on measures of intellectual ability were largely attributed to genetics. The belief had been widespread that African Americans, Mexican Americans, and Native Americans were cognitively deficient. In the early 20th century immigrants from Ireland and from eastern and southern Europe were similarly characterized (Laosa, 1984).

With the seminal work of Hunt (1961, 1964), Bloom (1964), and Bernstein (1961), however, the alternative-environmental explanation

came into currency. Hunt, for example, drew on Hebb's animal deprivation studies to argue that children who perform poorly on ability and
achievement measures are not genetically inferior but rather environmentally deprived. He supported his case with studies that demonstrated
the effects of different environments on children. A classic study of children moved from an orphanage to an institution for the mentally
retarded, for example, suggested that, when given love and attention,
children could make dramatic cognitive gains.

Such evidence provided a powerful rationale for "compensatory"
education. That is, if young children were in unstimulating home environments, they could still be provided with what they "lacked" and go on
to succeed. The poor scholastic performance of children was thus
blamed on "cultural deprivation" (e.g., Bloom, Davis, & Hess, 1965), a
theory that attributes low levels of achievement to inadequate childrearing practices. The deficiency formulation is registered in two ways: (1) in
the presumed lack of attributes or attitudes that are valued by members
of the "mainstream" (people thus are described as *dis*organized, *un*motivated, *un*stable), and (2) in the presumed acquisition of values and attitudes that are unacceptable to the "mainstream" (e.g., hedonistic, prone
to violence) (Howard & Scott, 1981).

Since environment is narrowly defined as what happens in the
home, policy initiatives grounded in this paradigm have focused on training mothers and other family members to interact with and stimulate
their children (e.g., Gray & Klaus, 1965; Levenstein, 1970) and on developing preschool programs such as Head Start that would provide children with educational experiences they would be unlikely to receive at
home. These assumptions have guided work with disadvantaged populations for nearly 30 years.

Anthropologists and sociologists were critical of the notion of cultural deprivation and supportive of claims made by members of "minority" groups that their cultures were not represented in schools. Wax and
Wax (1971), for example, called it a "vacuum ideology" (p. 6), one that
presumes that people have no culture, when, in fact, they simply have a
culture that differs. Other scholars provided examples of "difference, not
deficit."

Today most researchers and practitioners do not openly adhere to a
"deprivation" doctrine. However, a current, albeit subtle, manifestation of
the same assumptions appears in the form of the guidelines for developmentally appropriate practice (Bredekamp, 1987; sometimes referred to
as the DAP guidelines; National Association for the Education of Young
Children, 1986). Intended as directives for how young American children
should be cared for and educated, the guidelines are a description of

what constitutes "best practice" in early education programs for children birth through age 8. While the doctrine of cultural deprivation focuses on what is lacking, the DAP guidelines highlight what *should be present.*

Beneath the rhetoric of inclusion and "mentioning," the guidelines embody assumptions that are strikingly similar to those that have traditionally guided early education initiatives:

1. The belief that some cultural practices are preferable (and others, if not "deficient," certainly less desirable).
2. The focus on individuals (children and family members) in an effort to rectify social ills.
3. The intent to provide children with experiences they are not likely to get at home.
4. The commitment to share with parents the knowledge that they ostensibly lack.

For racial, ethnic, and linguistic minorities, it is a "kinder, gentler" version of an all too common refrain.

The limitations of this approach have begun to be realized. Derman-Sparks (1992), for example, calls attention to the fact that the "European-American culture-centered classroom" is not appropriate for all children and describes how practices might differ in classrooms of ethnically diverse children. Bowman (1992) likewise takes culture seriously and demonstrates eloquently how classrooms organized around dominant cultural practices can be out of sync with some children's acquired styles of learning and interacting. This chapter has a somewhat broader but related intent. Specifically, the "politicalization" of the DAP guidelines is addressed. The first section draws on research in the anthropology and sociology of education to explore how problems are defined and solutions proposed from three alternative perspectives. Work within these explanatory paradigms clarifies the importance of culture and the necessity of understanding how social inequity is maintained through practices that create status differentials between and among people and through ideologies that reify the knowledge most likely to be acquired by the dominant classes. I argue that the guidelines foster similar practices:

1. by defining dominant cultural practices as normal, positive, and universally applicable;
2. by claiming that it is incumbent upon those who are knowledgeable about "child development knowledge" to impart this knowl-

edge to parents (thereby setting up a "we/they" relationship
based on the privileged position of the professional); and
3. by focusing too narrowly on children and their families.

In the second section, the guidelines are examined to see how they
exemplify what Apple (1992) has called "the politics of official knowledge" and "the politics of cultural incorporation." The first focuses on the
rhetorical devices used to make the guidelines "official": the claim to universality, their legitimation through science, and the affirmation of a "professional-client" relationship between teachers and parents. The second
shows how efforts have been made to incorporate challenges to the
authority of the guidelines through compromise and the act of "mentioning." Finally, the issues are located within the broader arena of education policy in the United States and suggestions are made about what
might be different if linguistic and cultural diversity were taken seriously
in early education policy and practice.

PERSPECTIVES AND POSSIBILITIES

This section develops three alternative perspectives for explaining the
poor scholastic performance of disproportionate numbers of children
from ethnic, racial, and linguistic "minority" groups within American
society: the cultural, the institutional, and the structural. Representative
research literature grounded in each is then reviewed. A thorough discussion would require far more elaboration than space allows here.
Instead the examples are meant to be illustrative rather than exhaustive.

The Cultural Perspective

According to the cultural perspective, problems of poor school achievement lie in the mismatch between the culture of the school and that of
the children it serves. LeVine (1984) defines culture as "a shared organization of ideas that includes the intellectual, moral, and aesthetic standards prevalent in a community and the meaning of communicative
actions" (p. 67). Since values, meanings and behavior patterns differ for
members of different groups, "mainstream" teachers and "minority" children can experience "culture clash." Numerous studies have examined
continuities and discontinuities between the home and school experiences of children from diverse ethnic, racial, and social class groups
(e.g., Florio & Shultz, 1979; Ogbu, 1982; Philips, 1972, 1983) and the

polarized socialization, the "clash of cultures," children can experience in schools (e.g., Heath, 1982; Labov, 1982; Schofield, 1982; Shimahara, 1983). Observed cultural differences include: (1) dialect features in speech, (2) nonverbal behaviors that indicate attention and understanding, (3) accepted turn-taking practices, and (4) definitions of leading and following, adult and child roles, cooperation and competition, and humor and mock aggression (Erickson, 1986).

A study of the education of children on the Warm Springs Indian Reservation serves as one example of how children can be socialized to speak and interact in ways that differ from common schooling practices in the United States. Philips (1972) describes how (Anglo) teachers came to accommodate the predilection of Native-American children to work collaboratively in groups, rather than competitively as individuals. Comparing Native-American with non-Native-American classrooms at the first and sixth grade levels, she identifies four types of "participant structures." In the first type, the teacher directs the entire class, occasionally calling on individual students. In the second, the teacher works with a small group of students, again calling on individuals to respond to questions or to read. In the third, students work alone at their seats but may consult the teacher. In the fourth, students work together in small groups.

Philips found that Native-American children were reluctant to participate in the first two types of interactional structures: "'learning through public mistakes' is not a [value] the Indians share, and this has important implications for . . . understanding . . . Indian behavior in the classroom" (p. 381). Over time, the Native-American children were found to be willing to speak privately with the teacher, as in the third type. However, in the fourth type, in which children themselves run the groups, Native-American children were found to become deeply involved, to work closely with others, and to compete as a group with other groups. The Anglo children Philips observed were less comfortable with this type of structure, argued more, and were more likely to defer to an appointed chair.

Reservation teachers learned to reduce the number of occasions in which children would be asked to participate in teacher-directed activities or in situations in which they had to perform alone in front of others ("as in the ubiquitous 'show and tell' or 'sharing'") (p. 382). However, as a consequence, it became more difficult to assess what individual children knew, and later, when the children were bussed off the reservation for junior and senior high school, where these accommodations were no longer made, the Native-American children were found to fall silent and to refuse to participate.

Several educational reforms have been devised to minimize the cultural dissonance that some children experience. These efforts have three principal foci:

1. Helping the child to fit the school.
2. Helping the school to fit the child.
3. Helping the child to become bicultural.

One example of the first type appears in Shirley Brice Heath's (1983) classic educational ethnography, *Ways with Words*. The book provides insight into the subconscious rules followed by members of two cultural groups in the United States, describing in detail how children in Trackton, an African-American community, and Roadville, a white working class community, learn to use oral and written language (see chapter 3, this volume). These cultural practices are then contrasted with those of the neighboring middle-class "townspeople." Arguing that schools must lay the foundation for school-based literacy for children whose orientations to language and learning differ markedly from those assumed in schools, Heath chronicles many of the ways in which teachers learn to "build bridges" so that children can "learn school." For example, preschool teachers, formerly upset with children who did not behave as they expected, learned to revise and clarify implicit definitions of how time and space were to be used in their classrooms. They also learned to express requests directly, while providing opportunities for children to learn mainstream forms through story reading, the use of puppets, and other means.

An alternative response has developed under the rubric "culturally responsive education." Unlike the former effort, which aims to adapt the child to the school, this approach seeks, to the extent possible, to adapt the school to the child. This has been done by studying the learning strategies that are already familiar to children from particular groups and creating instructional formats that mirror their previous experience. Using this approach, the Kamahameha Early Education Project (KEEP) in Hawaii showed striking results in teaching native Hawaiian children to read. Within a year, the children in the initial study, whose reading achievement was among the lowest in the country, began to perform at levels above national norms (Calfee et al., 1981).

In the Kamehameha project, children set up the classroom themselves, because they were expected to be responsible for their living space at home. Since Hawaiian children are accustomed to learning from a variety of people, they frequently worked in peer groups. And they were allowed to use overlapping forms of speech while in reading groups. Native Hawaiians frequently co-narrate and overlap speech with a speaker (Au & Jordan, 1981).

A third emphasis has been to achieve a balance between home and school, through explicit efforts to help children to become bicultural and bilingual (e.g., Laosa, 1984; Soto, 1991; Wolf, 1992). Moll & Diaz (1987), in their case study of a bilingual program in which children were instructed in Spanish in one class and English in the other, examined how a teacher's methods hampered the full participation of Spanish speaking students in the classroom. The children's English proficiency was limited, causing the teacher to assume that their reading comprehension was poor. Thus the teacher focused on decoding the text for them. Researchers were able to demonstrate that the problem was not their comprehension, but rather their expressive language in English, which was not yet developed to the point where they could respond easily to the teacher's questions. By encouraging students to focus on comprehension and to use "bilingual communicative support" (p. 306) (i.e., switching to Spanish as necessary), the students, by the third lesson, were able to answer comprehension questions at grade level. In summary, an increasing number of educational programs are now taking culture into account, by teaching children new cultural practices, by conforming school practices to practices prevalent in the community, and by encouraging the use of both English and the language of origin.

The Institutional Perspective

From this perspective schools are seen to organize and serve their constituencies in ways that favor students from white and affluent backgrounds. A liberal version of the institutional perspective would state that schools hinder the success of some children because they have too few teachers from the same racial and ethnic groups, because they utilize unfamiliar or inappropriate teaching strategies, because they fail to elicit strong community involvement, and because, generally, they support policies and practices that are out-of-sync with the communities they serve. The underlying assumption of work from this vantage point is that, with a bit of insight or tinkering, schools can be made to better serve a wider range of students.

A more scathing critique of schooling has been mounted by those whose work is informed by a radical-critical perspective. Theories of *social reproduction, cultural reproduction,* and *cultural production* help illuminate how schools group, sort, and track children and make official the knowledge and values of the dominant culture. Members of disenfranchised groups have been shown to "resist" such practices.

THEORIES OF SOCIAL REPRODUCTION. Social reproduction theorists such as Bowles and Gintis (1976) argue that social relations within schools are strongly determined by the division of labor in the sphere of economic production. As Stanley Aronowitz (in Willis, 1977) states:

> The objective of public education [is] to produce workers at various levels of the capitalist labor process. Certain schools produce managers; others, technicians or professionals; the largest number generate industrial and clerical labor for the factories and offices of giant corporations. The curriculum, the authority relations, and the life in the classroom all conspire to persuade the working classes that, with few exceptions, their destiny [is] to remain on the bottom. (p. x)

The purpose of the school, in effect, is not to foster equality but to maintain inequality.

Social classes are believed to be reproduced in schools through differential funding (e.g., Kozol, 1991) and differential experience. Bowles and Gintis (1976) see a correspondence between the social relations of schooling and the social relations of work:

> Predominantly working class schools tend to emphasize behavioral control and rule-following, while schools in well-to-do suburbs employ relatively open systems that favor greater student participation, less direct supervision, more student electives, and, in general, a value system stressing internalized standards of control. (p. 132)

Anyon (1980) finds such differences in her study of classrooms for children of different classes. Working-class students were taught more by rote drill, while middle-class students were instructed in ways that encouraged discussion, analysis, and decision making.

Within schools, distinctions are also made that have the effect of stratifying children into groups and tracks according to their social class origins (e.g., Oakes, 1986; Rist, 1970; Wilcox, 1982). Oakes (1982), for example, shows how relationships in low tracks are characterized by punitiveness and alienation. Relational differences have consequences for how students come to perceive themselves (see the discussion of cultural reproduction that follows). High school seniors are more negative about themselves and their life chances than students in junior high. Thus, schools would seem to socialize students for different roles and influence the development of attitudes that correspond to those roles.

Another study illustrated how, in the United States, these effects are strongly mediated by race and ethnicity. McDermott and Gospodinoff (1981) used videotapes of reading time in a first grade classroom to show the different experiences students had in a classroom. The top group consisted of white children; the bottom group mainly of Puerto Rican children and one African-American child. In the top group, all of the children were readers, and the transition from one reader to another went smoothly. All were attentive, looking at their books, and in this postural configuration, they were not disturbed by other children. By contrast, the bottom group was more likely to look unfocused. Not all of the children in the bottom group could read, so the teacher had to decide who would take the next turn. Students vied for the teacher's attention. In the interactional dissonance that often ensued, the teacher often left the group to intercede. Students also disturbed the group by asking for the teacher's assistance. Over the course of the year, the children in the bottom group spent one third the amount of time reading as those in the top group, although they spent the same amount of time at the reading table. They fell further behind as the year progressed. The authors concluded: "If we wanted a mechanism for sorting each new generation of citizens into the advantaged and the disadvantaged, into the achieving and the underachieving, we could have done no better than to have invented the school system we have" (p. 229).

THEORIES OF CULTURAL REPRODUCTION. Cultural reproduction theories suggest how "a coherent field of rules and sets of relationships proclaiming itself as separate and objective dignifies, and makes 'official,' a culture that is actually the property of the dominant classes" (Willis, 1981, p. 54). What is presented as the cultural wealth and heritage of the entire society (e.g., literature, art, music) is, in fact, knowledge and experience that is differentially acquired by those who, because of their possession of *real* capital, are capable of appropriating it (e.g., Bourdieu, 1977).

Bourdieu attempts to provide an account of how power and privilege are transmitted through the educational system. He defines *cultural capital* as institutionalized knowledge and qualifications that serve to reproduce social class hierarchies (e.g., Bourdieu & Passeron, 1977) . According to this argument, the illusion is created that the social and educational systems are meritocratic. In fact, however, grading and testing are based on knowledge and skills that only the upper classes are likely to acquire. The construct is useful in understanding how schools and other dominant institutions define what counts as knowledge, set arbitrary standards, and serve particular interests.

Lareau (1989) explores how privileged social standing provides advantages that enable an individual to comply with the standards set by schools. She uses case studies to illustrate how upper middle-class and working-class parents relate differently to schools. Upper-middle-class parents know how to "work the system," how to use their "cultural cap-ital" to provide special advantage to their children. Thus, for example, a teacher would be likely to allow a child to join a higher reading group, if a middle-class parent requested it. Research drawing on this explana-tory framework suggests how ways of thinking and behaving are trans-mitted from one generation to the next, based on identifications with class (Willis, 1977, but see below) and race (e.g., Lareau, 1991; Ogbu, 1988).

THEORIES OF CULTURAL PRODUCTION. Theories of cultural production arose, at least in part, in reaction to the mechanistic, deterministic vision of human behavior presented in reproduction theories. Here individuals are not seen as mindless and passive, trapped in the processes of repro-duction like cogs in a machine; rather they stand in antagonistic and con-tested relation to authority (e.g., Everhart, 1983; Lubeck, 1988; Willis, 1977). The disadvantaged actively oppose the forms of domination they experience.

Perhaps the most celebrated study from this vantage point is the Willis (1977) classic, *Learning to Labor: How Working Class Kids Get Working Class Jobs.* The book is an ethnography of an English single-sex secondary modern school named Hammerstown Boys. Willis focuses on 12 working-class "lads" preliminary to their departure from school and 6 months after; he follows them, quite literally, onto the "shop floor." Through observation and participant observation, Willis comes to under-stand how the boys form an oppositional culture, or what he elsewhere refers to as "a creative collective self-making in the subordinate class" (Willis, 1981, p. 49).

Willis suggests that the "lads" achieve *partial penetration,* that is, they understand obliquely that qualifications have no real value, that upward mobility is, at best, unlikely, that the kind of work available to them is meaningless, and that, although individuals may "make it," the working class as a whole will not. The irony is that their very rebellion against a system stacked against them ultimately condemns them to rela-tively low-paid jobs with little opportunity for advancement. Willis' con-cept of "resistance" provides a counterpoint to theories of social and cul-tural reproduction by demonstrating "how human agency accommodates, mediates, and resists the logic of capital and its dominating social prac-tices" (Giroux, 1983, p. 282).

Theorists initially saw in the concept of resistance a way for subju-gated peoples to resist an oppressive social order. To mitigate the nega-tive effects of schooling for members of vulnerable groups, those oper-ating from this perspective argue that power differentials in schools need to be addressed, assessment and tracking practices need to be changed, and disenfranchised groups must organize and contest the policies and practices promoted by dominant groups.

The Structural Perspective

Research within the structural perspective explores the relationship between schooling and other dominant institutions and shows how the inequality some children experience in schools is endemic to the social order. Prejudice pervades, not only schools, but American institutions generally.

Ogbu (1978, 1981, 1987) has been the primary proponent of the theory that societies are organized into castelike systems (i.e., systems of social stratification based on group ascription) that privilege a dominant group and exclude and marginalize a minority group. He is critical of the deficit (environment) perspective and the difference (culture) perspective, because he sees both to be external definitions of home and community influences that fail to understand behaviors as strategies for survival (Ogbu, 1981, 1987).

In a study initiated in response to Jensen's hypothesis that compensatory education programs fail because black Americans are genetically inferior, Ogbu (1978) compared dominant and minority groups in three societies in which the groups were from the same "race" (India, Israel, and Japan) and dominant and minority groups in societies in which the races differed (Britain, New Zealand, and the United States). He found differences in school performance—and the same 15-point spread in IQ—in all the societies, regardless of race.

Ogbu's (1978) three-point alternative explanation has been the keystone of his research agenda for 15 years:

> Schools translate the inferior social and technoeconomic status of Blacks [and other castelike minorities] into inferior education; . . . caste barriers do not permit [them] to translate their academic skills into good jobs, income, and other benefits; and . . . both conditions result in [the fact that they develop] attitudes and skills less favorable to white middle-class type of school success. (p. 357)

Historically, schools or classes for some groups (African-Americans, Latinos, Native Americans) were segregated; today many exist in districts where the tax base is low, and classrooms are crowded, understaffed, and poorly equipped. Teachers of "minority" children frequently have low expectations for them, and many children come to be labelled as "problems." Also members of castelike minorities traditionally experienced a "job ceiling," that is, they were denied access to prestigious, well-paying jobs, even when they were qualified for them.

In response to this complex of factors, members of these groups can develop "secondary cultural differences . . . as a response to a contact situation" (Ogbu, 1987, p. 322). These have been characterized as differences in cognitive style or as a type of *cultural inversion* in which the values, meanings, and behaviors of one group (e.g., whites) are considered inappropriate for another group (e.g., blacks), and chosen values and behaviors are oppositional in nature: "distrust of white people and skepticism make it harder for them to accept and follow school rules and standard practices that enhance academic success" (p. 334).

For Ogbu, the problem lies in the society, and change is needed both in community values and in the "opportunity structure" of the school and of society more generally. In addition to community mobilization and school reform, therefore, broad societal reforms are necessary and implicit in Ogbu's position: anti-discrimination policies and policies that redistribute income and increase the life chances of members of oppressed groups.

In summary, the lack of school success experienced by disproportionate numbers of children from historically disenfranchised groups has been variously explained from different theoretical perspectives. In the heredity and environment conceptions, the problem is seen to reside "in" people, suggesting explicitly or by default that they are biologically or culturally inferior. In contrast, work from a cultural perspective recognizes culture as an important, shared, supraindividual phenomenon in human life and assumes that school personnel must take it into account (i.e., must deal with children as cultural beings). From an institutional vantage point, however, the school is more profoundly implicated. Where work from the cultural perspective can find that school administrators and teachers can be unfamiliar with or insensitive to children whose backgrounds differ from their own, work within the institutional perspective problematizes the "deep structure" of schools, in clarifying what knowledge has "cultural capital" and how practices such as tracking, grouping, grading, and testing serve to stratify children by social class, race, and ethnicity. Finally, the structural perspective lodges the problem in what Ogbu (1987) has called the "postschool opportunity structure." Society, school, and community fail children, particularly those with castelike or involuntary minority status. Solutions range from changing individuals to changing the conditions that affect their lives, from "doing good" to attempting to undo the social and economic inequity that constitutes disadvantage. In each case, the solution is guided by the problem that is defined. The answer, like a seed, is already contained within the question.

There are three principal features of the ideology of developmentally appropriate practice that are especially problematic with reference to children and families from traditionally disenfranchised groups. First, as currently formulated, DAP is an effort to teach dominant cultural practices to both teachers and parents, a retooled and repackaged variation of work within the broad purview of the environment perspective that has dominated early education initiatives since the 1960s. Exemplifying what Foucault (1980) calls "normalizing" practices, emphasis is no longer placed on what is defective or wrong but rather on what is defined as healthy and positive; at work on what is "productive" rather than "repressive" power.

Second, research within the institutional and structural paradigms discussed above illustrate ways in which children from certain groups are disproprotionately placed in low groups and tracks and how the knowledge they bring to school is devalued. These "systems" are not abstract entities, however, for as Outhwaite (1983) writes, social structure can more accurately be described as "the patterned relations among people" (p. 7). It is school personnel, acting in relation to those with less power, who decide what—and whether—children can learn. The DAP guidelines also favor certain knowledge and practice. Those with power have assumed the right to dictate "best practice" and to declare those with other values to be less informed. Like the more obvious practices discussed above, DAP serves to maintain the status quo.

Finally, DAP is too narrowly conceived to address the range of problems faced by ethnic, racial, and linguistic "minority" children and families. Rather a framework is needed that calls attention also to cultural concerns, institutional constraints, and broad-based social inequities. To do less is to perpetuate an early education practice that continues to focus on providing children and families what they "lack." It is not argued here that the guidelines are without value but rather that they are framed in a way that overstates their applicability and importance. It is to an analysis of the rhetorical devices used to support the claim that they are for *all* children that we now turn.

THE POLITICS OF
DEVELOPMENTALLY APPROPRIATE PRACTICE

Since the mid-1980s work on the politics of the curriculum has shifted from a concern with forces of reproduction and resistance to a focus on educational practice, particularly regarding issues of race, class, and gender (Pinar & Bowers, 1992). If politics is concerned with meaning, and power with the fact that some individuals and groups have greater authority in legitimating certain forms of knowledge or practice, the DAP guidelines can be investigated for ways in which alternative views have been silenced, coopted and incorporated. What follows is an examination of two somewhat interrelated ways in which the guidelines can be viewed as a political and politicized text. Borrowing from Apple (1992), the first involves "the politics of official knowledge" or how the guidelines are presented; the second deals with "the politics of incorporation" or how challenges have been incorporated and reconciled so that essential premises remain unchanged.

The Politics of Official Knowledge

Knowledge is never neutral. Rather it is socially constructed, reflecting the values and life orientations of a particular group. Education and power are inextricably linked. As Apple (1992) writes: "It is during times of social upheaval that this relationship of education and power becomes most visible. Such a relationship was and continues to be made manifest in the struggles by women, people of color, and others to have their history and knowledge included in the curriculum" (p. 4). It is in this context that the DAP guidelines deserve scrutiny.

The position statement for developmentally appropriate programs for children birth through age 8 (Bredekamp, 1987) states that all children will benefit from the same type of experiences, experiences that would be expected to vary only according to the age and "individuality" of children. Developmental appropriateness thus incorporates two central tenets: "there are universal, predictable sequences of growth and change that occur in children during the first 9 years of life," but "each child is a unique person with an individual pattern and timing of growth, as well as individual personality, learning style, and family background" (p. 2).

Certain conditions are held to facilitate development for all children:

- Children learn best through self-initiated, self-directed, and self-chosen activity (p. 7).
- The teacher facilitates children's learning by providing a variety of activities and materials and by talking with children about their play (pp. 3, 5, 7).
- Different types of activities and materials are appropriate for children of different ages (pp. 3–5).
- Children learn through play. Transformational materials (sand,

water, clay, blocks), puzzles, manipulatives, dramatic play
props, science equipment, books, records, paper, paint and
markers, etc. are all appropriate for early education classrooms
(p. 4).
- All children should be exposed to multicultural activities, materials, and equipment (p. 7).

There are three principal ways in which the guidelines are rendered
"official." First, they presume that all children develop in the same way.
Thus, a common (childrearing) practice is warranted. This view is challenged by cross-cultural research that shows how children adopt personality characteristics that are valued within their societies (e.g., Whiting &
Edwards, 1988; Whiting & Whiting, 1975), and how adults, particularly
women, play crucial socializing roles in helping children to adapt to distinctive living patterns and economic conditions (Minturn & Lambert,
1964).

Second, the guidelines are legitimated by proclaiming that they represent the "consensus" view of the profession and widespread dispersion
of and agreement with the ideas set forth (indeed 300,000 copies have
been sold), and also by claiming legitimation through science: "Human
development research indicates . . ." (Bredekamp, 1987, p. 2). Only a
cursory overview of the field of developmental psychology, however,
attests to the fact that there is widespread disagreement among developmentalists on a range of critical issues. And, increasingly, the entire edifice of conventional psychology is eroding as long-held tenets are being
called into question. Ingleby (1986) cites three themes that reflect a
broad-based critique:

1. Psychology was seen as propagating spurious norms of development: cultural values were presented as facts of nature . . . psychology "reified the status quo," transforming historical flux into
   timeless nature.
2. The second theme concerned the *individuation* of psychology.
   Because it focused on the single case, psychology tended to treat
   only the properties of the individual as variables; the culture
   became, in effect, a constant.
3. A third line of criticism, whose target was the "positivist" program
   of basing psychology on natural-science methods and concepts,
   concerned the "reification" of meaningful, purposive activity in a
   deterministic framework. . . . Positivism was attacked for its
   denial of *agency*. (pp. 299–300)

What Ingleby sees as the principal cause of disenchantment with conventional psychology is the realization that development cannot be studied in isolation from its social and historical context.

Finally, the guidelines have been rendered official through their strategic role in the formation of "professional-client" relationships. Those who are informed about the guidelines are presumed to be more knowledgeable about raising children. Therefore, teachers schooled in these principles are expected to advise family members on "child development knowledge, insights, and resources" (Bredekamp, 1987, p. 12). Parents, teachers, and other community members who may have different ideas about what children might need are summarily dismissed as uninformed. As Kessler (1991b) writes, however:

> What appears to be a debate between those who are well-informed by current research in child development and those who are not is, in reality, a debate between individuals who hold different values about the purposes of schooling, what counts as legitimate knowledge, and presumably the nature of the good life and the just society. (p. 193)

In the 1992 reformulation of the guidelines, Bredekamp and Rosegrant (1992) deemphasize "development" and instead assert that, "The dominant rationale for the kind of child-centered, experiential learning we advocate . . . is its consistency with democratic values" (p. 17). However, adults are not encouaged to draw on their experience to reflect critically on this type of practice. Adults are expected to listen to those who make claims to greater knowledge and authority.

Since the guidelines are presented as universal and immutable (requiring only minor adjustment or revision), they appear to be apolitical when, in fact, the dialogue has been "silenced" (Delpit, 1988). As such, they become hegemonic in the sense of a "'selective tradition' . . . which . . . functions to privilege certain sets and orders of knowledge over others" (Williams, cited in Pinar & Bowers, 1992, p. 169).

It was argued above that early education initiatives have typically been premised on the assumptions of the environmental perspective, one tenet of which is the belief that parents of "disadvantaged" or "at-risk" children will not or cannot provide their children what they need. Middle-class professionals then assume the responsibility of training parents in "correct" childrearing practices and in providing young children with "appropriate" preschool experiences. In the position statement for developmentally appropriate practice and in defense of it, however, this political agenda is obscured. Instead, the guidelines are elevated to

orthodoxy: "the principles guiding developmentally appropriate programs are universally applicable" (Kostelnik, 1992, p. 22) and "DAP is for
all children" (Bredekamp & Rosegrant, 1992, p. 5).

The Politics of Incorporation

In a recent discussion of "the politics of cultural incorporation," Apple
(1992) writes:

> Curricula aren't imposed in countries like the United States. Rather, they
> are the products of often intense conflicts, negotiations, and attempts at
> rebuilding hegemonic control by actually incorporating the knowledge
> and perspectives of the less powerful under the umbrella of the dis-
> course of dominant groups. (p. 8)

He notes how "Dominance is partly maintained . . . through compromise and the process of 'mentioning'" (p. 8). Therefore, the DAP guidelines and recommended curriculum strategies also can be analyzed to see
if or how they incorporate alternative perspectives and issues.

One example is the way in which culture, typically understood as a
supraindividual phenomenon, is reduced to the individual level. The fact
that children are members of different cultural groups is never
addressed. Within the DAP guidelines, for example, members of ethnic,
racial, and linguistic *groups* are not recognized as political stakeholders
in the formulation of curricula for their children. Instead, culture is
addressed by making it a characteristic of individuals, like a person's
needs or interests, or incorporated and subsumed, a programmatic add-
on, a mere component of an otherwise universalistic program: "Multicultural and nonsexist experiences, materials, and equipment should be
provided for children of all ages" (Bredekamp, 1987, p. 7). In these ways,
culture becomes a consideration in determining "individual appropriateness" or, alternatively, a type of "experience, material, or equipment."
However the conviction that the type of practice advocated can be
"adapted" to individual children misses the essential point. If culture is,
in fact, taken seriously, if parents and other community members have a
say in how their children will be educated, then the very nature of programs and the ontological and epistemological assumptions on which
they are based could differ.

A second way in which the political nature of the DAP guidelines
can be probed is by observing how challenges to their authority have
been managed. The guidelines appear to represent agreement among
early childhood professionals on issues of curriculum, adult-child interaction, home-school relations, and the assessment of children's develop-

ment and learning broadly defined. They have come under criticism, however, for a variety of reasons. Jipson (1991) uses the classroom journals and personal narratives of 30 early childhood educators to show how the guidelines represent cultural values that are not universally shared. She illustrates how teachers themselves frequently see the disjunture between professional and community notions of how children should be reared. For example, Alice, a Native American teacher, discusses how parents and tribal elders met with Head Start personnel to plan a program "that teaches the values, language, traditions, and practices of their tribal culture" (p.133), while Ann, a Euro-American teacher, worries that some African-American children are not learning in her developmentally appropriate classroom. Walsh (1991) argues that the guidelines present a false impression of consensus. Teachers express different views of development and researchers have different opinions on such questions as whether stages are, in fact, universal, whether development is an individual process or a socially mediated one, and whether development precedes or follows learning. Finally, Kessler (1991a & b) and Spodek (1988) make the case that "development" should not be the prime justification for early education practice.

The response to these critiques has largely been to incorporate them into the dominant discourse on developmentally appropriate practice. As Bredekamp (1991) writes in her response to Kessler (1991b), her purpose is, at least in part "to offer a justification, admittedly somewhat defensive, for the developmentalist perspective; and . . . to suggest an alternative argument for appropriate practice that draws on the strengths of these diverse perspectives" (p. 199).

In response to Jipson's concerns, it has already been noted how the cultural has been "mentioned," yet, in the process, trivialized and reduced. In response to Walsh's contention that the guidelines employ rhetoric that actually means different things to different people, Bredekamp and Rosegrant (1992) note that they may not represent the view of every practitioner, but that this and other NAEYC documents "result from a consensus-building process and reflect the views of the leadership of the association at the time of their adoption" (p. 3). Assuming a linear view ("knowledge expands and changes over time"), "the Association's positions must be reviewed and revised periodically to ensure their currency and accuracy" (p. 3). There is no recognition here that competing views exist. Rather the guidelines are presented as current and accurate to be changed only with time, as more information becomes available.

In lieu of a curriculum justified on developmental grounds, Kessler (1991b) advocates one that encourages "participatory democracy," emphasizing "the importance of the engagement of all individuals, not just a privileged few, in dialogue and action to create a community that collectively deliberates, creates, and resolves problems identified by the whole" (p. 194). In response, however, Bredekamp (1991) describes "the unsuccessful history of the arguments of the social reconstructionist perspective from John Dewey to John Holt" (p. 207). She argues instead for *linking* the two approaches in the hope that "real curriculum reform can result if the social reconstructionist and child-centered movements come together" (p. 208, emphasis added).

Through a continuing process of incorporation, the development of guidelines for practice suitable for *all* children has been an effort to achieve an ever-widening consensus, one focused on the common sharing of values and meanings, one which includes—and therefore silences— critical commentaries and alternative visions.

COMMONALITY VERSUS DIVERSITY

The issues raised in this chapter are at the heart of current debates within the education community. There are those who stress unity through commonality and thus propound a common curriculum (Bloom, 1987; Hirsch, 1987), a common set of goals and standards (e.g., National Commission on Excellence in Education, 1983), and a common view of the social ideal—a citizen who will adopt middle-class values, finish school, and get a job in the society as currently constituted (Margonis, 1992). There are others, however, who hold that curriculum should be tailored to the unique backgrounds and learning styles of students (e.g., Cazden & Leggert, 1981; Tharp & Gallimore, 1991), reflect multiple conceptions of excellence (e.g., Greene, 1984), and enable students to envision a society that is more open and equal than that which currently exists.

How a nation deals with issues of unity and diversity is one of the principal political questions of our time, for each agenda is problematic in its own right. A common set of goals and standards or a common curriculum obfuscates, but does not eliminate, the profound cultural diversity that exists within American society. Yet programs in culturally responsive education, bilingual education, and multicultural education will not, in themselves, guarantee a more egalitarian society. The root causes of the problems experienced by many children have been variously defined but, too often, education, particularly curriculum innovation, has been offered as a panacea for problems that have deeper roots and more profound implications.

What, then, might be different in an early education agenda that seriously took linguistic and cultural diversity into account? The keystone would be the dismantling of the power relations and rhetorical strategies that undergird the current effort and a framing of "problems" informed by cultural, institutional, and social understanding. The following "guidelines" are suggestive of such an altered agenda (recognizing, of course, that these are open to debate):

1. The DAP guidelines would be recognized for their role in supporting cultural, rather than universal, practice.
2. Teachers, parents, and community members would be able to speak openly about what is best for their children; professionals and community members would combine their "partial knowledge" in determining the practice that best fits a particular context or situation.
3. Teaching would encourage people to speak openly about their differing views, while teacher "training" would be dialogic rather than unidirectional.
4. There would be a recognition that practices could differ, depending on the values and beliefs of those involved.
5. Bridges would be built among homes, early education settings, and schools; educators would strive to devise culturally responsive pedagogy, and/or work actively to affirm both the culture of the school and the culture of origin.
6. The field of early childhood education would adopt a broad conception of practice, one which incorporated efforts to change policies that stratify and exclude.
7. Recognizing that the most basic changes needed to assist traditionally disadvantaged children and families are those that mitigate some of the most negative effects of a capitalist economic system, the over-arching early education agenda would involve efforts to effect profound structural change, specifically anti-discrimination and redistributive policies, such as a national health care plan, free pre- and postnatal care, universal immunization, job training for work that pays more than a minimum wage, parental leave and sick leave for all working parents, and full-day Head Start or day care on a sliding fee scale.

Early childhood educators are now working to transform assessment procedures and to change retention policies (e.g., Meisels, 1992), and the Children's Defense Fund and many early education professionals have campaigned actively for redistributive reforms. An expanded mandate thus serves to include efforts to restructure schooling and to redistribute income in a coherent agenda grounded broadly in democratic principles and enacted through democratic decision making.

Arguing that "curricula embody different *versions* of what is appropriate and good as well as different visions of how we, as a people, should live together in the future" (p. 137), Kessler (1991a) dismisses the notion of "development" because of its historic bias:

> Applying an ethical criterion to the metaphor . . . when the development of a relatively privileged segment of the population is used as the standard, leads one to conclude that this orientation toward curriculum results in ways of viewing students that foster a "deficit" perspective relative to the development of women, children of the working poor, and people of color, whose development may differ. (pp. 142–143)

She offers the alternative metaphor "schooling for democracy," because it has the potential to include the voices of those frequently excluded. In Kessler's view, curriculum needs to be recognized as a political text, and an early childhood curriculum needs to embody and reflect broader social ideals.

Today early childhood educators and members of traditionally disadvantaged groups, face a dilemma rife with paradox: how to prepare children to live in a society that cries out for fundamental change. Should children be schooled in "mainstream" values and communicative strategies or maintain culturally distinctive modes? How can "primary cultural" distinctions be separated from "secondary" ones that reflect a response to—or protest against—prejudice and injustice? How will we draw on the richness and diversity of our separate heritages to form a nation unified and strong? How can we re-create a society that Grubb and Lazerson (1982/88) describe as more in line with our espoused ideals, one "more egalitarian and less class-divided, a society that more nearly balances private interests with public responsibility, individual freedoms and collective decision making, liberalism, and democracy" (p. 296)?

The guidelines for developmentally appropriate practice are too narrowly conceived to adequately address such questions. It is time to move beyond the narrow confines of the environment paradigm and time to confront the irony of an idealized curricular approach that discourages critical reflection on—and fair and open dialogue about—practice. At issue is the question of whether cherished beliefs in pluralism and democracy will be manifest as rhetoric or as reality, a question of whether the distant voices of those too long silenced will be heard:

They told me my parents were wrong, their stories irrelevant. They told me to stop asking questions. They told me to stop putting the accent on my name. They told me to stop doing my math the way my father showed me. They told me that I should be more like the other boys and girls. They told me that my parents were wrong.
They never stopped to think that maybe they were wrong.

Mónica Byrne-Jiménez (1992, p. 18)

REFERENCES

Anyon, J. (1980). Social class and the hidden curriculum of work. *Journal of Education, 162,* 67–92.

Apple, M. (1992). The text and cultural politics. *Educational Researcher, 21* (7), 4–11.

Au, K., & Jordan, C. (1981). Teaching reading to Hawaiian children: Finding a culturally-appropriate solution. In H. Trueba, G. Guthrie, & K. Au (Eds.), *Culture and the bilingual classroom: Studies in classroom ethnography* (pp. 139–152). Rowley, MA: Newbury House.

Bernstein, B. (1961). Social class and linguistic development: A theory of social learning. In A. Halsey, J. Floud, & C. Anderson (Eds.), *Education, economy, and society* (pp. 288–314). New York: Free Press.

Bloom, A. (1987). *The closing of the American mind.* New York: Simon & Schuster.

Bloom, B. (1964). *Stability and change in human characteristics.* New York: John Wiley and Sons.

Bloom, B., Davis, A., & Hess, R. (1965). *Compensatory education for cultural deprivation.* New York: Holt, Rinehart, & Winston.

Bourdieu, P. (1977). Cultural reproduction and social reproduction. In J. Karabel & A. Halsey (Eds.), *Power and ideology in education* (pp. 487–511). New York: Oxford University Press.

Bourdieu, P., & Passeron, J. (1977). *Reproduction in education, society, and culture.* Beverly Hills, CA: Sage.

Bowles, S., & Gintis, H. (1976). *Schooling in capitalist America: Educational reform and the contradictions of economic life.* New York: Basic Books.

Bowman, B. (1992). Reaching potentials of minority children through developmentally and culturally appropriate programs. In S. Bredekamp & T. Rosegrant (Eds.), *Reaching potentials: Appropriate curriculum and assessment for young children* (Vol. 1, pp. 128–136). Washington, DC: National Association for the Education of Young Children.

Bredekamp, S. (Ed.). (1987). *Developmentally appropriate practice in early childhood programs serving children from birth through age 8.* Washington, DC: National Association for the Education of Young Children.

Bredekamp, S. (1991). Redeveloping early childhood education: A response to Kessler. *Early Childhood Research Quarterly, 6* (2), 199–210.

Bredekamp, S., & Rosegrant, T. (Eds.). (1992). *Reaching potentials: Appropriate curriculum and assessment for young children.* Washington, DC: National

Association for the Education of Young Children.

Bunce, V. (1990). The struggle for liberal democracy in Eastern Europe. *World Policy Journal, 395–430.*

Byrne-Jiménez, M. (1992, April). *Los solos: The education and experience of Latino children.* Unpublished master's thesis, The University of Michigan, Ann Arbor.

Calfee, R., Cazden, C., Duran, R., Griffin, M., Martus, M., & Willis, H. (1981). *Designing reading instruction for cultural minorities: The case of the Kamehameha Early Education Program.* Report to the Ford Foundation, New York.

Cazden, C., & Leggert, E. (1981). Culturally responsive education: Recommendations for achieving Lau remedies II. In H. Trueba et al. (Eds.), *Culture and the bilingual classroon: Studies in classroom ethnography* (pp. 71–86). Rowley, MA: Newbury House.

Delpit, L. (1988). The silenced dialogue: Power and pedagogy in educating other people's children. *Harvard Educational Review, 58* (3), 280–298.

Derman-Sparks, L. (1992). Reaching potentials through antibias, multicultural curriculum. In S. Bredekamp & T. Rosegrant (Eds.), *Reaching potentials: Appropriate curriculum and assessment for young children* (Vol. 1, pp. 114–127). Washington, DC: National Association for the Education of Young Children.

Erickson, F. (1986). Qualitative methods in research on teaching. In M. Wittrock (Ed.), *Handbook of Research on Teaching* (3rd ed., pp. 119–158). New York: Macmillan.

Everhart, R. (1983). *Reading, writing and resistance.* Boston: Routledge & Kegan Paul.

Florio, S., & Shulz, J. (1979). Social competence at home and at school. *Theory into Practice, 18,* 234–243.

Foucault, M. (1980). *Power/knowledge: Selected interviews and other writings 1972–1977.* New York: Pantheon Books.

Gee, J. (1990). *Social linguistics and literacies: Ideology in discourses.* London: The Falmer Press.

Giroux, H. (1983). Theories of reproduction and resistance in the new sociology of education. *Harvard Educational Review, 53,* 261–293.

Goodlad, J. (1981). *A place called school.* New York: McGraw-Hill.

Gray, S., & Klaus, R. (1965). An experimental preschool program for culturally deprived children. *Child Development, 36* (4), 887–898.

Greene, M. (1984). Excellence, meanings and multiplicity. *Teachers College Record, 86,* 283–297.

Grubb, N., & Lazerson, M. (1982/1988). *Broken promises: How Americans fail their children.* Chicago: The University of Chicago Press.

Heath, S. B. (1982). Questioning at home and at school: A comparative study. In G. Spindler (Ed.), *Doing the ethnography of schooling* (pp. 102–131). New York: Holt, Rinehart, & Winston.

Heath, S. B. (1983). *Ways with words: Language, life, and work in communities and classrooms.* Cambridge, England: Cambridge University Press.

Hirsch, E. D. (1988). *Cultural literacy: What every American needs to know.* New

York: Vintage Books.

Howard, A., & Scott, R. (1981). The study of minority groups in complex society. In R. Munroe, R. Munroe, & B. Whiting (Eds.), *Handbook of cross-cultural human development* (pp. 115–154). New York: Garland.

Hunt, J. M. (1961). *Intelligence and experience.* New York: Ronald Press.

Hunt, J. M. (1964). The psychological basis for using preschool enrichment as an antidote for cultural deprivation. *Merrill-Palmer Quarterly of Behavior and Development, 10* (3), 209–248.

Ingleby, D. (1986). Development in social context. In M. Richards & P. Light (Eds.) *Children of social worlds: Development in social context* (pp. 297–317). Cambridge, MA: Harvard University Press.

Jipson, J. (1991). Developmentally appropriate practice: Culture, curriculum, connections. *Early Education and Development, 2* (2), 120–136.

Kessler, S. (1991a). Early childhood education as development: Critique of the metaphor. *Early Education and Development, 2* (2), 137–152.

Kessler, S. (1991b). Alternative perspectives on early childhood education. *Early Childhood Research Quarterly, 6,* 183–197.

Kostelnik, M. (1992). Myths associated with developmentally appropriate practice. *Young Children, 47* (4), 17–25.

Kozol, J. (1991). *Savage inequalities: Children in America's schools.* New York: Crown Publishers.

Labov, W. (1982). Competing value systems in the inner-city schools. In P. Gilmore & A. Glatthorn (Eds.), *Children in and out of school: Ethnography and education* (pp. 148–171). Washington, DC: Center for Applied Linguistics.

Laosa, L. (1984). Social policies toward children of diverse ethnic, racial, and language groups in the United States. In H. Stevenson & A. Siegel (Eds.), *Child development: Research and social policy* (pp. 1–109). Chicago: University of Chicago Press.

Lareau, A. (1989). *Home advantage: Social class and parental intervention in elementary education.* London: Falmer Press.

Lareau, A. (1991, November). *'It's more covert today': The importance of race in shaping parents' view of the school.* Paper presented at the annual meetings of the American Anthropological Association.

Levenstein, P. (1970). Cognitive growth in preschoolers through verbal interaction with mothers. *American Journal of Orthopsychiatry, 40* (3), 426–432.

LeVine, R. (1984). Properties of culture: An ethnographic view. In R. Shweder & R. LeVine (Eds.), *Culture theory: Essays on mind, self, and emotion* (pp. 67–87). Cambridge, England: Cambridge University Press.

Lubeck, S. (1988). Nested contexts. In. L. Weis (Ed.), *Class, race and gender in American education* (pp. 43–62). Albany, NY: SUNY Press.

Margonis, F. (1992). The cooptation of "at risk": Paradoxes of policy criticism. *Teachers College Record. 94* (2), 343–364.

McDermott, R., & Gospodinoff, K. (1981). Social contexts for ethnic borders and school failure. In H. Trueba et al. (Eds.), *Culture and the bilingual classroom: Studies in classroom ethnography* (pp. 212–230). Rowley, MA: Newbury House.

Meisels, S. (1992). Doing harm by doing good: Iatrogenic effects of early child-
    hood enrollment and promotion policies. *Early Childhood Research Quar-
    terly, 7* (2), 155–174.
Minturn, L., & Lambert, W. (1964). *Mothers of six cultures: Antecedents of child
    rearing.* New York: John Wiley and Sons.
Moll, L., & Diaz, S. (1987). Change as the goal of educational research. *Anthro-
    pology and Education Quarterly, 18* (4), 300–311.
National Association for the Education of Young Children. (1986). Position state-
    ment on developmentally appropriate practice in programs for 4- and 5-year-
    olds. *Young Children, 41* (6), 20–29.
National Commission on Excellence in Education. (1983). *A nation at risk: The
    imperatives of educational reform.* Washington, DC: Department of Education.
Oakes, J. (1982). Classroom social relationships: Exploring the Bowles and Gin-
    tis hypothesis. *Sociology of Education, 55,* 197–212.
Oakes, J. (1985). *Keeping track: How schools structure inequality.* New Haven:
    Yale University Press.
Oakes, J. (1986). Tracking, inequality, and the rhetoric of school reform: Why
    schools don't change. *Journal of Education, 168,* 61–80.
Ogbu, J. (1978). *Minority education and caste.* New York: Academic Press.
Ogbu, J. (1981). *Schooling in the ghetto: An ecological perspective on community
    and home influences.* Washington, DC: National Institute of Education (ERIC
    #ED252270).
Ogbu, J. (1982). Cultural discontinuities and schooling. *Anthropology and Edu-
    cation Quarterly, 13* (4), 290–307.
Ogbu, J. (1987). Variability in minority school performance: A problem in search
    of an explanation. *Anthropology and Education Quarterly, 18,* 312–334.
Ogbu, J. (1988). Class stratification, racial stratification, and schooling. In L. Weis
    (Ed.), *Class, race, and gender in American education* (pp. 163–182). Albany,
    NY: SUNY Press.
Outhwaite, W. (1983). *Concept formation in social science.* London: Routledge &
    Kegan Paul.
Peshkin, A. (1992). The relationship between culture and curriculum: A many fit-
    ting thing. In P. Jackson (Ed.), *Handbook of research on curriculum* (pp.
    248–267). New York: Macmillan.
Philips, S. (1972). Participant structures and communicative competence: Warm
    Springs children in community and classroom. In C. Cazden, V. John, & D.
    Hymes (Eds.), *Functions of language in the classroom* (pp. 370–394).
    Prospect Heights, IL: Waveland Press.
Philips, S. (1983). *The invisible culture: Communication in classroom and com-
    munity on the Warm Springs Indian Reservation.* New York: Longman.
Pinar, W., & Bowers, C. (1992). Politics of curriculum: Origins, controversies, and
    significance of critical perspectives. *Review of Research in Education, 18,*
    163–190. Washington, DC: American Educational Research Association.
Rist, R. (1970). Student social class and teacher expectation. *Harvard Educa-
    tional Review, 40* (3), 411–450.
Schofield, J. (1982). *Black and white in school: Trust, tension, or tolerance?* New
    York: Praeger.

Shimahara, N. (1983). Polarized socialization in an urban high school. *Anthropology and Education Quarterly, 14,* 109–130.

Soto, L. (1991). Understanding bilingual/bicultural young children. *Young Children, 46* (2), 30–36.

Spodek, B. (1988). Conceptualizing today's kindergarten curriculum. *The Elementary School Journal, 89,* 203–211.

Tharp, R., & Gallimore, R. (1988–1991). *Rousing minds to life: Teaching, learning and schooling in social context.* Cambridge, England: Cambridge University Press.

U.S. Bureau of the Census. (1989). *The Hispanic population in the United States: March 1988 (final report).* Washington, DC: U.S. Government Printing Office.

Walsh, D. (1991). Extending the discourse on developmental appropriateness: A developmental perspective. *Early education and development, 2* (2), 109–119.

Wax, M., & Wax, R. (1971). Great tradition, little tradition, and formal education. In M. Wax, S. Diamond, & F. Gearing (Eds.), *Anthropological perspectives on education* (pp. 3–18). New York: Basic Books.

Whiting, B., & Edwards, C. (1988). *Children of different worlds.* Cambridge, MA: Harvard University Press.

Whiting, B., & Whiting, J. (1975). *Children of six cultures.* Cambridge, MA: Harvard University Press.

Wilcox, K. (1982). Differential socialization in the classroom: Implications for equal opportunity. In G. Spindler (Ed.), *Doing the ethnography of schooling* (pp. 268–309). New York: Holt, Rinehart, & Winston.

Willis, P. (1977). *Learning to labor: How working class kids get working class jobs.* New York: Columbia University Press.

Willis, P. (1981). Cultural production is different from cultural reproduction is different from social reproduction is different from reproduction. *Interchange, 12* (2–3), 48–67.

Wolf, L. (1992). Reaching potentials through bilingual education. In S. Bredekamp and T. Rosegrant (Eds.), *Reaching potentials: Appropriate curriculum and assessment for young children* (Vol. 1, pp. 139–144). Washington, DC: National Association for the Education of Young Children.

2

• • • • • •

Inclusive Policy, Practice, and Theory for Young Children with Developmental Differences

BRUCE L. MALLORY

The emergence of the discipline of early childhood special education over the past 25 years has been marked by both consensus and controversy. For those of us involved in the birth and development of this new field, we have seen enormous changes in the ways young children with developmental differences are treated in society at large and within the various learning environments in which they spend much of their time. While these changes have been discontinuous and uneven with respect to quality and distribution, we can nevertheless find steady progress that has led to improved lives for young children and their families. There have been several factors contributing both to the discontinuities and to the steady progress. In this chapter, those factors and their interrelationships will be discussed, and a convergent model for a more inclusive approach to developmentally appropriate practices for young children with special needs will be described.

HISTORICAL CHANGES IN
POLICY, THEORY, RESEARCH, AND PRACTICE

Change in educational practice is typically due to multiple factors converging within a particular historical context. In the case of the field of early childhood special education, a number of developments have occurred in the past three decades that have brought us to the present emphasis on inclusive practices. These developments are related to changes in social values, social policy, theoretical perspectives, research methodologies and findings, and practical applications of the expanding knowledge base. The evolution of these contributing factors may be characterized as transactional, that is, they influenced each other, and were interdependent, over time.

Core Social Values

Beginning with the War on Poverty and the civil rights movement of the early to mid 1960s, two major social values have emerged that support inclusive practices for young children with developmental differences. The first of these is the underlying constitutional and ethical commitment to equal opportunity for all citizens. *Brown v. Board of Education* (1954), and the many consequent court decisions and legislative actions that nullified the traditional "separate but equal" doctrine, firmly established the concepts of equal opportunity and equal access for previously disenfranchised citizens as core values, in fact inalienable rights, in our society. The initial application of these values to African-Americans was soon extended to other minority groups, women, and, more recently, Americans with disabilities. While there have been various practical means used to achieve the principles of equal opportunity and access (referred to as compensatory, remedial, affirmative, and so forth), the aim of social policy has been to redress the inequities associated with living on the margins of the core culture, or being excluded entirely.

One of the central characteristics of social welfare policy in the early stages of this movement was a concern with reducing "cultural disadvantage." The guiding assumption seemed to be that children belonging to minority groups were inherently disadvantaged, or deprived, in comparison to children growing up in white, middle-class families. This generalization had obvious stigmatizing consequences. While efforts were made in later years to emphasize *economic* disadvantage rather than *cultural,* in order to reduce the judgmental aspects of the latter, the notion of "bootstrapping" minorities into mainstream culture remains an implicit goal in social policy (e.g., note the ongoing debate about bilingual versus English-only education for children with limited English proficiency [Wong-Fillmore, 1991]).

The notion of *cultural* disadvantage also has implications for the field of special education, where the claim has been made that children with disabilities lack the social competence and adaptive behaviors necessary for acceptance into the mainstream or core culture. Often, a child's disability is directly related to the demands of social discourse, as is the case with hearing impairments, speech and language impairments (the most common diagnosis among children below school age [Mallory & Kerns,

1988]), and affective disorders such as autism. When a child is unable to participate in the natural flow of conversation due to sensory, motor, cognitive, or social-emotional impairments, this has powerful effects on the ability to become a fully integrated member of the community.

As Gliedman and Roth (1980) have noted, individuals with disabilities are an "unexpected minority" and are subject to prejudice and exclusion in forms that are similar to those experienced by individuals from racial and ethnic minorities. Consequently, much of special education curriculum is intended to teach "socially acceptable" or "adaptive" behaviors in order to foster full integration into the core (behavioral) culture. In this way, the ideal of equal opportunity can be realized for those who had been previously excluded because they lacked the physical or behavioral wherewithal.

The second value associated with the War on Poverty was known as the principle of "maximum feasible participation" and became a guiding tenet of the community action arm of anti-poverty legislation. The goal of maximum feasible participation is to include the beneficiaries of social action programs in decisions about their design and operation. Its contemporary moniker is "empowerment." The expression of this value is manifest when program participants are enlisted as volunteer board members or paid staff members in order to include the perspectives of intended recipients and to improve their career opportunities. The Head Start Policy Councils, with their mandated parent majorities, are a prime example. Subsequently, the consumer rights movement of the 1970s and 1980s built upon this concept, resulting in the strong emphasis in special education legislation on parent participation in decision making, to the point of guaranteeing due process to parents who believe that the rights of their disabled children are being abrogated.

These two core values—equal opportunity and maximum feasible participation—have served as a foundation for our contemporary commitment to full inclusion in society for people with disabilities. In this perspective, people with disabilities have a constitutional right to unfettered participation in all social institutions, and their voices are to be paramount in decisions affecting their lives. This view extends to all people with disabilities, from the newborn infant in the intensive care unit (whose parents assume the role of consumer advocate) to the adult who has a right to live out his or her life in socially valued and meaningful roles.

Social Policies and Young Children with Special Needs

The values described above have been articulated in various social policies enacted since the 1960s which focus on children with educational disabilities. In 1968, Congress passed the Handicapped Children's Early Education Act (HCEEA; PL 90-583), that created a national "First Chance Network" to support innovative programming, parent involvement, program replication, systematic evaluation, and local adoption after a federally-funded demonstration period (DeWeerd, 1981). Built into this legislation was a desire to create planned variation models that could illustrate the most cost efficient and effective ways to improve the development of young children with disabilities and those who were deemed to be "at risk" for school failure.

Simultaneous with the implementation of the HCEEA, Congress funded the Head Start Planned Variation initiative. This was another systematic effort to compare various models of early education for children from economically disadvantaged backgrounds who were assumed to be likely candidates for school failure. While the results of the Head Start Planned Variation models were mixed (Datta, 1975), a number of diverse service delivery approaches emerged that remain part of Head Start and its offshoots (e.g. Home Start, Healthy Start, Even Start).

In the early 1970s, Congress amended the Head Start legislation to require that 10% of program enrollments consist of children with diagnosed handicapping conditions (PL 92-924 and PL 93-644). While such children had not been excluded from Head Start previously, this step signified a conscious effort to integrate young children with special needs, particularly those with severe disabilities who had traditionally not been served in Head Start classrooms (Allen, 1984). One consequence of this action was to concentrate in a national early childhood program children from families with the lowest socioeconomic status and children with severe disabilities. It may not be too harsh to suggest that one effect of this policy has been to "ghettoize" low income and disabled children, especially when we consider that two thirds of Head Start children are members of racial and ethnic minorities.

The landmark federal special education legislation enacted in 1975, known as PL 94-142, gave the strongest support to date for achieving the goal of integrating children with disabilities. As Allen (1984) noted, "A free, appropriate education in the least restrictive environment became, at long last, the right of every handicapped child" (p.13). However, Cohen, Semmes, and Guralnick (1979) observed that PL 94-142 contained a "flawed mandate" in that it did not require states to serve children below 6 years old. This choice was left to the discretion of each state. The result was an uneven distribution of preschool special education services, so that by 1987, 40 states mandated services to children between 3 and 5 (7 of which extended that mandate down to birth or the initial diagnosis [Garwood, 1987; Mallory & Kerns, 1988]).

This flaw was corrected, at least partially, with the passage of PL 99-457 in 1986. Under the new legislation, all states are required to serve children with diagnosed disabilities as well as children who are "delayed" or "at-risk for delay" between the ages of 3 and 21 (each state may still determine the definition of "delay" and may decide whether or not to include "at-risk" preschoolers in the eligible population). In addition, the law authorizes expenditures for services to children from birth through 2 years who have conditions likely to lead to developmental and educational disabilities (with individual states again having the option to participate in this aspect of the legislation, known as "Part H").

PL 99-457 is also noteworthy because it strengthens the "maximum feasible participation" concept by requiring that services for children below 3 years old be broad enough to address family needs and goals. Rather than developing an Individual Education Plan (IEP), required for children from 3 to 21, program staff, in consultation with family members, must write an Individual Family Service Plan (IFSP) that is based on social support needs identified by parents, who are the primary caregivers for young children with special needs. Thus, parents are given greater authority and choice in the provision of early intervention services. PL 102-119, adopted in 1991, extended family-centered services to older children by allowing Individual Family Service Plans, rather than IEP's, for the 3- to 6-year-old population, at local or state discretion.

Beginning with PL 94-142 and continuing to the present, a core requirement of federal and state policy has been the mandate that *appropriate* educational services be provided in the least restrictive settings. This early use of the term appropriate with reference to special education helped create a context for its use by the National Association for the Education of Young Children (NAEYC) in the late 1980s. However, soon after the federal law took effect in 1978, considerable litigation occurred over the interpretation of what is "appropriate" for any given child. Often, courts were asked to adjudicate disputes over what was "appropriate" versus what was "restrictive." In some cases, public school personnel argued that individually appropriate services could only be provided in a setting other than the mainstream, due to the particular nature and severity of a child's disability. Courts generally sustained this argument, and opted for appropriateness over greater integration, when forced to make a choice. Thus, a precedent has been established that exclusionary practices may be justified when a beneficial service can only be provided outside of the mainstream. This precedent hardly settles the debate; it only exacerbates the tension created when the multiple goals of equal opportunity, remedial or compensatory education, and individualized instruction are simultaneously embraced.

PL 99-457 continues to emphasize the provision of services in least restrictive environments. But the evidence so far is that states are interpreting this concept quite conservatively. Burton, Hains, Hanline, McLean, and McCormick (1992) write,

> The policy changes achieved under the law thus far appear somewhat circumscribed as compared to the original congressional intent. . . . Many states have met the letter of the law by providing preschool services to 3- to 5-year-olds with special needs, yet stopped short of the law's spirit in relation to such issues as family involvement, least restrictive environment, and noncategorical labeling (Division for Early Childhood, 1987). For instance, some states authorize only self-contained ECSE programs in public schools, thereby meeting the least restrictive environment requirement but missing opportunities to build upon existing community or school-based early childhood programs. (pp. 55–56)

Theoretical Perspectives

Paralleling the evolution of social policy since the 1960s, there have been a number of theoretical paradigms affecting practice in the field of early childhood special education. These paradigms have been sometimes competitive, sometimes conflicting, and other times complementary. They include maturational models associated with early writers such as Rousseau and more recently with Gesell and his followers; behavioral models developed by Watson, Skinner, Bijou, Englemann, and others; cognitive-developmental models articulated by Piaget, Vygotsky, Bruner, Kagan, and others; and ecological models proposed by Bronfenbrenner, Hobbs, Cochran, and Dunst.

These various perspectives have at times been viewed as mutually exclusive, particularly when applied to different populations of young children. That is, it is assumed that different "treatments" should be applied to children with different characteristics, especially if their development deviates from what is defined as the norm. Typically developing, middle-class preschoolers are expected to thrive in an environment that is non-intrusive and allows expression of individual differences (the maturational or romantic environment). Young children who have experienced social disadvantage or developmental impairments are more likely to be exposed to behavioral interventions (for example, Englemann's [1969] DISTAR curriculum). Recent claims about best practices, however, suggest the need to reconceptualize these models in order to generate more inclusive theory and practice, based on both integrated theory and new paradigms of development and early intervention (Berkeley & Ludlow, 1989; Dunst et al., 1987; Mallory, 1992; McDonnell & Hardman, 1988). A fundamental question is whether diverse theoretical models should be seen as competing with one another, which requires that they be viewed as discrete and mutually exclusive; or, whether they should be seen as potentially complementary, so that particular approaches based on particular theories are viewed as options from which to choose, depending on the characteristics of individual children and the circumstances in which they exist.

Another strategy in the search for inclusive practice would be to articulate the overlapping constructs of existing theories in order to develop a more cohesive approach to enhancing the development of young children with disabilities. This could lead to a more convergent paradigm. The attraction of such an approach is that it would reflect the aim of inclusive education—convergent theory would undergird inclusive practices. There is a fidelity in such a model that should be explored for its usefulness. The convergence of theories that have traditionally been viewed as discrete and competing will be addressed more fully in the second half of this chapter, and is also examined in chapter 5 by Ludlow and Berkeley. In any case, the value of either existing theoretical models, or convergent ones, requires empirical analysis in order to understand the effectiveness of our current and future efforts.

Empirical Understanding of Inclusive Early Education

The theoretical frameworks referred to above, as well as the evolution of social policy, have stimulated a significant number of empirical studies concerned with the efficacy of early education for children with disabilities or who are believed likely to experience school failure. These studies have also been concerned with finding effective means for integrating typical and atypical children in early childhood programs. It is beyond the scope of this chapter to review even a representative sample of those studies. However, three general categories of research will be summarized to cast light on our contemporary understanding of inclusive early education.

RESEARCH ON PLANNED VARIATIONS. One of the largest and most comprehensive longitudinal studies of early intervention for preschool children with poor developmental prognoses was the Developmental Continuity Consortium study (Lazar & Darlington, 1979), which examined the effects of 12 different preschool models over a period of a decade and a half. The models served children from 3 months to 5 years old in both center and home-based environments, for periods ranging from 1 to 5 years. The children served were primarily from low-income families, were African American (92%), and had undereducated parents (mothers averaged 10 1/2 years of schooling); 36.4% of the children were in father-absent homes; and a majority had three or more siblings. Mean measured IQ at the time of program entry was 89.82 (n = 820). In general, the enrolled children did not have diagnosed disabilities. That is, they were identified as "delayed" or "at-risk" children, to use today's parlance, rather than disabled.

What is most important about the Consortium's work for the present discussion is the use of diverse curriculum models in an attempt to find those theoretical and practical approaches that would make the most difference for this population of young children. The Consortium was an example of "planned variation" on a large scale, and seemed to be an opportunity to discover what works best with children living in circumscribed environments. It was assumed that the ability to detect positive changes in such children as a result of early intervention, and to link those changes to specific curriculum models, would have important implications for improving the early childhood knowledge base and for designing more effective social policies.

As it turns out, claims about child outcomes based on precise distinctions among curriculum models are hard to make. There are simply too many confounding factors, and our evaluation technologies, especially during the period of the Consortium's studies, have been too limited to serve as the basis for drawing such conclusions. In reviewing the Consortium studies and other similar investigations, Farran (1990) writes,

> It is currently popular to argue that studies such as those just reviewed provide strong evidence for the value of early intervention for children who are disadvantaged by poverty and/or social disorganization. . . . In truth, there is little support for statements that are either so absolute, so long term, or so inclusive regarding the effects of early intervention. Available data suggest a range of potential benefits from carefully planned and well-implemented early intervention efforts. (p. 512)

On the other hand, general statements about the outcomes of early intervention with low-income, minority children who are regarded as likely candidates for school-age special education can be made. While long-lasting *cognitive* differences were not found for target children, there were *performance* and *social indicator* differences. For example, participating children were significantly less likely to be retained in elementary school, less likely to be placed in special education programs, and more likely to graduate from high school.

> The consortium studies suggested that even if measured intelligence gains declined as children progressed in elementary school, behavioral manifestations of cognitive ability and attitude indicated important and positive effects of program participation. (Hobbs et al., 1984, p. 104)

Perhaps the most important lesson learned as a result of the Consortium work was the finding that parent-focused programs were more likely to produce long-term gains than child-focused programs. High parent involvement was correlated strongly with positive outcomes for children's cognitive and behavioral development. And, programs that involved parents as educators of their own children and in other roles as decision makers and active participants were more cost effective (Hobbs et al., 1984). The timing of these findings was crucial. In the 15 years since their release, additional research and practice have confirmed the necessity of working with families in the delivery of early intervention services. Thus, by this point in our history, the value of family-based services, with both "high risk" and disabled young children, has been well established (Bronfenbrenner, 1974; Dunst, Trivette, & Deal, 1988; Thurman & Widerstrom, 1990).

METAEVALUATIONS OF RESEARCH ON EARLY INTERVENTION. If the 1970s was the era of planned variations and longitudinal studies of programs for disadvantaged children, the 1980s was the era of program implementation and evaluation for children with diagnosed disabilities. However, comparability across studies is even more problematic in this arena, given the tremendous variability among subjects, program sites, assessment and curriculum approaches, and intended outcomes (Meisels, 1985). The controversies surrounding the work of metaevaluation specialists at the Utah State University Early Intervention Research Institute illustrate this difficulty. When the Institute reported, based on pooled analyses of 447 studies, minimal cognitive gains for disabled children, and no significant differences when parents are involved or not involved (e.g., Castro & Mastropieri, 1986), the reaction from the early intervention community was predictable. Critics were later mollified when Shonkoff and Hauser-Cram (1987) conducted a separate analysis and found significant effects for family involvement and earlier program entry for children less than 3 years old and with less severe biological impairments (Farran, 1990).

In a recent review of 42 projects serving preschool children with disabilities (Farran, 1990), the overall summary reached was "that precise solutions for the most appropriate form of intervention for children with disabilities have not been found" (p. 530). Because of the weak evaluation methodologies used, variability in program quality, and the heterogeneous nature of the children, families, and staff involved, general conclusions are difficult to glean.

Little information is available in these studies that would support focusing intervention on any one of the approaches tried over the others. As

Simeonsson (1985) pointed out, the enthusiasm of proponents for one type of intervention or another is not matched by data supporting their efforts. (Farran, 1990, p. 530)

RESEARCH ON EFFECTIVE MEANS TO PROMOTE SOCIAL INTEGRATION. The third area of empirical inquiry to be discussed here is the work exemplified by Guralnick, Strain, Odom, and many other contemporary investigators concerning effective ways to promote positive social interactions among typical and atypical preschool children. In a recent review of this body of work, Demchak and Drinkwater (1992) identify the key variables for successful integration. These include adequate preparation of classroom teachers and support staff (both attitudinal and practical training), appropriate modification of the physical environment and the use of nonintrusive materials that elicit peer interactions, teaching nonhandicapped peers to respond to and reinforce social interactions with their disabled counterparts, and focusing intervention on social-communicative exchanges through skill enhancement in children with disabilities (Dunst et al., 1987; Strain, 1984).

Demchak and Drinkwater (1992) make an important point with respect to program evaluation models when social integration is a primary goal. When designing intended outcomes for early intervention programs, factors other than cognitive competence must be included. Reminiscent of the earlier critiques of overly narrow outcome measures, it is argued that:

> Evaluation efforts should be expanded to include the impact of integration on children's self-esteem, on nonhandicapped children's acceptance, and on participation in life experiences (Campbell, 1991). Inclusion of these additional variables mirrors the current holistic emphasis in education of children with special needs. Examination of other relevant factors that define successful integration efforts are as equally important as noting progress in development of children with disabilities. (p. 77)

SUMMARY. Empirical studies have focused on the effectiveness of diverse intervention approaches for young children living in conditions of environmental risk, on the pooled results of efficacy studies that cut across child and context variables, and on the enhancement of social interactions (as well as other areas of inquiry not described here). In light of the methodological problems raised by the critics, should we conclude that early intervention does not make a difference for young children and their families? Of course not. The lesson, rather, is that we do not yet know enough about what does work, with what groups of children, under what circumstances, to claim that a particular theoretical or pedagogical method is the one right system. And we are still trying to determine what our outcome questions should be in the first place. This is not a disappointing or discouraging situation. It allows for continued diversity of approaches, accompanied by careful, systematic evaluation of effects, over time. We certainly know enough about development and family systems and the effects of both nature and nurture to give some guidance. We know that programs that focus only on children are not as likely to make a difference. We know that programs that measure only cognitive gains, and aim their interventions only at cognitive skills, are not likely to show dramatic differences. We know that high quality, sustained efforts based on our best understandings of both child development and social conditions will make a difference in important areas such as school success and later achievement. However, continuing confusion over the fundamental theoretical premises of early intervention and the design of evaluation methodologies that are socially and ecologically valid requires that we examine the basic assumptions and theories that underlie programs for young children with developmental disabilities or delays.

A CONVERGENT THEORETICAL MODEL FOR EARLY CHILDHOOD SPECIAL EDUCATION

In light of the core values, social policies, theoretical frameworks, and empirical studies described above, how can we improve services without continuing to operate from an overly narrow knowledge base or simply throwing up our hands and claiming that anything goes? One approach is to continue the kind of planned as well as de facto variation that has characterized the field of early childhood special education for the past two decades. Such a strategy would allow us to test different theoretical and empirical models of intervention with particular groups of children, defined for, example, by age, diagnosis, geographic location, or socioeconomic status. That is, *pluralistic* notions of treatment and outcome would hold sway.

An alternative approach would be to find the *common* aspects of existing models and then derive a *convergent* set of principles in order to expand the present conceptualization of appropriate practices in early childhood education. The intent of this approach is to create theoretical congruence or fidelity between what we believe and what we do. That is, if our aim is to create inclusive practices and policies, then one means to that end is to create more holistic, encompassing theory to guide those practices and policies.

There is an inherent dilemma in this that should be acknowledged.

Shouldn't programs for diverse children draw upon diverse theoretical and practical frameworks? Isn't it a violation of the ideological values of democracy and diversity to suggest that a more unified, overarching model be applied regardless of diagnostic category or some other child-specific trait? These are legitimate concerns. But I believe that experience has shown that previous reliance on multiple (even competing) approaches, based on child-specific characteristics and narrow conceptions of "typical" development, has led to inconclusive evidence of efficacy and has perpetuated the exclusionary practices that young children with disabilities have been exposed to so frequently. If early education programs could be guided by inclusive theory, they might be more apt to engage in inclusive practices. If in the past we have judged that some children do not "fit" in particular early childhood settings, perhaps it is time to expand the parameters within which those settings operate in order to assure that there is room for everyone.

An inclusionary, or convergent, paradigm of appropriate practice in early childhood education draws upon developmental-interactionist, functional (historically referred to as behavioral), and biogenetic models of human growth and change. Each of these models will be summarized below, and convergent principles will be suggested.

Current Models of Growth and Change

The developmental-interactionist model characterizes the present definition of "developmentally appropriate practice" (Bredekamp, 1987). The DAP guidelines focus on curriculum, adult-child interactions, and relations between home and program. Cutting across each of these concerns is a commitment to age appropriateness and individual appropriateness, themes that also appear in the functional and biogenetic models (the latter also emphasizes the concept of "maturationally appropriate"). Also of central importance is the role of play. "Child-initiated, child-directed, and teacher-supported play is an essential component" of DAP (Bredekamp, 1987, p. 3). The primary theoretical framework that undergirds this model is cognitive-developmental theory associated with the work of Piaget and Bruner, among others. Terms used to describe this approach might include *holistic, interactive, concrete, responsive, choice-driven, contingent, error-inclusive,* and *emotionally supportive.* The primary goal of the model is to move children into higher levels of development, enabling them to become increasingly independent (decentered) in their thinking, social skills, and physical abilities. Assessment is often concerned with the achievement of cognitive and linguistic milestones, using normative criteria for interindividual comparisons. Bidell (1992) has referred to this perspective as the "ladder-of-progress" metaphor which comes from earlier evolutionary and historiographic theories. Development is linear, progressive, and cumulative.

The functional model shares some of these attributes (including age and individual appropriateness) and departs on others. The emphases on systematic or direct instruction, error-free learning, instilling adaptive behaviors, and designing curricula to match specific social contexts and the behaviors needed to negotiate those contexts are departures from the developmental-interactionist model. The functional model has been central to special education in general, and often has provided a basis for practice in early childhood special education (Graham & Bryant, 1993).

An example of the differences between the developmental-interactionist and functional models is found in the use of the term "domain." In the former, domain refers to the areas of cognition, communication, social-emotional skills, and motor ability. In the latter, domain refers to the general settings in which different tasks are performed—domestic, leisure/recreation, community, and vocational (Snell, 1987). Note that the latter three of these are settings into which young children gradually move, depending on cultural and chronological expectations. Much of young children's early experience centers on domestic settings and activities, even when they are in out-of-home programs. This difference in the definition of domain reflects an underlying difference in epistemology. The developmental-interactionist model emphasizes the internal processes associated with individual maturation and development, processes subject to both genetic and experiential factors. The functional model, with its roots in behavioral theories, emphasizes the external cues and contingencies that shape a child's repertoire of skills. It is the power of these external forces that most affects a child's competence. The more severe a child's disability, the more powerful and carefully planned these external forces must be.

The biogenetic model is the third leg of the stool. The history of this model precedes that of the developmental-interactionist and functional approaches. Since Darwin and Galton described individual variations and they and their peers analyzed the interplay of ontogeny and phylogeny, biogenetic explanations for development and behavior have played a central role in human science. As medical technology allowed premature and sick newborns to survive, beginning in the early part of this century, the foundation was laid for a biogenetic or maturational perspective. The early influence of the Darwinian paradigm is reflected in the emphasis on adaptation (or homeostasis) that has become the central focus of this model. The primary concern is with the biogenetic status of the young child as she or he adapts and responds to environmental stimuli. This adaptation is manifested, for example, in the ability of the young child to acquire stable and regular states of sleep, arousal, and wakefulness. As the child grows, innate characteristics such as activity level (metabolism), temperament, and drives for arousal, satisfaction, and social interaction supersede earlier sensorimotor responses. Primitive, involuntary reflexes are replaced by voluntary and increasingly differentiated movements that parallel cognitive and linguistic maturation. Appropriate and varied stimuli are needed for central nervous system development, and are associated with dendritic expansion in the cortex. Individual differences in rates and quality of development are attributed to constitutional rather than environmental factors, especially if those differences persist through the preschool years (Korner, 1971, 1989; Korner et al., 1985). Thus, this model has been applied particularly to premature and low birth weight infants, and has affected practices in newborn nurseries and early intervention programs for infants and toddlers with developmental disabilities and chronic illness.

A Triangulated Model

These three perspectives evolved separately and have been applied differentially depending on the nature of the children being served and the training of the professionals working with those children. But it is possible to think of them as complementary rather than mutually exclusive. It has been argued (Mallory, 1992) that the three models share common attributes. These include an emphasis on independent mastery of tasks, adaptation to environmental demands, the value of a contingently responsive social context, the aim of achieving social competence in young children, and a concern for individualized intervention. These commonalities provide conceptual bridges across what have been seen as discrete models.

In addition, the models are related in a "nested" fashion to each other. At the first level, the biogenetic model of growth and maturation articulates necessary prerequisites in terms of the basic ability of the infant and young child to maintain some constitutional stability, stamina, and adaptability to environmental demands. Without these building blocks for later growth, successful development will be retarded. Next, the developmental-interactionist model is concerned with the ways in which the basic biogenetic attributes of a child are expressed in the form of cognitive, communicative, motoric, and psychosocial qualities. The expression of these qualities depends on characteristics of the social and material environment and the quality of the child's interaction with those characteristics. Finally, the functional model encompasses the specific and discrete behaviors that are expressed as a result of physical, social, and intellectual development. Put simply, biogenetic factors prepare the child for coping with the world, developmental factors mediate the child's understanding of that world, and functional abilities enable the child to succeed in varying and increasingly complex social environments.

Such a "trialectic" allows for a broader understanding of children's needs, and ways to meet those needs, than the narrow theoretical and pedagogical assumptions found in the present definitions of DAP. This broader understanding is necessary when children with atypical characteristics are served in an early childhood setting. The DAP guidelines assume a fairly narrow range of variability in children, and therefore a fairly narrow range of appropriate teaching practices. (These shortcomings are already being addressed, at least partially, in NAEYC's recent review of appropriate curriculum and assessment practices [Bredekamp & Rosegrant, 1992].) Children who have seizure disorders, sensory or motor impairments, limited communicative abilities, or unpredictable, impulsive behavior need greater support than those who do not. This support comes in the form of more direct teacher intervention (modeling, prompting, reinforcing), more direct environmental cues (clearer choices, close-ended as well as open-ended problem solving, fewer distracters, peer modeling), and more direct physical intervention (positioning, guided assistance, adapted furniture and toys, directed lighting). The addition of these kinds of approaches to the present conception of developmentally appropriate practice would make the model itself more inclusive, and therefore would help practitioners to create more inclusive early childhood settings.

CONCLUSION

Significant and substantial changes have occurred in the field of early childhood education over the past 30 years. These changes have been related to social policies (which have reflected fundamental political and cultural values), empirical research, and the emergence of new theoretical paradigms. The discipline of early childhood special education is one result of these historical developments. In light of these changes, there is a need for an expanded conceptualization of developmentally appropriate practice that can accommodate the particular characteristics and needs of young children experiencing developmental difficulties. This expanded understanding must be based on the essential ethic of inclusion. Inclusion refers to theoretical, social, and curricular means for assuring that all children are fully accepted members of the learning communities in which they participate.

The value of inclusion is supported by our constitutional and legislative guarantees for equal opportunity and access to resources for all citizens, regardless of economic status, ethnicity, gender, or abilities. Supporting these values, and making their realization more likely, is the principle of "maximum feasible participation." The full and meaningful participation of all people affected by social welfare programs as policy makers and informed consumers has become a central feature of public initiatives to enfranchise people who have been marginalized in our society. Such participation is seen as a means to sustain diversity while encouraging democratic solutions to common problems.

Social policy efforts have reflected these values, particularly with respect to children with educational disabilities. There have been increasing efforts to extend special education services to very young children, and to include their families as both recipients and equal partners in service delivery. Although the ideal of full inclusion has yet to be achieved, social policies continue to emphasize least restrictive services in order to increase opportunities for children to succeed in mainstream social contexts.

Given an evolving empirical knowledge base, there is a need to use what we already know and then design new forms of early intervention that build on current and emerging developmental, cultural, and behavioral models. A convergent or triangulated theoretical framework was suggested as the basis for high quality early childhood programs. Drawing on principles of biogenetic maturation, developmental-interactionist theory, and functional learning, this framework allows teachers and administrators to plan programs that can meet the needs of a diverse population. In turn, improved programs will generate new empirical information that can lead to refined theory and responsive social policy. The recognition of this transactional relationship between values, policy, theory, and practice will make a significant contribution to our ability to do what is right for *all* young children and their families.

REFERENCES

Allen, K. E. (1984). Federal legislation and young handicapped children. *Topics in Early Childhood Special Education, 4* (1), 9–18.

Berkeley, T. R., & Ludlow, B. L. (1989). Toward a reconceptualization of the developmental model. *Topics in Early Childhood Special Education, 9* (3), 51–66.

Biddell, T. R. (1992). The constructive web: Diversifying conceptions of development. *Paper presented at the annual meeting of the Jean Piaget Society,* Montreal, Quebec.

Bredekamp, S. (1987). *Developmentally appropriate practice in early childhood programs serving children from birth through age 8.* Washington, DC: National Association for the Education of Young Children.

Bredekamp, S., & Rosegrant, T. (Eds.). (1992). *Reaching potentials: Appropriate curriculum and assessment for young children* (Vol. 1). Washington, DC: National Association for the Education of Young Children.

Bronfenbrenner, U. (1974). *Is early intervention effective? A report on longitudinal evaluations of preschool programs* (Vol. 2). Washington, DC: Office of Child Development, Department of Health, Education, and Welfare.

Brown v. Board of Education 347 U.S. 483, 74 S. Ct. 686, 98 L. Ed. 873, (1954).

Burton, C. B., Hains, A. H., Hanline, M. F., McLean, M., & McCormick, K. (1992). Early childhood intervention and education: The urgency of professional unification. *Topics in Early Childhood Special Education, 11* (4), 53–69.

Castro, G., & Mastropieri, M. (1986). The efficacy of early intervention programs: A meta-analysis. *Exceptional Children, 52,* 417–424.

Cohen, S., Semmes, M., & Guralnick, J. J. (1979). Public law 94-142 and the education of preschool handicapped children. *Exceptional Children, 45* (4), 279–285.

Datta, L. E. (1975). Design of the Head Start planned variation experiment. In A. M. Rivlin & M. P. Timpane (Eds.), *Planned variation in education: Should we give up or try harder?* Washington, DC: Brookings Institution.

Demchak, M., & Drinkwater, S. (1992). Preschoolers with severe disabilities: The case against segregation. *Topics in Early Childhood Special Education, 11* (4), 70–83.

DeWeerd, J. (1981). Early education services for children with handicaps—Where have we been, where are we now, and where are we going? *Journal of the Division for Early Childhood, 2,* 15–24.

Dunst, C. J., Lesko, J. J., Holbert, K. A., Wilson, L. L., Sharpe, K. L., & Liles, R. F. (1987). A systemic approach to infant intervention. *Topics in Early Childhood Special Education, 7* (2), 19–37.

Dunst, C. J., Trivette, C. M., & Deal, A. G. (1988). *Enabling and empowering families: Principles of guidance for practice.* Cambridge, MA: Brookline Books.

Engleman, S. (1969). *Conceptual learning.* San Rafael, CA: Dimensions.

Farran, D. C. (1990). Effects of intervention with disadvantaged and disabled children: A decade review. In S. J. Meisels & J. P. Shonkoff (Eds.), *Handbook of early intervention* (pp. 501–539). Cambridge, England: Cambridge University Press.

Garwood, S. G. (1987). Political, economic, and practical issues affecting the development of universal early intervention programs for handicapped infants. *Topics in Early Childhood Special Education, 7* (2), 6–18.

Gleidman, J., & Roth, W. (1980). *The unexpected minority: Handicapped children in America.* New York: Harcourt, Brace, Jovanovich.

Graham, M. A., & Bryant, D. M. (1993). Developmentally appropriate environments for children with special needs. *Infants and Young Children, 5* (3), 31–42.

Hobbs, N., Dockecki, P. R., Hoover-Dempsey, K. V., Moroney, R. M., Shayne, M., & Weeks, K. H. (1984). *Strengthening families*. San Francisco: Jossey-Bass.

Korner, A. F. (1971). Individual differences at birth: Implications for early experience and later development. *American Journal of Orthopsychiatry, 1* (4), 608–619.

Korner, A. F. (1989). Infant stimulation: The pros and cons in historical perspective. *Zero to Three, 10* (2), 11–17.

Korner, A. F., Zeanah, C. H., Linden, J., Kraemer, H. C., Berkowitz, R. I., & Agras, W. S. (1985). Relation between neonatal and later activity and temperament. *Child Development, 56* (1), 38–42.

Lazar, I., & Darlington, R. (1979). *Lasting effects after preschool*. Washington, DC: U. S. Department of Health and Human Services.

Mallory, B. L. (1992). Is it always appropriate to be developmental? Convergent models for early intervention practice. *Topics in Early Childhood Special Education, 11* (4), 1–12.

Mallory, B. L., & Kerns, G. M. (1988). Consequences of categorical labeling of preschool children. *Topics in Early Childhood Special Education, 8* (3), 39–50.

McDonnell, A., & Hardman, M. (1988). A synthesis of "best practice" guidelines for early childhood services. *Journal of the Division for Early Childhood, 12* (4), 328–341.

Meisels, S. J. (1985). The efficacy of early intervention: Why are we still asking this question? *Topics in Early Childhood Special Education, 5,* 1–11.

PL 90-583, Handicapped Children's Early Education Assistance Act, 1968.

PL 92-924, Economic Opportunity Act Amendments, 1972.

PL 93-644 Economic Opportunity Act Amendments, 1974.

PL 94-142 Education for All Handicapped Children Act, 1975.

PL 99-457 Education of the Handicapped Act Amendments, 1986.

PL 102-119 Individuals with Disabilities Education Act Amendments, 1991.

Shonkoff, J. P., & Hauser-Cram, P. (1987). Early intervention for disabled infants and their families: A quantitative analysis. *Pediatrics, 80,* 650–658.

Simeonsson, R. (1985). Efficacy of early intervention: Issues and evidence. *Analysis and Intervention in Developmental Disabilities, 5,* 203–209.

Snell, M. (Ed.). (1987). *Systematic instruction of persons with severe handicaps* (3rd ed.). Columbus, OH: Merrill.

Strain, P. S. (1984). Efficacy research with young handicapped children: A critique of the status quo. *Journal of the Division for Early Childhood, 9,* 4–10. 32

Thurman, S. K., & Widerstrom, A. H. (1990). *Young children with special needs: A developmental and ecological approach* (2nd ed.). Newton, MA: Allyn & Bacon.

Wong-Fillmore, L. (1991). When learning a second language means losing a first. *Early Childhood Research Quarterly, 6* (3), 323–346.

PART II

Critical Perspectives on Theory

• • • • • •

In the four chapters of this section, the authors directly question the appropriateness of our almost exclusive reliance on the current child development knowledge base to inform sound early childhood pedagogy. The section begins and ends with critiques of the ethnocentric biases which currently characterize the discipline's depiction of appropriate adult caregiving behavior and optimal child development outcomes. Chapter 3 draws upon the field of cross-cultural child development research to identify specific examples of parent and teacher behavior as well as interpretations of children's development that are counter to those portrayed in child development texts and espoused in current views of developmentally appropriate practice. Drawing upon her observations of an exemplary early childhood program in Reggio Emilia, Italy, New argues for a revised conceptualization of the role of the teacher as collaborative researcher, utilizing interactions with parents and observations of children in classroom settings to assist in determining appropriate educational goals and practices.

In chapter 4 the theoretical and methodological paradigm associated with the study of parent-infant dyadic interactions is described as a tool for illustrating the relationship of individual differences to the social contexts of teaching and learning. McCollum and Bair identify a number of myths that characterize current efforts with young children with disabilities, and offer specific recommendations for appropriate practice with young children with disabilities based on the emerging research on the social contexts of early development and learning. In particular, they draw upon the theoretical construct of scaffolding to illustrate developmentally appropriate strategies of teaching and intervention for the special needs child.

The call for theoretical revision appears again in chapter 5, where Ludlow and Berkeley challenge the traditional depiction of normative child development as outmoded and inadequate. They propose a new theoretical view of development "that is holistic, dynamic, and transactional." Noting the need to adopt a more process-oriented view of development, the authors propose the salient response model as one viable alternative means to such a theoretical expansion. In particular, they highlight that theoretical model's ability to be utilized by professionals from a variety of disciplines as they attempt to identify and implement developmentally appropriate practices for young children with disabilities.

In chapter 6 Bowman and Stott continue the refrain of chapter 3, examining the role of current child development theory in the definition of DAP. They critique decontextualized views of development, noting that, for example, developmental milestones "take on their meaning only in the context of social life"; and the failure to include culture in sources of knowledge about children has compromised educational practice. The authors go on to propose a new conceptual framework for understanding the relationship between culture and development, and then describe how that framework might be applied in early childhood classrooms. They conclude their chapter—and this section—by reiterating the role of reflection in teachers' efforts to determine developmentally appropriate practices.

3

• • • • • •

Culture, Child Development, and Developmentally Appropriate Practices
Teachers as Collaborative Researchers

REBECCA S. NEW

As this volume makes clear, the publication of NAEYC's (National Association for the Education of Children) guidelines for developmentally appropriate practice (Bredekamp, 1987) did not put an end to the debate about early educational goals or practices. Nonetheless, the guidelines sparked a renewed commitment on the part of early childhood educators to relate educational practice to our current knowledge about how young children grow and learn. Yet both the knowledge base and related recommendations for practice reflect norms and values primarily associated with white middle-class America. As such, there is a built-in rationale for considering the accumulating body of knowledge based on work with young children from culturally diverse populations in the articulation of sound pedagogical practice in early education. Indeed, the changing ethnic and racial composition of U.S. classrooms has resulted in a resounding mandate to reexamine current theories of development as they influence our conceptions of educational goals as well as what constitutes "developmentally appropriate practice."

The purpose of this chapter is to respond to that mandate in the following threefold fashion: to examine the role of child development theory and research in the determination of early educational goals and practice; to critique the field and its research base from a comparative, cross-cultural perspective; and to illustrate a new interpretation of the teacher's role as a collaborative researcher with parents in determining developmentally appropriate goals and practices in culturally diverse early childhood settings. The stance to be assumed in this task reflects:

- a critical perspective in the consideration of the strong linkages between child development research that is ethnocentrically narrow and biased (LeVine, 1980), and the determination of developmentally appropriate practices for classrooms that are culturally and linguistically diverse;
- the belief that educational goals and practices must be responsive to a broader interpretation of "developmental appropriateness" than is currently held, one that considers the developmental needs of adults as well as the larger societal contexts within which young children live;
- the value of both cross-cultural and teacher research in gaining a better appreciation of the range and complexity of human behavior, as well as recognition of the multiple and complex ways in which environmental features—including cultural values, beliefs, and goals—influence behavior and development.

It will be argued, in the discussion to follow, that it is only through examining and attempting to understand cultural interpretations of development that we can begin to redress the limitations of current Western theories of development *and* their use as a predominant source of influence in the determination of appropriate early educational goals and practices. Specific reference will be made to the Italian community of Reggio Emilia, whose early child care and education program has received international acclaim, to illustrate the potentials in a new interpretation of the role of the teacher.

SOCIETAL CONCERNS AND EDUCATIONAL RESPONSES

Contemporary theory and practice in early childhood education is securely wed to the field of child development (Bloch, 1991), an affiliation established early in the century as early childhood educators seeking to be recognized as professionals were urged to become more "scientific" in their endeavors (Bloch, 1987). Educational policies and programs also reflect contemporary views of the young child as well as popular and political interpretations of society's responsibility to that child (e.g., current efforts to teach young children how to detect "friendly" and "unfriendly" strangers; see also chapters 1 and 2 by Lubeck and Mallory, respectively, this volume). A common thread connecting the knowledge base to social policy priorities is the view of education as a means to solve society's problems (Weber, 1987).

Thus it would seem that any determination of "developmentally appropriate practice" would ideally reflect both the available theoretical and empirical knowledge as well as the sociohistorical concerns of the time. Sometimes, however, these sources of influence are at cross purposes, as can be seen in the competing solutions proposed in recent school reform efforts.

Several major contemporary educational concerns in the United States involve cultural differences. The first is characterized by an increasing pessimism regarding the nation's competitive status in economic and technological domains (United States Department of Education, 1983), hence a growing pressure to "fix the schools" such that they are more like those of our international competitors (United States Department of Education, 1984). Related school reform efforts emphasize a unified core curriculum that—because of its revised content and high standards—would presumably benefit all students, including those of minority as well as majority status (Bennett, 1988; Hirsch, 1988). A second problem facing U.S. educators focuses directly on our growing numbers of culturally and linguistically diverse classrooms. Considerable rhetoric and an almost palpable sense of frustration characterize discussions regarding the most effective, equitable, and efficient means of responding to the nation's diverse population. Many multicultural school reform efforts propose to modify curriculum goals and teaching strategies to correspond to culturally salient learning styles and content, in what is regarded by some to be a futile attempt to compensate for societal inequities by minimizing home/school cultural incongruities (Ogbu, 1992). A third and related problem is the growing number of incidents of racial violence (in and out of schools) perpetuated within and against minority populations. Educational responses to this last and most frightening of our society's ills range in the extreme.

Within the field of early childhood education, current efforts at addressing issues of diversity are based on principles of social equity, even as concerns continue to focus on the fact that the school achievement of many minority children remains problematic at best. In addition to compensatory entitlement programs, typical early childhood strategies include the incorporation of anti-bias and multicultural aims and materials within the curriculum. While the definitions of multicultural education vary (Sleeter & Grant, 1987), common interpretations emphasize tangible aspects of cultural diversity within the curriculum (Williams, Gaetano, Harrington, & Sutherland, 1985). Antibias strategies promote the social value of inclusion (Derman-Sparks & the A.B.C. Task Force, 1989).

These additions to the standard early childhood fare are necessary and admirable, yet they are an inadequate response to the complexity of the problems noted above, and they don't compensate for the narrow interpretation of child development reflected in the current guidelines for developmentally appropriate practice. Collectively, such concerns challenge the early childhood education field's dependence upon our limited understanding of children's normative development as the primary determinant of sound pedagogical practice.

SO WHAT'S THE PROBLEM?
CULTURAL BIAS IN DEVELOPMENTAL RESEARCH

In spite of the numerous, recent school reform efforts focused on issues of diversity, an ethnocentric bias continues to characterize most of Western developmental psychology. The field of child development was built upon a predominance of studies conducted on white, middle-class American children. This ethnocentric bias has remained in spite of several decades of studies—inspired by the work of Margaret Mead and operationalized by Beatrice and John Whiting (1975)—that have demonstrated significant cultural variability in the structuring and interpretation of children's development. The insular view of the field was still apparent in the late 1970s when less than 10% of all studies found in a 5-year review (1974–1978) of major child development journals (*Child Development, Human Development, Developmental Psychology,* and *Merrill-Palmer Quarterly*) included other than Caucasian American subjects. Less than 3% of all studies were conducted on children in the non-Western societies of Latin America, Africa, Asia, and Oceania—where a majority of the world's children reside (LeVine, 1980). These findings highlight the failure of American social scientists to acknowledge the cultural diversity inherent in both child rearing contexts and developmental consequences throughout the non-Western world. Few seemed to consider the risks of relying upon studies primarily focused on the white American middle-class child to inform contemporary developmental theory and practice.

A more recent review of studies published in *Child Development* from 1986 to 1990 (New, 1992a) found that studies on culturally or linguistically diverse populations (within or outside the United States) remain in the minority (9.3% of the total). Even fewer studies considered the home environment or any indices of cultural identity as a part of the research design, and little or no mention was made of ethnographic material that would allow for the consideration of results within a cultural context. While special issues and articles devoted to the study of minority children appeared to be on the increase (c.f., Spencer, 1990), studies of children developing in cultures outside the United States again represented less than 3% of all studies published in the second-half of the so-called International Decade of the Child. Clearly, data on non-Anglo children in indigenous settings, such as Puerto Ricans in Puerto Rico, or Italians in Italy, are still not considered essential to the determination of child development norms or the evaluation of developmental theories.

This lack of representation in the research literature of studies on culturally diverse populations is particularly alarming given the fact that the American early childhood classroom increasingly mirrors the diverse demographics of our complex society. Efforts to address this theoretical and empirical deficiency are being made by advocates of a cross-cultural perspective, who call for the incorporation of cultural variability into contemporary theories of child development as well as the determination of educational goals and practices.

CROSS-CULTURAL RESEARCH IN CHILD DEVELOPMENT

The nonrepresentational view of child development that is currently depicted in mainstream developmental research literature and standard child development texts belies the extant knowledge base. The steady rise in cross-cultural investigations of child development conducted over the past two decades has resulted in diverse and compelling challenges to current beliefs regarding normative child development processes as well as optimal child development settings. Such studies have also contributed to our understanding of ideological bases of behavior, and the significance of the sociocultural context in interpreting and structuring the child's development (Bronfenbrenner, 1979; LeVine, 1974; Rogoff & Wertsch, 1984; Super & Harkness, 1986).

Expanded Views of Developmental Possibilities and Pathways

One of the primary benefits of comparative research is that it forces us to reflect upon our own beliefs and practices (White, 1987) and to rethink the extent to which current ideas of normative and optimal development place limits on our work with young children. Examples of studies in four broad domains will be presented to support the contention that current views of child development are ethnocentrically narrow, and thus not sufficiently informed to guide educational practice for a culturally diverse population.

CULTURAL DIFFERENCES IN PARENTAL ROLE INTERPRETATION. Cross-cultural studies of mothering—such as among the Efe, where newborns are nursed and cared for by numerous individuals other than their mothers (Tronick, Morilli, & Winn, 1987); and in northeastern Brazil, where sickly young children are selectively left to die (Scheper-Hughes, 1987)—challenge the biologically based interpretation of optimal maternal behavior. Less dramatic but equally convincing comparative studies of maternal behavior in diverse cultures make clear that significant differences exist in caregiving patterns and priorities throughout childhood, variations that are associated with cultural belief systems as well as environmental constraints (Goodnow & Collins, 1990; Richman et al., 1988; Whiting & Whiting, 1975). Results of these and other studies not only support the notion of cultural variability in human child care, but are consistent with other observations that contemporary Western patterns of infant care deviate along a continuum from moderate to extreme from that believed to be prototypical of the human species (Lozoff & Brittenham, 1979).

While some of the differences alluded to above may be attributed to parents allocating their attention to children in direct proportion to the availability of subsistence resources, other differences in the psychological dimensions of parenting—including conceptions of parental indulgence and control—also vary as a function of cultural beliefs and expectations (Bornstein, 1991). In numerous settings in sub-Saharan Africa, children grow up without hearing parental praise for their efforts or accomplishments (LeVine, 1989). That such children exhibit no expectation of recognition for their good behavior challenges response-reinforcement theories, and illuminates the ethnocentric nature of American virtues of parental consistency and child self-esteem. Japanese parents provide psychological support for their children during periods of difficulty—such as during school examination time—but they also assign value to children's experience of such hardships (White & LeVine, 1986). At the same time, Japanese teachers and parents make few explicit behavioral demands on children, and rarely enforce their requests when children resist. These strategies—which contribute to Japanese children's internalization of parental, group, and institutional values—are in direct conflict with American notions of the need for firm control and rule enforcement (Lewis, 1984).

CULTURAL STRUCTURING OF DEVELOPMENTAL PROCESSES. Belief systems influence not only parental or caregiving behavior, but developmental processes as well. Studies of African infants in Western Kenya challenge the notion of genetically determined patterns of motor development (Super, 1981). Philips' (1983) study of the Warm Springs Indian reservation illustrates the many ways in which a young child's attention structure and regulation of turns differ from Anglo expectations. My own work with Italian parents and children as well as other studies on the mediating role of cultural norms in child language acquisition raise important questions about the reciprocal model of communicative exchanges and its relation to language acquisition and development, and the notion of the dyad as the natural human relation (New, 1984, in preparation; Schieffelin & Ochs, 1986).

Cultural variation in the socialization of young children is apparent in numerous studies on children's peer relations (e.g., Corsaro's work with Italian nursery school peer cultures, 1985; Corsaro & Eder, 1990); as well as in conceptions and structuring of children's play and domestic activities in settings around the world (Roopnarine & Johnson, in press; Whiting & Edwards, 1988). These and related studies, especially among traditional societies such as the Kalahari San, suggest that concepts such as "collective monologue," "peers," and "parallel play" are merely terms used by Western developmental psychologists to explain behaviors associated with the particularly Western phenomenon of same-age play groups, rather than in response to some pan-cultural feature of children's social activity (Konner, 1977).

CULTURAL INTERPRETATIONS OF OPTIMAL DEVELOPMENT. Perhaps not surprisingly, such cultural differences in the organization, structuring, and interpreting of children's behavior have also been associated with variations in developmental outcomes. A large body of research supports the hypothesis that cognitive abilities vary as a function of environmental demands. For example, a study of Israeli children raised in either the kibbutz or in urban families illustrates the possibility that different competence profiles and developmental paths result from different forms of childrearing, each with its own set of adaptive functions (Levy-Shiff, 1983). Cultural variation has also been established in the domains of emotional display and affect (Harkness & Super, 1983), moral development (Snarey, 1985), gender role differentiation (Whiting & Edwards, 1988), and even conceptions of selfhood (Katz, 1981). In each case, developmental processes conform to contextual demands, including cultural values as well as socioeconomic circumstances, such that the very concept of optimal development appears negotiable. Indeed, the claim has been made that much of what is considered to be the result of "natural" laws of human behavior is, in fact, culture-bound (Jahoda, 1986).

Cultural interpretations of developmental outcomes not only vary in terms of defining optimal development, but developmental discord as well (Super, 1987). These interpretations vary with regard to the overall significance of the developmental delay or difficulty, as well as the attribution of cause related to the disability (Stevenson, Lucker, Lee, & Stigler, 1987). Views on disability as well as attitudes regarding the significance and mutability of physical, mental, and emotional deviance are subject to the same sociohistorical factors and cultural values that come to bear on the definition of more optimal forms and expressions of development (Mallory, 1993).

CHILD DEVELOPMENT NORMS AND PEDAGOGY. A related challenge to current guidelines for developmentally appropriate practice that draws on cross-cultural research is the cultural variation in interpretations of the conceptual linkages between child development norms and sound pedagogy. These variations are apparent even in settings where the basic developmental characteristics of young children are similarly acknowledged. For example, young children's difficulty at sitting still and focused for long periods of time is well known among American preschool teachers. Equally well-accepted is the presumption that this "short attention span" precludes the young child's ability to remain involved, with sustained interest, with a topic of investigation for any length of time. Young Italian children appear no more skilled at sitting still and attending quietly over any length of time. Yet observations within the schools of Reggio Emilia suggest that the attainment of specific developmental milestones—such as those associated with increasing physical maturity—is not seen as a necessary precursor to the child's involvement in long-term projects characterized by intense intellectual engagement (New, 1993). Italian responses to and expectations of children's social competencies also vary as a function of cultural values (Edwards & Gandini, 1989), as does their facilitation of autonomous behavior. Few Italian 2-year-olds have been taught how to put their coats on unassisted; adults in Reggio Emilia enjoy the opportunity to assist children, even as they encourage children to also help one another.

Similarly, challenges to American conceptions of and responses to the young egocentric child may be found in Japanese settings. In preschool classrooms, large building blocks—too heavy for one child to carry alone—and purposefully limited supplies are seen as essential strategies for the encouragement of cooperative and altruistic behavior (Lewis, 1984). Origami tasks involving prolonged periods of concentration are seen as appropriate means of fostering the culturally valued trait of persistence (Tobin, Wu, & Davidson, 1989). In Japanese and American toddlers' interactions with their mothers during a teaching task, cooperation, autonomy, and competence are differentially fostered and expressed (Messinger & Freedman, 1992).

Cross-Cultural Challenges to Developmental Psychology

To date, however, findings from these and related cross-cultural studies have remained on the periphery of the child development field, and have had little impact on the hegemony of developmental psychology. One explanation for the insular nature of the field of child development draws upon a primary feature of the parental field of general psychology, in which both theory and research are aimed at establishing and explaining supposed central and inherent processing mechanisms. Such a Platonistic undertaking—based on the long-held belief that people are basically the same—was perpetuated during the 1960s at the time of cognitive psychology's impact on the field (Shweder, 1990). The effect has been translated into a set of heuristics for Western developmental researchers whereby they continue to look for abstract means to represent central processing systems. This focus allows researchers to ignore both the content of behavior *and* any exterior and extrinsic features such as the sociocultural environment, because what is "really real" is within the individual. Even in the quest for universal laws, the mantra is "don't think about anything that can't be controlled and measured in a lab" (Shweder, 1990, p. 20).

Motivations to view contrary evidence as consistent with the view of universality include the positivist belief that there is one best pathway of development. Other factors that have enabled researchers to discount cross-cultural challenges to contemporary developmental theory include the belief in endogenous development—in which the sturdiness of maturational patterns preserves the onset of major trends while environmental factors merely influence the timing and range of expression—and the primacy of methodological rigor, reflected in the assumed need to restrict our view of what is known to replicated research studies under controlled conditions (LeVine, 1989). The power of these tacit assumptions is reflected in the extent to which cross-cultural challenges are still not being taken seriously.

Implications for Educational Theory and Practice

Cross-cultural research in child development provides ample supporting evidence for more recent culturally informed theories of development that have yet to be well utilized by educators in the determination of educational goals or practice. The acceptance by developmental psychologists of Vygotskian notions of constructivist theory has provided a basis for a culturally oriented view of development (Vygotsky, 1978). Indeed, a growing number of scholars now view development as a collective process in which children help to shape and share in their own developmental experiences through their participation in everyday cultural routines (Bruner, 1986; Rogoff, 1990; Schieffelin & Ochs, 1986; Tharp & Gallimore, 1988; Wertsch, 1985). From this point of view, human thinking cannot be disentangled from the historical and cultural contexts in which it plays a "co-constituting part" (Shweder, 1990, p. 13). Yet constructivist research relies primarily on the principle of individualism, and is characterized by an "overwhelming concern with the endpoint of development" (Corsaro & Eder, 1990, p. 199). These principles and priorities, in turn, continue to characterize even the most contemporary interpretations of educational goals and strategies.

In sum, cross-cultural research has demonstrated significant differences in parental goals and strategies, developmental norms and processes, and interpretations of "appropriate" educational responses to child development norms. Cumulatively, such studies have much to contribute to current theories dominating the child development discourse, and challenge the idea of any single optimal approach to early care and education. Yet, at a time when even mainstream child development research is moving to new interpretations of the interplay of sociocultural and cognitive processes, guidelines for developmentally appropriate practice remain heavily influenced by genetic epistemology, with the individual-child-as-active-learner the typical unit of discussion (O'Loughlin, 1991; Walsh, 1991).

TEACHERS AS COLLABORATIVE RESEARCHERS

As currently conceived, principles of developmental theory, with classificatory stages and assumptions of normal development, are presented as unequivocable (O'Loughlin, 1991). Carefully detailed descriptions of practices that are categorically labeled "appropriate" or "inappropriate" follow suit (Bredekamp, 1987), and leave little room for alternative interpretations. As such, NAEYC's guidelines for developmentally appropriate practice reinforce uncritical thinking and teaching; and contribute to a static view of both child and adult development.

Such a view of the teacher—as an actor following a script for "appropriate practice"—is inconsistent with our knowledge of adult development (Oja, 1991), our understanding of constructivist theory (Fosnot, 1989), and our view of the teacher as reflective practitioner (Duckworth, 1987; Schön, 1983). Such a didactic strategy for defining good practice also makes teachers more vulnerable to the previously described limitations of the child development knowledge base. On the other hand, alternative strategies—that encourage teachers to inquire about children's development and put that knowledge to good use—empower teachers in their work with young children, and contribute to their own professional development.

Engaging in Research

As the heterogeneity of American classroooms increases, so, too, does the imperative that teachers wait no longer for the field of child development to broaden its scope in contributing to a better understanding of the full range and processes of human potential. One strategy by which teachers can begin to address this issue while responding to the demands of the classroom is to consider three variations on the theme of teacher as researcher: that of epistemologist, classroom ethnographer, and cultural anthropologist.

The first two forms of teacher research are drawn from ongoing work with the community-based infant/toddler and preprimary program in Reggio Emilia, Italy. This commmunity's early childhood program has provided strong incentives to examine contemporary American early childhood practices (New, 1990). Key elements of the program, such as the project approach, the use of symbolic languages, and the process of teacher development, are described elsewhere (Edwards, Gandini, & Forman, 1993). Pertinent to this discussion is the Reggio Emilia model of teacher development, one that views teachers as learners and collaborative researchers-in-action.

Teachers in Reggio Emilia function as *classroom ethnographers,* conducting formal and informal observations of children at work and play in the school setting. These observations, facilitated by documentation in the forms of photographs, video and tape recordings, and samples of children's work, are directly linked to curriculum decisions. Teachers take notes, recording conversations as they occur within the context of ongoing classroom activities. These recordings and observations, in turn, are shared and clarified in a variety of ways with children, parents, and other teachers. Through the practice of documentation and exhibition of children's thinking and project work, *all* of the teachers—and a good many parents—gain a better understanding of their children's development, and the means by which they can contribute to that development.

A second type of research, one that also characterizes the work of Reggio Emilia teachers, is that of *teacher as epistemologist.* Teachers in Reggio Emilia hypothesize about and experiment with diverse strategies, materials, and activities in their efforts to promote and facilitate children's learning. They prepare provocative materials and structure groups according to a feature of interest such as groups of one sex, and then another; groups of mixed ability versus homogeneous grouping; groups of experienced players with children who are new to the activity. In each case, teachers arm themselves with tape recorders, paper and pencil, observing and recording the various responses and outcomes of children's behavior. These observations, often accompanied by slides or actual samples of children's work, are then shared in staff meetings where teachers debate among themselves the relative merits and shortcomings of their teaching strategies. Staff development opportunities build upon these experiences throughout the school year.

A third strategy by which teachers can inform their own practice is through the role of *teacher as anthropologist*. One of the most direct ways in which teachers can contribute to their own understanding of the cultural heritage of children in their classrooms is to gain an understanding of each child's "developmental niche" (Super & Harkness, 1986). As outlined, the developmental niche serves as a framework within which to consider the interface between culture and an individual child's development. As envisioned by a classroom teacher, the niche consists of three dimensions: the physical and social characteristics of the child's life outside the classroom; the patterns of care and interaction that characterize the child care environment; and the "psychology" of his or her caregivers, including not only their views of development, but their aims and expectations of schooling. By enacting the role of anthropologist, teachers can inform themselves of the basic characteristics of the child's out-of-school life, as well as the extent to which environmental features—including parental beliefs about development—are idiosyncratic or exist as part of a larger ideological system.

This strategy for "unpackaging" (Whiting, 1976) so-called independent variables (such as social class and family demographics) has characterized recent ethnographic efforts aimed at understanding cultural effects on classroom learning. In studies of two working class communities in the southeastern U.S. (Heath, 1983), as well as ongoing efforts with native Hawaiians in the KEEP project (Tharp & Gallimore, 1988), anthropologists have emphasized the importance of selectively responding to cultural differences of educational significance, rather than assuming the need for totally embracing a culture's norms. Such studies also underscore the critical need to avoid cultural explanations of diversity that might result in further stereotypic treatment of individuals, particularly minorities (Heath, 1990; Ogbu, 1981; Weisner, Gallimore, & Jordan, 1988).

Collaborating with Parents

Critical to the success of each of these three types of research is the inclusion of parents as rightful participants in meaningful ways in their children's early education. In Reggio Emilia, parental concerns are directly addressed in curriculum planning and evaluation. Parental involvement in the identification and interpretation of teachers' foci of study (e.g., children's fascination with war toys) not only supports the rights of parents to advocate on behalf of their young children, it also provides a means of assistance in the interpretation of consequential familial differences as opposed to those that are merely divergent. Teacher attitudes regarding their own professional development enable them to benefit from multiple points of view, and parents see their role as valued and significant. Throughout, these adults repeatedly emphasize the importance of asking questions and being forced to reexamine their positions as contributors to their own learning.

Supporting the Role of Teacher as Learner

This conception of teacher as learner finds considerable support in recent research on teachers and teaching, which emphasizes the importance of enlarging the focus from what works best for children to include the relationship between how teachers teach and what teachers need (Duckworth, 1987; Fosnot, 1989; Yonemura, 1986). Such a view of teacher as collaborative and action-oriented researcher not only contributes to the determination of developmentally appropriate practices with young children, but provides a vehicle for teacher development as well. In that light, it is also clear that such a new interpretation of the role of the teacher will not take effect automatically, unsupported, or in isolation. To begin, teachers' views of their own professional expertise and development will require modification. The implementation of strategies of collaboration and negotiation with parents and other teachers clearly requires administrative acknowledgement and assistance. Teachers need both "opportunities and time for disciplined inquiry" (Lieberman & Miller, 1990, p. 10). None of these changes are modest; indeed, they represent a dramatic departure from the typical modus operandi of teachers and schools. The challenges of change appear well worth the effort, however. Teacher inquiry into the contexts of children's lives, informed by genuine and ongoing conversations with parents, is clearly useful in making classrooms compatible to children of various cultural groups. The insights that come from such collaborative and cooperative activity give new meaning to the teachers' efforts; and acquaint them with the human consequences of contemporary economic and sociopolitical conditions. These are no small gains.

CONCLUSION

An expanded understanding of developmental appropriateness must take into account not only the lives of children, and the course of their development, but also the lives of adults (both teachers and parents), and the cultural and societal contexts in which those children and adults live. That is, development is not a phenomenon limited to young children. Rather, it is a process also experienced by adults and by society in general. Children *and teachers* require learning environments that allow them to hypothesize, investigate, experiment, and construct new understandings of themselves and others with whom they work (New, 1992b; Seefeldt, 1993). Parents must have opportunities to participate in educational decisions and the design of educational programs that affect their children. Societal development requires that cultural diversity be allowed to flourish, and that social institutions be responsive to the needs of individuals as well as group differences.

The inclusion of comparative and cross-cultural research findings into the child development knowledge base will not solve all of the problems facing our nations' schools. The peaceful coexistence of competing value structures in our society (Shigaki, 1983) will require more than effective parent-teacher relationships. The goal of reducing cultural incongruities and home/school inequities is made all the more challenging by school ethnographers who warn against the misapplication of group level cultural generalizations to individuals (Tharp, 1989; Weisner, Gallimore, Jordan, 1988; Zueli & Floden, 1987). Critical theorists relentlessly point to the need for a transformative political agenda if school reform efforts—especially those associated with multiculturalism—are to be successful (Estrada & McLaren, 1993; Ogbu, 1992; Sleeter & Grant, 1987). That we are still wondering how to best provide an education for young children living beyond the middle-class mainstream (Schweinhart & Weikart, 1988) may be because we aren't yet asking the right questions. Our consistent failure to fully understand the range and significance of cultural differences in children's lives and their parents' educational expectations has resulted in a silencing of ideas rather than an educational exchange (Delpit, 1986, 1988), with far too many unfulfilled expectations (Snow, Barnes, Chandler, Goodman, & Hemphill, 1991).

A new interpretation of developmentally appropriate practices that is dynamic and responsive to teachers' observations of and interactions with the children they teach could go a long way toward redressing the inequities and insufficiencies apparent in the schooling of culturally diverse children. A conception of teachers as collaborative researchers empowers teachers to not only seek out opportunities to learn from the diverse children in their classrooms, but also to

- incorporate parents into a partnership affiliation that is denied by such concepts as "parent education";
- work with other teachers in the laboratory of the school setting; and
- view current theories of child development with a healthy skepticism.

These partnerships with children, parents, and other teachers, in turn, serve to encourage and support teachers' reflections on the relationship between their efforts and the needs of the larger society. By so doing, we can avoid the institutionalization of knowledge about childhood as we discover multiple possibilities for responding appropriately to young children's diverse competencies, needs, and potentials.

REFERENCES

Bennett, W. (1988). *American education: Making it work.* A report to the President and the American people. Washington, DC: Department of Education.

Bloch, M. (1987). Becoming scientific and professional: An historical perspective on the aims and effects of early education. In T. Popkewitz (Ed.), *The formation of school subjects: The struggle for an American institution.* Bristol, PA: Falmer Press.

Bloch, M. (1991). Critical science and the history of child development's influence on early education research. *Early Education and Development, 2* (2), 95–108.

Bornstein, M. (Ed.) (1991). *Cultural approaches to parenting.* Hillsdale, NJ: Erlbaum.

Bredekamp, S. (Ed.) (1987). *Developmentally appropriate practice in early childhood programs serving children from birth through age 8.* Washington, DC: National Association for the Education of Young Children.

Bronfenbrenner, U. (1979). *The ecology of human development.* Cambridge, MA: Harvard University Press.

Bruner, J. (1986). *Actual minds, possible worlds.* Cambridge, MA: Harvard University Press.

Corsaro, W. A. (1985). *Friendship and peer culture in the early years.* Norwood, NJ: Ablex.

Corsaro, W. A. & Eder, D. (1990). Children's peer cultures. *Annual Review of Sociology, 16,* 197–220.

Delpit, L. D. (1986). Skills and other dilemmas of a progressive Black educator. *Harvard Educational Review, 56* (4), 379–385.

Delpit, L. D. (1988). The silenced dialogue: Power and pedagogy in educating other people's children. *Harvard Educational Review, 58* (3), 280–298.

Derman-Sparks, L., and the A.B.C. Task Force (1989). *Anti-bias curriculum: Tools for empowering young children.* Washington, DC: National Association for the Education of Young Children.

Duckworth, E. (1987). *The having of wonderful ideas & other essays on teaching & learning.* Cambridge, MA: Harvard University Press.

Edwards, C. P., & Gandini, L. (1989). Teachers' expectations about the timing of developmental skills: A cross-cultural study. *Young Children, 44* (4), 15–19.

Edwards, C. P., Gandini, L., & Forman, G. (Eds.) (1993). *The hundred languages of children: The Reggio Emilia approach to early education.* New Jersey: Ablex.

Estrada, K. & McLaren, P. (1993). A dialogue on multiculturalism and democratic culture, *Educational Researcher, 22* (3), 27–33.

Fosnot, C. T. (1989). *Enquiring teachers, enquiring learners: A constructivist approach for teaching.* New York: Teachers College Press.

Goodnow, J. J., & Collins, W. A. (1990). *Development according to parents: The nature, sources, and consequences of parents' ideas.* Hillsdale, NJ: Erlbaum.

Harkness, S., & Super, C. (1983). The cultural construction of child development: A framework for the socialization of affect. *Ethos, 11* (4), 18–23.

Heath, S. B. (1983). *Ways with words: Language, life, and work in communities and classrooms.* Cambridge: Cambridge University Press.

Heath, S. B. (1990). The children of Trackton's children: Spoken and written language in social change. In J. W. Stigler, R. A. Shweder, & G. Herdt (Eds.), *Cultural psychology: Essays on comparative human development.* New York: Cambridge University Press.

Hirsch, E.D. (1988). *Cultural literacy: What every American needs to know.* New York: Random House.

Jahoda, G. (1986). A cross-cultural perspective on developmental psychology. *International Journal of Behavior and Development, 9,* 417–437.

Katz, R. (1981). Education as transformation: Becoming a healer among the !Kung and Fijians. *Harvard Educational Review, 51* (1), 57–78.

Konner, M. (1977). Relations among infants and juveniles in comparative perspective. In M. Lewis & L. Rosenblum (Eds.), *Friendship and peer relations.* New York: John Wiley and Sons.

LeVine, R. A. (1974). Cultural values and parental goals. *Teachers College Record, 76,* 226–239.

LeVine, R. A. (1980). Anthropology and child development. *New Directions for Child Development, 8,* 71–86.

LeVine, R. A. (1989). Cultural environments in child development. In W. Damon (Ed.), *Child development today and tomorrow.* San Francisco: Jossey-Bass.

Levy-Shiff, R. (1983). Adaptation and competence in early childhood: Communally raised Kibbutz children versus family raised children in the city. *Child Development, 54,* 1606–1614.

Lewis, C. C. (1984). Cooperation and control in Japanese nursery schools. *Comparative Education Review, 28* (1), 69–84.

Lieberman, A., & Miller, L. (1990). Teacher development in professional practice schools. *Teachers College Record, 92* (1), 105–122.

Lozoff, B., & Brittenham, G. (1979). Infant care: Cache or carry. *The Journal of Pediatrics, 95* (3), 478–483.

Mallory, B. (1993). Changing attitudes toward disability in developing countries: Social and historical factors. In monograph #53, *Attitudes toward disability in developing countries.* International Exchange of Experts and Information in Rehabilitation. Durham, NH: University of New Hampshire.

Messinger, D., & Freedman, D. G. (1992). Autonomy and interdependence in Japanese and American mother-toddler dyads. *Early development and parenting, 19* (1), 33–38.

New, R. (1984). Italian mothers and infants: Patterns of care and social development. Unpublished dissertation, Harvard Graduate School of Education.

New, R. (1990). Excellent early education: A town in Italy has it. *Young Children, 45* (6), 4–10.

New, R. (1992a, April). Babies and the bathwater: Uses and abuses of child development research and developmentally appropriate practice. Paper presented at the American Educational Research Association, San Francisco.

New, R. (1992b). The integrated early childhood curriculum: New interpretations based on research and practice. In C. Seefeldt (Ed.), *The early childhood curriculum: A review of current research.* 2nd edition. New York: Teachers College Press.

New, R. (1993).Cultural variations on developmentally appropriate practice. In C. Edwards, L. Gandini, & G. Forman (Eds.), *The hundred languages of children: The Reggio Emilia approach to early childhood education.* New Jersey: Ablex.

New, R. (in preparation). *Bello, bravo, buono: Italian early childhood.* New York: Guilford Press.

Ogbu, J. U. (1981). School ethnography: A multilevel approach. *Anthropology and Education Quarterly, 12* (1), 3–29.

Ogbu, J. U. (1992). Understanding cultural diversity and learning. *Educational researcher, 21* (8), 5–14.

O'Loughlin, M. (1991, October). Rethinking early childhood education: A sociocultural perspective. Paper presented at Conference on Reconceptualizing Research in Early Childhood Education, Madison, WI.

Oja, S. N. (1991). Adult development: Insights on staff development. In A. Lieberman & I. Miller (Eds.), *Staff development for education in the 90's.* New York: Teachers College Press.

Philips, S. U. (1983). *The invisible culture: Communication in classroom and community on the Warm Springs Indian Reservation.* New York: Longman.

Richman, A. L., LeVine, R. A., New, R. S., Howrigan, G. A., Welles-Nystrom, B., & LeVine, S. (1988). Maternal behavior to infants in five cultures. In R. A.

LeVine, P. M. Miller, & M. M. West (Eds.), *Parental behavior in diverse societies. New Directions for Child Development* (40), 81–97.

Rogoff, B. (1990). *Apprenticeship in thinking: Cognitive development in social context.* New York: Oxford University Press.

Rogoff, B., & Wertsch, J. (Eds.) (1984). *Children's learning in the zone of proximal development.* San Francisco: Jossey Bass.

Roopnarine, J. & Johnson, J. (in press). *Children's play in diverse cultures.* Albany, NY: SUNY Press.

Scheper-Hughes, N. (1987). "Basic strangeness": Maternal estrangement and infant death—A critique of bonding theory. In C.M. Super (Ed.), *The role of culture in developmental disorder.* London: Academic Press.

Schön, D. A. (1983). *The reflective practitioner: How professionals think in action.* New York: Basic Books.

Schieffelin, B., & Ochs, E. (1986). Language socialization. *Annual Review of Anthropology, 15,* 163–191.

Schweinhart, L. J., & Weikart, D. P. (1988). Education for young children living in poverty: Child-initiated learning or teacher-directed instruction? *Elementary School Journal, 89* (2), 213–227.

Seefeldt, C. (1993). Social studies: Learning for freedom. *Young Children, 48* (3), 4–9.

Shigaki, I. S. (1983). Child care practices in Japan and the United States: How do they reflect cultural values in young children? *Young Children, 38*(4), 13–24.

Shweder, R. (1990). Cultural psychology—what is it? In J. W. Stigler, R. A. Shweder, & G. Herdt (Eds.), *Cultural psychology: Essays on comparative human development.* New York: Cambridge University Press.

Sleeter, C., & Grant, C. (1987). An analysis of multicultural education in the United States. *Harvard Educational Review, 57,* 421–444.

Snarey, J. (1985). Cross-cultural universality of socio-moral development: A critical review of Kohlbergian research. *Psychology Bulletin, 97,* 202–232.

Snow, C., Barnes, W., Chandler, J., Goodman, I., & Hemphill, L. (1991). *Unfulfilled expectations: Home and school influences on literacy.* Cambridge, MA: Harvard University Press.

Spencer, M. B. (1990). Development of minority children: An introduction. *Child Development, 61,* 267–269.

Stevenson, H. W., Lucker, G. W., Lee, S., & Stigler, J. W. (1987). Poor readers in three cultures. In C. M. Super (Ed.), *The role of culture in developmental disorder.* London: Academic Press.

Super, C. M. (1981). Behavioral development in infancy. In R. H. Munroe, R. L. Munroe, & B. B. Whiting (Eds.), *Handbook of cross-cultural human development.* New York: Garland.

Super, C. M. (Ed.) (1987). *The role of culture in developmental disorder.* London: Academic Press.

Super, C. & Harkness, S. (1986). The developmental niche: A conceptualization at the interface of child and culture. *International Journal of Behavioral Development, 9,* 545–569.

Tharp, R. (1989). Psychocultural variables and constants: Effects on teaching and learning in schools. *American Psychologist, 44* (2), 349–359.

Tharp, R. G. & Gallimore, T. (1988). *Rousing minds to life: Teaching, learning, and schooling in social context.* Cambridge: Cambridge University Press.

Tobin, J., Wu, D. H. Y., & Davidson, D. (1989). *Preschool in three cultures: Japan, China, and the U.S.* New Haven, CT: Yale University Press.

Tronick, E., Morilli, G., & Winn, S. (1987). Multiple caretaking of Efe (Pygmy) infants. *American Anthropologist, 89,* 96–106.

United States Department of Education (1983). *A nation at risk: the imperative for educational reform: a report to the nation and the Secretary of Education.* Washington, DC: National Commission on Excellence in Education.

United States Department of Education (1984). *The nation responds: recent efforts to improve education.* Washington, DC.

Vygotsky, L. (1978). *Mind in society.* Cambridge, MA: Harvard University Press.

Walsh, D. J. (1991). Extending the discourse on developmental appropriateness: A developmental perspective. *Early Education and Development, 2* (2), 109–119.

Weber, E. (1987). *Ideas influencing early childhood education: A theoretical analysis.* New York: Teachers College Press.

Weisner, T. S., Gallimore, R., & Jordan, C. (1988). Unpackaging cultural effects on classroom learning: Native Hawaiian peer assistance and child-generated activity. *Anthropology and Education Quarterly, 19,* 327–353.

Wertsch, J. (Ed.) (1985). *Culture, communication, and cognition: Vygotskian perspectives.* NY: Cambridge University Press.

White, M. (1987). *The Japanese educational challenge: A commitment to children.* New York: Free Press.

White, M., & LeVine, R. (1986). The good child. In R. Stevenson, H. Azuma, & K. Hakuta (Eds.), *Child development and education in Japan.* (pp. 55–62). New York: Freeman.

Whiting, B. B. (1976). Unpackaging variables. In K. Riegel & J. Meacham (Eds.), *The changing individual in a changing world.* Chicago: Aldine.

Whiting, B. B., & Edwards, C. P. (1988). *Children of different worlds: The formation of social behavior.* Cambridge, MA: Harvard University Press.

Whiting, B. B., & Whiting, J. W. M. (1975). *Children of six cultures: A psycho-cultural analysis.* Cambridge, MA: Harvard University Press.

Williams, L., Gaetano, Y., Harrington, C., & Sutherland I. (1985). *Alerta: A multicultural, bilingual approach to teaching young children.* Reading, MA: Addison-Wesley.

Yonemura, M. V. (1986). *A teacher at work: Professional development and the early childhood educator.* New York: Teachers College Press.

Zueli, J. S., & Floden, R. E. (1987). Cultural incongruities and inequities of schooling: Implications for practice from ethnographic research? *Journal of Teacher Education, 38* (6), 9–15.

4

• • • • • •

Research in
Parent-Child Interaction

*Guidance to Developmentally Appropriate Practice for
Young Children with Disabilities*

Jeanette A. McCollum and Helen Bair

In the world of early childhood special education, as in the substantially
overlapping world of early childhood education, developmentally appropriate practice (DAP) (Bredekamp, 1991) is considered an important standard against which everyday practice in programs for young children is
evaluated as worthy or unworthy, helpful or harmful, good or bad. In a
nutshell, practices advanced by this standard are those that facilitate active,
independent exploration and problem solving by young children. Based
on a constructivist model of early development drawn primarily from the
work of Piaget, these broad goals have been translated into a set of guidelines for the development and implementation of early childhood programs
that support children's natural curiosities and approaches to learning.

HOW APPROPRIATE IS
DEVELOPMENTALLY APPROPRIATE PRACTICE?

As might be expected, applying DAP to populations of children with very
diverse characteristics has led practitioners and researchers in both early
childhood education and early childhood special education to question
its broad applicability as a sufficient standard for judging the quality of
programs for young children (Mallory, 1990). We have only to think of
ourselves to know that strategies used to teach us to play tennis must differ from those used to increase our understanding of the opera. Appropriate teaching practices must be determined not only by the differing

84

cognitive and motor components of each task, but also by the level of skill we hope to attain in this task, by the specific component currently being emphasized within the overall task, by how much skill we may already have, and by our individual strengths as learners. Our motivation to pursue and practice this goal, moreover, will be influenced by how important this particular task is to us in our everyday lives, as well as by how much competence we experience in the initial stages of learning.

Few would argue that the supports provided for our learning and development should differ substantially based on what is appropriate for each particular configuration of task and person. Yet it is the inability to account for just such complexity that appears to stand in the way of applying the premises of DAP to intervention with young children with disabilities. Individualization, a concept of critical importance in these cases, and one encompassed within the DAP guidelines, has been lost.

Among early childhood practitioners, concern has been expressed about the myths that have come to dominate the field as the apparently straightforward standard of DAP has been applied too simply, broadly, and unquestioningly (Kostelnik, 1992; Walsh, 1991). Additional concerns have arisen as DAP has been applied to early childhood special education. New myths have taken root, resulting in new dilemmas for early childhood special educators attempting to reconcile the guidelines of DAP with the principles of individualization that form the backbone of special education law, policy, and practice. One myth we have heard is that individual objectives are incompatible with child-directed activities. Yet existing research with young children with disabilities indicates that individual objectives are one of the clearest markers of successful intervention (Wolery, Strain, & Bailey, no date). Another myth is that direct teaching of knowledge and skills is not developmentally appropriate because it negates the perspective of child as active learner. Yet we have only to refer to our lessons in tennis and the opera to know that one model does not fit all goals or situations, nor will one model be applicable to all learners. "Active learner" does not necessarily mean "alone." Rather, the development of many areas of skill, knowledge, and values depends on transmission from someone else.

A particularly pernicious myth is that the most developmentally appropriate practice is that which is appropriate for a child who is at the same developmental age as the child with disabilities (Goodman, 1992). The implication is that the most developmentally appropriate practice is to wait until the child with disabilities is "ready," i.e., reaches a certain developmental age, before introducing particular tasks. This myth is based on the assumption that at a given developmental age, two children will be characterized by the same abilities, regardless of their chronological ages. Research presents strong evidence that young children with disabilities may manifest not only delays, but also differences, potentially influencing how individual development is structured (Cicchetti & Beeghly, 1990a). Simple assumptions of delay do not recognize qualitative differences in development and learning that may be inherent in some etiologies (e.g., Down syndrome), and they ignore the history of environmental experience that may result. Individual differences may influence both the quantity and quality of the child's experiences, with consequences for what the child brings to interactions in terms of motivation, basic exploratory skills, cognitive strategies, knowledge, and self efficacy. Thus, knowledge of normal development and the processes that support it may be inadequate as the sole guide to intervention.

A developmental perspective on young children with disabilities requires that we attend not only to the sequence of development, but to its organization within the individual child at that particular point. Developmental and learning goals may differ for each child. Moreover, specific modifications may be needed in the processes required for their attainment. Recognition and knowledge of differences (as well as similarities) may result in the development of different goals, as well as in different strategies that better match the styles of environmental interaction that each child exhibits.

Early childhood special education is, first and foremost, intervention: The underlying purpose and hope is to change the trajectory of development from what it would have been without intervention. Therefore, an important research issue is to define teaching processes to support this ambitious purpose. It is not our intent in this chapter to contrast developmentally based practice with systematic instruction, nor to place value on one over the other. Clearly, general teaching practices derived from both DAP and special education are useful. However, even together, they are not enough unless placed within the context of the individual child and situation. We hope to show that our choice of particular strategies would depend on the combination of task (the goal that has been selected based on its developmental or functional relevance) and person (what the child brings to the task in terms of individual abilities and differences). We believe that developmental theory that emphasizes the transactions between child and environment provides a framework to accomplish this.

Four areas of research appear to have particular relevance for understanding and defining practice that is developmentally appropriate for young children with special needs. One is the emerging evidence of differences in development, referred to above. Models of child-environment interaction provide a second critical body of literature, since a developmentally appropriate environment will provide different supports at different points in development, changing to match emerging developmental abilities and tasks that form the individual child's developmental agenda (Wachs & Gruen, 1982). With respect to young children with disabilities, the environmental specificity hypothesis also would indicate that we must attend to the implications of these differences for providing optimal physical and social environments for each child.

The third area of literature of particular relevance is that which assumes that development is embedded within, and inseparable from, the social context. Based on Vygotsky's (1978) concept of the zone of proximal development, more skilled partners provide the child with opportunities to experience and practice more advanced performance, thereby exerting a "push/pull" on development (Bruner, 1990; Lockman & Hazen, 1989; Rogoff, 1991). Viewed in combination with the two bodies of literature already noted, we might expect that, for young children with disabilities, the social mediator's role would assume primary importance. Research on parent-child interaction in dyads in which the child has disabilities, the fourth area, lies squarely at the intersection of these three literatures, and clearly highlights their intertwining.

In the remainder of this chapter, we hope to utilize research from these last two areas to illustrate the importance of employing a theory base that incorporates knowledge of individual differences within the social nature of the individual teaching/learning process. First, we will provide a brief overview of the major conclusions to be drawn from research on parent-child interaction, with clear evidence of the importance of adaptations to developmental differences in young children who have disabilities. We will use this literature as a basis for understanding the transactions that occur between adults (whether parent or interventionist) and very young children with disabilities. Parallels have been drawn by previous writers between characteristics of good parenting as derived from the parent-infant interaction literature, and qualities of good teaching as derived from the premises of developmentally appropriate practice (Mahoney, Robinson, & Powell, 1992). It is significant that researchers of parent-infant interaction and proponents of DAP have both devoted attention to the role of the adult in responding to the child's interactions with the social and physical environments. What has been learned about parent-child interaction when young children have disabilities potentially has much to offer in developing a more comprehensive definition of developmentally appropriate practice. Following this necessarily brief review, we will then interpret what we have learned from this literature within the context of emerging research that examines the social contexts of early development and learning. This research, like

that on parent-child interaction, indicates that the adult's role as supporter of the child's emerging competencies, manifested in interactions
with the environment, is of primary importance. Finally, we will draw
implications for developmentally appropriate practice as it applies to
young children with special needs.

INTERACTION BETWEEN PARENTS AND YOUNG CHILDREN WITH DISABILITIES

Interactions between very young children and their caregivers provide a
powerful context for early learning and development, and in many ways
set the stage for what comes later. It is within this context that children
first develop views of themselves and others that are carried forward to
later relationships (Field, 1986). Here, too, the child develops strategies,
propensities, and perceptions of self that influence heavily how future
social and physical environments are approached and engaged. Early
interactions play a crucial role across multiple domains of development
as the child learns about self, others, the physical environment, and the
cultural contexts within which these occur. Although much of the
research in the areas of caregiver-infant interaction has been done with
parents, this is by no means universally true. In addition, the processes
described apply equally to all social partners who serve the same functions. Because we are ultimately drawing conclusions for the role of the
teacher, we have used several terms interchangeably throughout this
chapter, including "adult," "caregiver," and "parent." We have not dealt
with peers in this chapter, yet they too may provide some of these same
functions.

Three converging trends within this research are especially instructive for developing a view of developmentally appropriate practice that
is also individually and ecologically appropriate. The first has been a
movement away from the study of relationships between global parental
or familial characteristics (such as race or socioeconomic status) and
broad child outcomes (intelligence) toward the study of more specific
characteristics of parental behavior (characteristics of parental language),
and more narrowly defined developmental outcomes in children (mean
length of utterance, or MLU); to the study of the interaction process itself
(dyadic roles); thence to the influence that particular characteristics of
one or both partners (gender, disability) may have on the structure of the
interaction; and finally back to a broader but now more informed view
of the interrelationships between interactions and their individual, familial and cultural contexts.

The second trend has been away from a main effects model, in which predictions about development are based solely upon some characteristic of the environment (mother's education) or child (prematurity); to a bi-directional model, in which both child and parent are seen as having characteristics that influence the quality of the interaction; and finally to a transactional model, in which characteristics of each partner not only influence the character of the interaction, but also require that each partner adapt to individual differences in the other (Sameroff & Chandler, 1975). The transactional model predicts that interactions in which the individual engages will differ across partners as members of each unique dyad adapt to one another. Thus, interactions that the young child experiences will differ depending on who the partner is, the purpose of the interaction, and what the child, as a partner, brings to the interactive situation at different points in development. In turn, the child will be shaped by these interactions, influencing what the child brings to future ones. This second trend has led to increased understanding of the child's potential influence on the interactions experienced. It also has highlighted important aspects of the broader social and physical environment that affect the child's develomental trajectory, even in cases where the child displays biological differences or delays. The "continuum of caregiving casualty" as defined by Sameroff & Chandler (1975) may in fact be of more critical importance for these children than for those without biological differences, who may be more resilient and adaptable (Walker & Crawley, 1983).

Both of these trends in parent-infant interaction research have been facilitated by yet a third: the gradual move toward studying populations who differ from the average, with the goal of highlighting the processes of normal interaction and development through better understanding of how specific individual differences impact the quality and quantity of the interaction (Cicchetti, 1984; Walker & Crawley, 1983). Thus, as researchers began to describe the structures of early interactions between infants and caregivers, the inclusion of non-average populations of caregivers and children began to test the limits of theory. Clearly, this literature is important for interventionists' understanding of parent-child interaction as an important context for early development. In addition, it has direct relevance for understanding interventionist-child interaction as developmentally appropriate practice.

The Achievement and Functions of Synchrony

Interactions between parent and infant are achieved and maintained through the regulation and synchronization of each individual's separate acts. The nature of synchrony and how it is achieved in the parent-infant dyad have been approached from a number of different perspectives. First, it is evident that with very young infants, the content of the interaction, the "topic" of conversation, is the emotion that is shared by parent and child. Face-to-face games, both traditional and idiosyncratic to the dyad, predominate (Field, 1978; Stern, 1974). As the infant passes the midpoint of the first year, this topic begins to give way to the objects and events in the infant's environment, mirroring not only the infant's growing interest in the world, but also an increasing ability to shift attention between object and social partner, and finally to combine both within the same arena of attention (Bakeman & Adamson, 1984).

Caregivers interpret this interest as "trying to find out" (Bruner, 1975), and respond by elaborating on what the infant is attending to (Collis, 1977). Looks at the caregiver's face during object play also are likely to elicit a comment. Thus, the infant's developing interest in the world is reflected in a shift in the topic of conversation between parent and infant.

This process illustrates a second focus taken in this research, the changing but continually reciprocal nature of the roles of the two partners. Reciprocity implies that each individual's actions are predictable from those of the other (Gottman, 1979) and are integrated into a nonrandom pattern. For example, during social play, mutual gaze is more likely than gaze by either partner alone (Stern, 1974), whereas alternating vocalizations are more likely than vocal overlaps in caregivers and their 1–2-year-olds (Schaffer, Collis, & Parsons, 1977). This predictable structure occurs without conscious effort by either member. Rather, infants and their caregivers appear to be preadapted to interaction, effortlessly achieving mutuality (Stern, 1974), although each dyad of infant and primary caregiver soon builds beyond preadaptation, based on each partner's growing personal understanding of the other (Trevarthan, 1977). With development, the child gradually takes a more active role in initiating and maintaining the interaction, yet preserving the underlying nonrandom structure. It is important to note that this gradual role shift is not only supported by the infant's growing competence, but also by the predictable and responsive structure that is provided by the caregiver, freeing the infant to focus his energies on learning, and then fitting into, this structure. This allows the blending of two separate behavior streams into one interaction, providing a scaffold for the infant's increasingly reciprocal role.

Interactions are not all "theme," but rather are characterized by "theme and variation" (Stern, Beebe, Jaffe, & Bennett, 1977), allowing the child not only to experience anticipation, intention, and contingency, but also to be challenged and to develop and test hypotheses about the environment. Bruner and Sherwood's (1976) description of the development of the "peek-a-boo" game between one infant and her mother beautifully illustrates each of these perspectives. The game begins in very early infancy in a form that takes advantage of the child's innate responsiveness to looming objects (in this instance, a face), as well as of innate biological rhythms underlying cycles of attention and withdrawal. Gradually the game evolves into a hiding game, first of the infant's face and then the mother's. As the baby develops, the role of "hider" is transferred from mother to child. Building on her daughter's natural responses to elements of surprise, and utilizing an underlying repetitive structure, the mother forms a consistent set of rules, thereby providing the infant with ample opportunity to practice the roles emerging at each successive level of complexity. Through this rule structure, the mother achieves a delicate balance for maintaining the child in an anticipatory mode, neither sure of the outcome nor overloaded by too wide a range of possibilities. As the game evolves over time, it gradually incorporates the many variations possible within its rules. In the view of the researchers, patterned variation within a set of constraining rules, and matched to the child's current understanding, is crucial to the development and mastery of both competence and generativeness.

Clearly, the child is experiencing the effect of his own actions upon the environment in a form that makes sense to him. Within this framework of interaction are combined and experienced components of emotional (Isabella, Belsky & von Eye, 1989), motivational (Belsky, Good & Most, 1980), communicative (Dunst, 1985), and cognitive competence (Rogoff & Gardner, 1984). The caregiver's role is to adapt the form of the game (both within and across sessions) and the strategies used to maintain it, matching the child's emerging skills and abilities while keeping the game continually interesting and challenging. Clearly, too, because each infant has different lower and upper thresholds for stimulation (Field, 1980), interactions will be most satisfactory for both partners if the caregiver is a good reader of cues, adapting not only to increasing competence, but to individual differences in temperament, preferences, and capabilities, and to the efforts of the infant within the particular interaction. Nevertheless, it is the child's ability to respond to the rule structure, to learn it, and to assume responsibility for it that turns the game into the elegantly scaffolded activity that it is. Thus, both partners have important roles to play in the ongoing development of the game.

Disabilities as Individual Differences

All young children are dependent on their caregivers not only for access to and interpretation of the larger environment but as supporters of interactions with that environment. This dependency may be especially evident in young children with biological differences that may influence the ways in which they approach and engage their environments. In addition, individual differences in their abilities as interactors may result in their being less able to create their own developmentally supportive interactions, thereby violating a key assumption of DAP.

It is apparent that characteristics of interactions with caregivers are dependent on the history and ecological contexts of the particular child-caregiver relationship. As we might predict, they also are dependent on the capabilities and characteristics of each individual partner (Walker, 1982). Each partner must be self-regulated to the extent that patterns of behavior are predictable to the other. Furthermore, each must respond to the other's behaviors in a manner that makes it clear that the partners are sharing the same experience. Finally, each partner must be capable and willing to adapt behavior patterns to the extent necessary to mesh them into synchronous units with multiple partners in multiple situations. Hence, clarity of signals, or "readability" (Dunst, 1985; Goldberg, 1977), plays a major role in accomplishing synchrony between the partners. Conversely, "readability" also plays a significant role (McCollum, 1991) as each partner attends and adapts to the other.

It might be expected that extreme individual differences, such as those that may be associated with disabilities in young children, would present unique challenges to their interactive partners. There is now a substantial body of research indicating that young children with various disabilities, as well as those born prematurely or with other biologically based conditions, do display differences in their interactions with others and with their physical environments that may make it more difficult for their partners to engage them and to support their participation (Field, 1980). Visual impairment, for instance, influences one of the major modalities through which early communication occurs, as well as the child's ability to interact independently with the physical environment. Infants with cerebral palsy may be less able to regulate their own levels of excitement, or as they get older, to move to objects of interest or organize their abilities for exploring various facets of their environments. These differences will in turn influence the interactive roles of their caregivers.

Whereas in cases such as sensory or motor impairment differences in interaction may be at least partially predictable, in others they may be more subtle. For instance, as social partners, infants with Down syndrome demonstrate differences and delays in the development of affective expression (Cicchetti & Sroufe, 1976), including longer latencies to expression and more subdued affect (Emde, Katz and Thorpe, 1978). Jones (1977) documented disruptions in burst-pause patterns of vocalization, as well as in eye contact. As children with Down syndrome grow beyond infancy, they continue to exhibit differences in communicative systems, as well as in cognitive areas that form the basis of parent-child interactions, including problem solving, memory, exploration, goal directed behavior, and attentional processes (see Cicchetti & Beeghly, 1990a, 1990b). However, etiologies provide only part of the answer: There also are differences in style of interaction that appear to be more general across disabilities. As a group, children with biologically based disabilities and other conditions have been described as less readable, less responsive, and as taking less initiative during social interaction (Field, 1980; Fraiberg, 1974; Jones, 1977).

These differences have broad implications not only for children's ability to engage their physical and social environments, but for the roles of their caregivers in supporting these interactions. Thus, if mutual pleasure and intersubjectivity are to be achieved, we would expect compensatory differences in parental interaction styles as well. Research describing the interactive characteristics of parents with their infants with disabilities, as well as with other biologically based differences such as prematurity, has yielded fairly consistent results. Compared to parents of infants who are biologically intact, these parents tend to provide more stimulation, to be more directive, and to assume more dominant roles in guiding the interaction (Marfo, 1991).

Interpreted within a main effects model of development, and bolstered by results from more mainstream interaction research that indicated a correlation between these same characteristics and poorer outcomes in children, the initial interpretation was that the caregiver's behavior was causing the children's delay. Directiveness was defined not only as undesirable, but as harmful. However, later work indicates that the relationship between directiveness and development is much more complex.

In a recent review of research on parental directiveness during interactions with young children with disabilities, Marfo (1991) traced the beginnings of the common assumption that directiveness is undesirable to research in normal language development, where variations in parental behavior have been related to variations in children's linguistic competence. Marfo summarized the fallacies underlying this argument. Although there does appear to be a relationship between parental interactional styles and individual differences in children's linguistic competence, one major flaw in the interpretation that certain characteristics of parental language are thereby undesirable is that these conclusions have been derived most often from correlational studies; these may show a relationship between variables without supporting any valid interpretation of direction of effects. A second logical flaw is the direct application of this interpretation of directiveness as inherently problematic to dyads in which the infant may bring substantial interactional differences to the interactive situation. Less than a handful of studies have examined this relationship directly. As Marfo notes, this argument fails to account for the transactional nature of interaction, yet, as we have seen, it is essential that the infant's role in the interaction be an important determiner of the caregiver's.

Few studies have examined individual differences in caregivers' interactions in relation to individual differences in children's behavior during the interaction. These few studies indicate that the dimension of "directive-nondirective" must be differentiated from the dimension of "responsive-intrusive," as the two may define very different and potentially orthogonal qualities. Thus, a caregiver may be both responsive and directive (Crawley & Spiker, 1983; Tannock, 1988), with responsiveness being defined in relation to the particular child in the particular situation. The social and object directed behavior of the child during the interaction, rather than diagnostic status, may be the stronger determinant of maternal directiveness (Tannock, 1988).

A transactional model of development would predict that individual differences in infants, such as those related to having a disability, would be related to differences in their caregivers as well. Further, rather than placing a value on these differences, this model would cause us to ask "why" the differences occur and what they accomplish for that dyad. However, a transactional interpretation of dyadic differences has emerged only recently. Bell (1968) was instrumental in bringing to our attention the child's role in the interaction, resulting in a major shift in the interpretations of interaction research. In 1980, Field published a summary and analysis of research describing the qualitative and quantitative differences that had emerged from this work for children with biological differences and their parents. Of particular interest was her discussion of the combination of potentially higher thresholds of activation for these infants, requiring caregivers to "work harder" to obtain a response, and lower thresholds of over-stimulation, requiring caregivers to achieve a sensitive balance between enough and too much. Goldberg (1977) and Dunst (1985) provided useful models of the transactional process and its implications when one member of a dyad has characteristics that make him a more difficult partner. The competent infant is instrumental in establishing those social conditions that support his own development. Equipped with a repertoire of behaviors that capture adult attention and facilitate interaction, the infant indirectly also facilitates his own early social relationships. Caregivers, in turn, evaluate the effectiveness of their own interactions on the basis of how the infant responds. When the infant's cues are easy to read, adjustments are readily made that engender feelings of success. When the infant is more difficult to read, adjustments are more difficult to make, and may be less successful, potentially engendering feelings of failure. Thus, the readability of the infant plays a major role not only in what the infant experiences during the interaction, but in the feelings that the caregiver may develop about interaction with her child (Dunst, 1985; Goldberg, 1977).

There is more than sufficient evidence that children with disabilities and other biological differences may present significant interactive challenges to their caregivers, both during early face-to-face interactions and as they develop over time. Emerging from the transactional perspective is a clear indication that, in order to support the interactions between infants with disabilities and their social and physical worlds, caregivers may have to assume a more active role, carrying more of the burden not only for structuring the environment, but for supporting the child's interactions with it. For synchrony to be achieved to the extent that interaction will serve its important functions in early development, extraordinary sensitivity, "readability," and adaptability may be required of caregivers (McCollum, 1991).

Currently, the theoretical perspective that offers the most useful framework for incorporating this information into a redefinition of developmentally appropriate practice is one that places development and learning squarely within its social context, with careful examination of the role of the social partner in supporting the child's role within the situation being examined. Clearly, this framework, defined by the zone of proximal development and the caregiver's role as a scaffolder, fits neatly within a transactional perspective (Marfo, 1991). We believe that this model, in addition to helping us understand early development, also provides explicit guidance for the role of the caregiver as supporter of the child's development and learning. Thus, it has direct relevance for defining developmentally appropriate practice in a manner that goes beyond overreliance on a constructivist theory of early development.

INTERACTIONS AND ADAPTATIONS AS SCAFFOLDING

Scaffolding as Developmental Support

The seminal study of "scaffolding," and the one that introduced the metaphor, was done by Wood, Bruner and Ross (1976). Observing a natural tutoring situation, a child working with an adult on a block construction task, the researchers sought to describe how children of different chronological (and therefore presumably developmental) status responded to different kinds of assistance. The tutor's assistance varied from presenting the goal (model) and the materials, to providing verbal instruction, to completing steps of the construction herself. The 3-year-olds could do little on their own, and the roles of the tutor included recruiting the child to the task, providing materials, and jointly completing the construction. But 5-year-olds, once they knew the goal, completed the task relatively independently, and the tutor's role was to confirm or check the construction. The behavior of the middle group, the 4-year-olds, was the most difficult for the tutor. Because these children proceeded on a "try it and see" basis, it was hard for the tutor to match support to the child's behavior. This matching, equivalent to the adaptations we see with parents, depends on the child's progression through the task, as well as on an understanding of the child's learning patterns and history with the task. It is of note that the match became most critical when learning was taking place not at either end of a child's zone of proximal development, as with the 3- and 5-year-olds, but in the middle, where the necessary level of graded support or challenge is not as immediately evident, or in the terminology of the interaction literature, where readability was more difficult.

In an earlier study, Wood and Middleton (1975) had observed that the children most successful at independent construction by the end of an observation session were those whose mothers followed the pattern of, "If the child succeeds, offer less help when next intervening; if the child fails, offer more help." Wood and Middleton inferred that the critical aspect of scaffolding was sensitivity to the child's level of ability with that task, mirroring the importance of caregiver responsiveness as defined in the research on parent-child interaction. From their observations, and consistent with their theory, Wood, Bruner and Ross (1976) described six functions that have come to define "scaffolding":

1. The tutor must recruit the learner to the task by obtaining interest in solving the problem or acquiring the skill. Though seemingly simple, this is a crucial aspect of the tutor's role, because it is in this recruitment that caregiver and child begin to develop their mutual understanding of the purpose of the task.
2. The tutor must simplify the task so that the child can perform all of the subtasks that he can manage. The tutor is in control of the total task, provides subtasks for the child to try, and fills in around the child's efforts.
3. Throughout the process the tutor maintains the child's interest in what has been accomplished, as well as in the next step.

4. The tutor must "mark discrepancies" between what the child has produced and what would be acceptable. In this way, the tutor provides feedback that the child can use to adjust his performance so that it becomes progressively closer to successful independent completion.
5. The child's frustration must be controlled by correction that is supportive of his progress.
6. The tutor provides models of successful task completion, not just by a successful performance, but by modelling the process or by finishing an attempt of the learner's.

From the perspective of Rogoff (1991) and others (e.g., Wertsch, 1985), our understanding of development in young children has gone beyond the Piagetian focus on the individual's construction of reality, and has come to encompass the broader functions and contexts of human development. In particular, the social context of development and the cultural provision of practices in which to embed social interactions are now viewed as crucial to understanding the collaborative nature of human development. All young children are indeed active participants in their own progressively complex adaptations to their environments, but their participation is guided by an adult's sensitive provision of information, explanation, models, roles, and goals. Goals are of particular importance, since they provide focus and purpose to both joint and individual activity. Children do not produce performance that is error free, and adults use errors to adjust the type and extent of the scaffold (Greenfield, 1984). Within this theoretical framework, it does not make sense to partial out the adult's behavior from the child's. Rather, the unit of interest and analysis is the pattern of collaboration.

Several researchers have found that different types of tasks elicit different scaffolding strategies. Sorsby and Martlew (1991), compared features of mother-child conversation during book reading and Play-doh modeling, and found that mothers used different kinds of utterances in the two tasks with their 4-year-old children. When engaged in joint reading, mothers used utterances that were at a higher level of abstraction than during the modelling task. During the modelling task, mothers provided more acknowledgement of the child's activity. A study by Sigel and McGillicuddy-Delisi (1984) also found that different strategies were used in two different tasks, reading and paper folding. Parents seemed to use a more demanding conversational mode in the paper folding task, noting, however, that parents appeared to regard this task as more of a teaching task, in which we would expect them to use more instructive or demanding discourse. This is consistent with a study by McDonald and

Pien (1982), who found that the mother's intent significantly influenced the nature of her requests to the child.

There is substantial evidence from this literature that parents systematically vary and adapt their levels of challenge and support within and across interactive situations to match the child's capacities and patterns and to scaffold the child's participation in the interaction. These variations and adaptations appear to be based on the parent's sensitivity to the child's immediate performance, coupled with understanding of various characteristics of the child, the demands of the task, and the parent's own goal for the outcome of the interaction. Parental variations provide compelling evidence that the developmental appropriateness of any practice must be tailored to the child, the task, and the child's previous experience with the task. Presumably, by supporting practice and acquisition of the behaviors necessary for successful engagement and performance, the child is helped to develop an understanding of the process of his involvement, and begins to internalize this process, thereby becoming capable of performing the task alone. It is this internalization of process that exerts the "push/pull" for development.

Scaffolding and Young Children with Disabilities

Like the literature reviewed above on early reciprocal interactions, scaffolding studies demonstrate the delicate balance in roles that is achieved as the adult initially and progressively modifies strategies to achieve an interface between task and person that is most likely to result in the child's acquiring the components, and eventually the whole, of the task. Based on research on interactions with young children with disabilities, in which partners may be required to observe and adapt more carefully and consciously to idiosyncratic capabilities and patterns of the child, we also would expect that the interactional processes involved in scaffolding might be more difficult with these children. This hypothesis is in line with the finding mentioned earlier (Wood, Bruner & Ross, 1976) that the more uncertainty in the system, the less readily evident may be the necessary balance of support and challenge.

In defining the functions of scaffolding, Wood, Bruner, and Ross (1976) pointed out that recruitment to the task is particularly important because it organizes and establishes the mutuality of the task. If we assume that children are major initiators, recruitment may require little work on the part of the adults. For children who may initiate interactions less frequently, such as those with Down syndrome or visual impairment, the adult's role may require more aggressive recruitment. Knowing that early involvement with a new task, or working on a task in the upper range of a child's zone of proximal development, requires more support, and knowing that children with Down syndrome prefer easier tasks (Harter, 1977), we would expect that adults, in recruiting and simplifying a task, would need to provide greater support in the form of subtask completion, information, repetitions, and provision of models. Thus, for the child with a disability, the appropriate balance of support and challenge may look quite different from that which is appropriate to a child who frequently initiates and independently pursues encounters with objects or events in his environment.

Few studies have attempted to directly link specific parental strategies to specific individual differences in children's responses during the process of the interaction. The potential of this type of research for identifying the adaptive value of matching scaffolds to child and task within the interaction is particularly important. For instance, Landry and Chapieski (1989) studied the ability of 12-month-olds to attend to and explore their environments in interaction with their mothers, using a comparison between infants with Down syndrome and developmental-age-matched, high-risk preterm infants. In both groups, higher levels of object play were obtained when mothers matched the infant's focus of attention, rather than redirecting it. However, infants with Down syndrome were less attentive to the task in general: Therefore, their mothers had to use more attention-directing strategies. When required to shift attention between two toys, the infants with Down syndrome were never successful in becoming involved with the new toy, whereas those who were preterm were sometimes able to accomplish this shift with their mother's support. Moreover, different strategies elicited toy interaction in the two groups. In the group of infants with Down syndrome, higher level responses were achieved when mothers directly demonstrated the toy. In the group of preterm infants, this higher degree of structure was not necessary in order to achieve the same levels of play. Simply directing attention or reorienting the baby toward the toy was sufficient. Thus, not only were scaffolds needed to serve different purposes in the two groups, but there was a qualitative difference in what worked.

Although research does not yet provide information on long-term developmental outcomes that may be related to caregiver adaptations, it does indicate that those parents who are better able to match their children's needs for support within the interaction may be more successful at setting the stage for participation, practice, and ultimately, development. While limited, this research points to the conclusion that the strategies used by caregivers (whether parent or interventionist) must be examined from the perspective of their adaptive value for that dyad, in that particular situation, and at that particular point in development (Heckhausen,

1987). Just as adaptations are made as the developing child achieves new levels of competence, so too must adaptations be made for young children who differ substantially in their ability to engage their physical and social environments. It is apparent that these adaptations may provide the child with increased opportunities for pleasurable contingency experiences, thereby setting the stage for further development.

DEVELOPMENTALLY APPROPRIATE PRACTICE FROM AN INDIVIDUAL PERSPECTIVE

DAP, as defined by National Association for the Education of Young Children (Bredekamp, 1991), is organized around child directed play, with emphasis on child choice and interests, expressed in independent actions on the environment. When a child has disabilities, assumptions made with regard to any or all of these components may or may not hold true. Therefore young children with disabilities provide a unique opportunity to reexamine the basic tenets of DAP:

- How can "development" be defined in a way that makes sense with children who exhibit extreme heterogeneity both within and across etiologies, or whose developmental status across domains may differ?
- How do we ensure compatibility between purely developmental goals and those that define functional skills that the child needs to fully participate in home, school, and community environments?
- Can we influence how young children with disabilities experience their environments, and what they are able to gain from these interactions, and thereby influence their development?
- Is what is developmentally appropriate for one child necessarily appropriate for another, and how is this played out in content (goals) and in the teaching environments and processes designed to support development and learning?

To date, answers to these questions, as applied to children with disabilities, are not clear.

In this chapter, we elected to focus on caregiver-child interaction as a microcosm within which to examine the potential effects of a disability on what the child brings to interactions with his environments, and therefore on the supports that may be required from the caregiver to optimize these interactions. All transactions, including scaffolding transactions, are built around the reciprocal roles of caregiver and child, adjusted across task, child, and time. This review indicates that developmentally appropriate practice may be most usefully examined from the perspective of what the individual child brings to the particular task at hand, and the level and types of support needed by the child to focus attention on salient aspects of the particular situation, obtain feedback on his own participation, and interact successfully with the task. To achieve this, children with disabilities may require both more, and different types of, support. Thus, these literatures have focused our attention on the potentially adaptive value of caregiver differences, including differences in directiveness, as they interact with and support these children. The critical variable, distilled from both the interaction and the scaffolding literatures, is the feedback that the child receives from the environment as to the effectiveness of his efforts during the interaction process.

Interpretation of difference as beneficial, like interpretation of difference as harmful, requires careful examination. Given different degrees of readability and readerability within any specific dyad, adjustments may not occur automatically, or when they do occur, may not necessarily be optimally supportive of the child's involvement and participation, or of further development. For instance, energetic physical stimulation of a less responsive infant may achieve a momentarily pleasurable interaction. However, if used to the exclusion of other modes of interaction, it may limit the infant's ability to take an increasingly reciprocal role. Thus, the worth of any particular strategy must be evaluated within the context of individual and task, with the critical variables being the balance between this context on the one hand, and the type and extent of support provided on the other.

Careful study of interactions from a transactional perspective can lend itself to developing more developmentally appropriate adaptations. For instance, Tannock (1988) noted that caregivers may need to learn to adjust the pace of their interactions to compensate for the slower response time of the infant with Down syndrome. Based on her experience with families in which the infants were blind, Fraiberg (1974) was able to help parents provide more developmentaly appropriate situations assisting them to be better readers of their childrens' alternative, subtle cues. As more research of this kind becomes available, it will allow us not only to recognize developmentally appropriate adaptations, but to consciously improve the quality of our own adaptations.

The notion of scaffolding in no way negates the importance of child as active participant, but rather recognizes that optimal activity on the child's part may be directly related to the supports provided to facilitate the match between his own abilities and the task. What is important is what recruits, maintains, and facilitates this child as an active participant in the particular task. Such a definition has the advantage of making derivative teaching practices more easily translatable to the non-cognitive learning domains that may assume relatively more explicit emphasis in early childhood special education than in early childhood education. By recognizing the developmental appropriateness of a more active role for the interventionist as a supporter of the child's interactions, it also has the added advantage of increasing the compatibility between teaching procedures that at times have been characterized as polar opposites: developmental practice and direct instruction. The abilities, needs, and individual differences present in a particular child, in combination with the goal, will determine the nature of the transaction between interventionist and child. Individual differences also may influence the goals selected as important for that child, whether they be developmental, functional, or informational (Campione, Brown, Ferrara, & Bryant, 1984).

Educators have come to understand the necessity of forging a partnership with parents to strengthen any child's learning environment. Most of these partnerships have been based on the idea that parents can be included in the work of the school. The literature reviewed in this chapter takes us in another direction, and we would do well to import into the classroom the knowledge that can be gained of developmentally supportive transactions between adult and child that have evolved in family environments. By focusing on the match between task and child, and on the adult's role in achieving this match over microgenetic and ontogenetic development, scaffolding provides an alternative, useful way of examining developmental appropriateness.

In many ways, the movement toward DAP as a primary standard for practice has thrown a smokescreen on progress in early childhood special education, distracting our attention from the broader issues:

- Understanding the development of young children with special needs and the theories that may increase our understanding of appropriate intervention practices.
- Understanding the ecological contexts of development and how these may be employed in support of development.
- Understanding the impact of what the adult brings to the interaction in terms of individual differences.
- Better defining the zone of proximal development for children with disabilities, in terms of both etiological groups and individual differences.
- Exploring and better defining the types of scaffolding that may be employed to support children's interactions.
- Exploring the implications of the scaffolding process for

classroom practices beyond interactions between child and interventionist.

The issue is not whether practice should be developmentally appropriate: clearly it should. Rather, the issue is to define a developmental approach that makes sense for diverse children, and to determine whether the guidelines of DAP, as currently formulated and applied, lead to practice that is developmentally appropriate for a particular young child with special needs. As in the study of development, in which research with children with disabilities has taught us much about normal development (Cicchetti, 1984; Walker & Crawley, 1983), it is likely that careful examination of DAP as a standard of practice with children with disabilities will teach us much about the definition of intervention practices that are developmentally appropriate for all children. We believe that what will be learned is that the definition lies not in particular practices, but in the match between a particular child, a particular task, and the balance of challenge and support provided.

REFERENCES

Bakeman, R., & Adamson, L. (1984). Coordinating attention to people and objects and mother-infant and peer-infant interaction. *Child Development, 55,* 1278–1289.

Bell, R. Q. (1968). A reinterpretation of the direction of effects in studies of socialization. *Psychological Review, 75,* 81–95.

Belsky, J., Goode, M., & Most, R. K. (1980). Maternal stimulation and infant exploratory competence: Cross-sectional, correlational and experimental analyses. *Child Development, 51,* 1168–1178.

Bredekamp, S. (1991). *Developmentally appropriate practices in early childhood programs serving children from birth through age eight* (expanded ed.). Washington, DC: National Association for the Education of Young Children.

Bruner, J. (1990). *Acts of meaning.* Cambridge MA: Harvard University.

Bruner, J. (1975). The ontogenesis of speech acts. *Journal of Child Language, 2,* 1–19.

Bruner, J., & Sherwood, V. (1976). Peekaboo and the learning of rule structures. In J. S. Bruner, A. Jolly, & K. Sylva (Eds.), *Play: Its role in development and evolution* (pp. 277–285). New York: Basic Books.

Campione, J., Brown, A., Ferrara, R., & Bryant, N. (1984). The zone of proximal development: Implications for individual differences and learning. In B. Rogoff & J. Wertsch (Eds.), *Children's learning in the "zone of proximal development"* (pp. 77–91). San Francisco: Jossey-Bass.

Cicchetti, D. (1984). The emergence of developmental psychopathology. *Child Development, 55,* 1–7.

Cicchetti, D., & Beeghly, M. (1990a). An organizational approach to the study of Down syndrome: Contributions to an integrative theory of development. In D. Cicchetti & M. Beeghly (Eds.), *Children with Down syndrome: A developmental perspective* (pp. 29–62). Cambridge, England: Cambridge University Press.

Cicchetti, D., & Beeghly, M. (1990b). *Children with Down syndrome: A developmental perspective.* Cambridge, England: Cambridge University Press.

Cicchetti, D., & Sroufe, L. A. (1976). The relationship between affective and cognitive development in Down syndrome infants. *Child Development, 47,* 920–929.

Collis, G. M. (1977). Visual co-orientation and maternal speech. In H. R. Schaffer (Ed.), *Studies in mother-infant interaction* (pp. 355–375). London: Academic Press.

Crawley, S. B., & Spiker, D. (1983). Mother-child interactions involving two-year-olds with Down syndrome: A look at individual differences. *Child Development, 54,* 1312–1323.

Dunst, C. J. (1985). Communicative competence and deficits: Effects on early social interactions. In E. T. McDonald & D. L. Gallagher (Eds.), *Facilitating social-emotional development in multiply handicapped children* (pp. 93–140). Philadelphia: Michael C. Prestegord.

Emde, R. N., Katz, E. L., & Thorpe, J. K. (1978). Emotional expression in infancy: II. Early deviations in Down syndrome. In M. Lewis & L. Rosenblum (Eds.), *The development of affect* (pp. 351–360). London: Plenum.

Field, T. (1986). Models for reactivity and chronic depression in infancy. In E. Z. Tronick & T. Field (Eds.), *Maternal depression and infant disturbance.* San Francisco: Jossey-Bass.

Field, T. (1980). Interactions of high-risk infants: Quantitative and qualitative differences. In S. B. Sawin, R. C. Hawkins, L. O. Walker, & J. H. Penticuff (Eds.), *Exceptional infant: Psychosocial risks in infant-environment transactions,* (Vol. 4, pp. 120–143). New York: Brunner/Mazel.

Field, T. (1978). The three Rs of infant-adult interactions: Rhythms, repertoires, and responsivity. *Journal of Pediatric Psychology, 3* (3), 131–136.

Fraiberg, S. (1974). Blind infants and their mothers: An examination of the sign system. In M. Bullowa (Ed.), *Before speech: The beginnings of interpersonal communication* (pp. 149–169). Cambridge, England: Cambridge University Press.

Goldberg, S. (1977). Social competence in infancy: A model of parent-infant interaction. *Merrill-Palmer Quarterly, 23* (3), 163–177.

Goodman, J. (1992, January 7). Wrong way to educate the handicapped. *Washington Post,* Op Ed page.

Gottman, J. (1979). Time series analysis of continuous data in dyads. In M. E. Lamb, S. J. Suomi, & G. R. Stephensen (Eds.), *Social interaction analysis: Methodological issues.* Madison, WI: University of Wisconsin Press.

Greenfield, P. (1984). A theory of the teacher in the learning activities of everyday life. In B. Rogoff & J. Lave (Eds.), *Everyday cognition: Its development in social context* (pp. 117–138). Cambridge, MA: Harvard University Press.

Harter, S. (1977). The effects of social reinforcement and task difficulty level on the pleasure derived by normal and retarded children from cognitive challenge and mastery. *Journal of Experimental Child Psychology, 24,* 476–494.

Heckhausen, J. (1987). Balancing for weaknesses and challenging developmental potential: A longitudinal study of mother-infant dyads in apprenticeship interactions. *Developmental Psychology, 23* (6), 762–770.

Isabella, R. A, Belsky, J., & von Eye, A. (1989). Origins of infant-mother attachment: An examination of interactional synchrony during the infant's first year. *Developmental Psychology, 25,* 12–21.

Jones, O. (1977). Mother-child communication with prelinguistic Down's syndrome and normal infants. In H. R. Schaffer (Ed.), *Studies in mother-infant interaction* (pp. 379–401). New York: Academic Press.

Kessler, S. A. (1991). Early childhood education as development: Critique of the metaphor. *Early Education and Development, 2* (2), 137–152.

Kostelnik, M. J., (1992). Myths associated with developmentally appropriate programs. *Young Children, 47* (4), 17-23.

Landry, S. H., & Chapieski, M. L. (1989). Joint attention and infant toy exploration: Effects of Down syndrome and prematurity. *Child Development, 60,* 103–118.

Lockman, J. J., & Hazen N. L. (1989). *Action in social context: Perspectives on early development.* New York: Plenum.

Mahoney, G., Robinson, C., & Powell, A. (1992). Focusing on parent-child interaction: The bridge to developmentally appropriate practices. *Topics in Early Childhood Special Education, 12* (1), 105–120.

Mallory, B. L. (1990, May). *Developmental, functional, and biological models for early intervention: A convergent perspective.* Paper presented at the annual meeting of the American Association on Mental Retardation, Atlanta, GA

Marfo, K. (1991). The maternal directiveness theme in mother-child interaction research: Implications for early intervention. In K. Marfo (Ed.), *Early intervention in transition: Current perspectives on programs for handicapped children* (pp. 177–203). New York: Praeger.

McCollum, J. A. (1991). At the crossroad: Reviewing and rethinking interaction coaching. In K. Marfo, (Ed.), *Early intervention in transition: Current perspectives on programs for handicapped children* (pp. 137–176). New York: Praeger.

McDonald, L., & Pien, D. (1982). Mother conversational behavior as a function of interactional intent. *Journal of Child Language, 9,* 337–358.

Rogoff, B. (1991) *Apprenticeship in thinking: Cognitive development in social context.* New York: Oxford University Press.

Rogoff, B., & Gardner, W. P. (1984). Guidance in child development: An examination of mother-child instruction. In B. Rogoff & J. Lave (Eds.), *Everyday cognition: Its development in social context* (pp. 95–116). Cambridge, MA: Harvard University Press.

Sameroff, A., & Chandler, M. (1975). Reproductive risk and the continuum of caretaking casualty. In F. Horowitz (Ed.), *Review of child development research* (Vol. 4). Chicago: University of Chicago Press.

Schaffer, H. R., Collis, G. M., & Parsons, G. (1977). Vocal interchange and visual regard in verbal and pre-verbal children. In H. R. Schaffer (Ed.), *Studies in mother-infant interaction* (pp. 291–324). London: Academic.

Sigel, I., & McGillicuddy-Delisi, A. (1984). Parents as teachers of their children: A distancing behavior model. In A. D. Pelligrini & T. D. Yawkey (Eds.), *The development of oral and written language in social context* (pp.71–91). Norwood, NJ: Ablex.

Sorsby, A., & Martlew, M. (1991). Representational demands in mothers' talk to preschool children in two contexts: Picture book reading and a modeling task. *Journal of Child Language, 18,* 373–395.

Spodek, B. (1991). Reconceptualizing early childhood education: A commentary. *Early Education and Development, 2* (2), 161–167.

Stern, D. (1974). Mother and infant at play: The dyadic interaction involving facial, vocal and gaze behaviors. In M. Lewis & L. Rosenblum (Eds.), *The effect of the infant on its caregiver* (pp. 187–214). New York: John Wiley and Sons.

Stern, D. N., Beebe, B., Jaffe, J., & Bennett, S. L. (1977). The infant's stimulus world during social interaction: A study of caregiver behaviors with particular reference to repetition and timing. In H. R. Schaffer (Ed.), *Studies in mother-infant interaction* (pp. 177–202). London: Academic Press.

Tannock, R. (1988). Mothers' directiveness in their interactions with their children with and without Down syndrome. *American Journal on Mental Retardation, 93* (2), 154–165.

Trevarthen, C. (1977). Descriptive analysis of infant communicative behavior. In H. R. Schaffer (Eds.), *Studies in mother-infant interaction* (pp. 227–270). London: Academic Press.

Vygotsky, L. (1978). *Mind in society: The development of higher psychological processes.* Cambridge, MA: Harvard University Press.

Wachs, T.D., & Gruen, G.E. (1982). *Early experience and human development.* New York: Plenum.

Walker, J. A. (1982). Social interactions of handicapped infants. In D. D. Bricker (Ed.), *Intervention with at-risk and handicapped infants* (pp. 271–232). Baltimore: University Park Press.

Walker, J. A., & Crawley, S.B. (1983). Conceptual and methodological issues in studying the handicapped infant. In S. G. Garwood & R. R. Fewell (Eds.), *Educating handicapped infants: Issues in development and intervention* (pp. 25–68). Rockville, MD: Aspen.

Walsh, D. J., (1991). Extending the discourse on developmental appropriateness. *Early Education and Development, 2* (2), 109–119.

Wertsch, J. V. (1985). *Vygotsky and the social formation of mind.* Cambridge, MA: Harvard University Press.

Wolery, M., Strain, P. S., & Bailey, D. B. (no date). *Applying the framework of developmentally appropriate practice to children with special needs.* Pittsburth: Allegheny-Singer Research Institute.

Wood, D., Bruner, J. S., & Ross, G. (1976). The role of tutoring in problem solving. *Journal of Child Psychology and Psychiatry, 17,* 89–100.

Wood, D., & Middleton, D. (1975). A study of assisted problem-solving. *British Journal of Psychology, 66,* 181–191.

5

• • • • • •

Expanding the Perceptions of Developmentally Appropriate Practice
Changing Theoretical Perspectives

BARBARA L. LUDLOW AND TERRY R. BERKELEY

With the proclamation of developmentally appropriate practice (DAP) as the foundation for curriculum development and program design in early childhood education, teachers and other professionals are urged to arrange the environment to provide numerous opportunities for young children to explore and to direct their own learning through hands-on experiences (Bryant, Clifford, & Peisner, 1991; Elkind, 1990; Yonemura, 1986). Proponents of DAP argue that failure to provide education that is appropriate to a young child's development may contribute to learning and behavior problems since children may be asked to "learn what they cannot understand" (DeVries & Kohlberg, 1990, p. 18). The notion that education for young children should be developmentally appropriate can hardly be questioned; the challenge remains to interpret the meaning of age appropriateness and individual appropriateness with respect to children who exhibit delays, disabilities, and other developmental differences.

Considerable controversy has arisen over the application of DAP to early intervention and early childhood special education programs. Some professionals have advocated DAP as a foundation for best practice for children with disabilities or those who are at risk for developmental delays between birth and 6 years of age (Connor, Williamson, & Siepp, 1978; Holdgrafer & Dunst, 1986; Norris, 1991), while others have singled out DAP as a threat to quality programming and services for this same group of children, since it may not provide sufficient direct, intensive instruction in specific skills (Carta, Schwartz, Atwater, & McConnell,

1991; Odom & McEvoy, 1990). Some authors have argued that DAP curriculum guidelines conflict with the behaviorist instructional methods of most intervention programs (Klein & Campbell, 1990), but others have asserted that DAP facilitates the integration of children into mainstream preschools and kindergartens (Deiner, 1993).

Most agree that DAP constitutes a reasonable and organized point of departure from the developmentally inappropriate, atheoretically based programming often found previously, and sometimes seen even now in child care centers, early childhood programs, public school kindergartens, and early elementary grade classrooms. While we are convinced that practice must be appropriate to the development of the child, existing notions of DAP may themselves not be appropriate insofar as they are based on an outmoded conceptualization of development. As we have argued elsewhere (Berkeley & Ludlow, 1989, 1992), all of us who work in the fields of early childhood education and intervention must reexamine present practices in the light of new understandings of child development. For us, this means adopting a theoretical view of development that is holistic, dynamic, and transactional, thus expanding the present boundaries of our thinking about developmental processes.

PROMPTINGS FOR CHANGE

In his address to the Biennal Institute of the National Center for Clinical Infant Programs upon receipt of its Dolly Madison Award, Urie Bronfenbrenner (1992) offered a provocative retrospective and challenge to those who work in the field of early childhood education. He stated,

> Recently, I had the occasion to examine what current textbooks, and their counterparts in the nation's bookstalls, have to say about the conditions and processes that foster, or undermine, children's development. Once one gets beyond the new demographics of family forms, two-wage-earner households, gender roles, child care, poverty, and minorities—as important as those are—the discussion of what goes on (or should go on) *within* any of these settings is mostly a rather sparse, dull, and curious mix of facts and ideas from the 1960s and 1970s. It's still "ages and stages," with occasional doses of behavior modification. Nothing important that needs to be done takes longer than just a few minutes—Sesame Street style. The processes mentioned are always one-way, with no turns allowed. There is more talk of parental discipline than of joint activities of parents with their children. Genetics only happens to twins, and they produce effects all by themselves. Objects and symbols are things used in tests. And the only times that children develop are when they're with somebody else. (p. 33)

Here Bronfenbrenner shows his impatience with the field's continued dependence on outmoded notions of developmental stages, milestones, and domains to support the design of programs and procedures. He calls upon us to formulate new conceptualizations of development that recognize the unique reciprocal relationship between each child and the environment.

Shonkoff (1992) also has advocated for meaningful and thoughtful shifts in our thinking about development, specifically to devise an updated theory that incorporates the most recent data. He said, "Even our best assessment of child . . . functioning [is] limited, and the challenges of interpreting data on human development and adaptation over time are monumental" (p. 9). Meisels (1992) agreed, stressing the need to move beyond current understandings through critical analysis and innovation. "We have gone beyond the 'discovery' of the family and the rejection of single causal models as adequate explanations of delay, disorder, and disability. Now we must accept the responsibility to create new early intervention approaches that are sensitive to our current contexts" (p. 5). Mallory (1992) suggested a need to completely refocus DAP to emphasize a convergence of biological, functional, and developmental frameworks, because it is important "to synthesize best practices from each into a coherent whole" (p. 11).

Such prompts for change are neither new nor unique. In fact, there is a considerable history in the child development literature urging us to move beyond the "stages and ages and phases" endlessly discussed by so many researchers, curriculum designers, and program providers. The so-called "universals" of development were called into question nearly 25 years ago (Feldman, 1980). In an interview with Biringuier (1980), Piaget stated, "My . . . ambition is that the hypotheses one could oppose to my own will finally be seen not to contradict them but to result from a normal process of differentiation" (p. 143). Bruner (1983), too, argued compellingly that child development researchers needed to move away from what he described as "singular systems of thought". To shortchange this process of theory building, research, translation, program design, implementation, evaluation, and review will not be beneficial to children, to their families, or to program providers, either in the short term or in the long. If programs are implemented to stimulate developmental change in children, then the procedures, strategies, and methods used to bring about that change must be grounded in a sound basis of theory, fact, estimation, testing, and review, all of which has been explicated and considered *prior to as well as during* the implementation of early childhood education and intervention. We believe that it is now critical to discuss the viability and applicability of a different approach to development, thereby leading to alterations in how DAP is perceived and how programs for young children are designed, developed, operated, and evaluated.

A PROCESS-ORIENTED VIEW OF DEVELOPMENT

By development we mean the process of individual change that proceeds due to maturation (physiological growth under the influence of genes) plus learning (direct and/or mediated interactions with the environment in time and space). Development is *holistic* (each organism operates as an irreducible whole); *dynamic* (a continuously evolving process); and *transactional* (the individual changes the situation even as it changes her or him). Development is *not* fragmented (domain-specific); static (outcome- or stage-oriented); or unidirectional (representing a one-way effect by either individual or environment). Developmental changes cannot be captured by observing specific behaviors at isolated times; rather they can be understood only by analyzing patterns of actions over time and across settings.

Until now, in most conceptualizations, development has been represented as discrete bits of information about the organism at specific times. The traditional image is a set of stairsteps up which a child must climb; or a series of snapshots suspending the child in a sort of "developmental space" whether through developmental domains, developmental tasks or milestones, or a set of normative standards that focus on changes as they are expected to occur rather than as they happen.

These nonintegrated views of development may have been fostered by traditional research designs and methods (Schickendanz, Hansen, & Forsyth, 1990). That is, positivist research paradigms have focused our attention on overt behavior observable by others rather than on the individual's understanding that underlies the behavior. Group designs have been most effective in examining a few easily controlled variables instead of the interrelated complexity of factors that necessarily comprise development. Cross-sectional investigations have analyzed data from many children at specific instants rather than studying the changes of a few children over long periods of time. And research has been conducted primarily in contrived laboratory settings to control or eliminate natural variation. In our view, such approaches to research about child development have emphasized simplicity of explanation, application of general principles, and a search for homogeneity, all at the expense of richness of detail and applicability to individual circumstances.

To refocus theory and research about children's development to embrace and embody the complexity inherent in the human organism, we would begin with a simple assumption: development, in and of itself, cannot be seen directly but must be inferred from changes. As Sroufe (1979) suggested, development is a process rather than an outcome. An updated image of development would envision it as a videotape reflecting changes in the child in time, space, and perspective—with a focus on the tape's continuity, its wholeness, rather than the specific components within individual frames.

This changing perspective of development is made possible, in part, by recent changes in scientific paradigms for the study of human characteristics. The shift from a model of stability to a model of change (Haywood & Switzky, 1986; Jensen, 1990) encourages researchers to employ longitudinal designs that capture, over time, differences in behavior and traits that reflect the course of individual development. An idiographic orientation to empirical investigation (Frank, 1986) assumes that the accumulation of evidence from individual cases is essential to the formulation of general principles. The need to study the "whole child" (Zigler, 1990) has led investigators to explore a broader range of variables and the effect of their interactions on development. And, growing use of qualitative methodology (Stainback & Stainback, 1990) has facilitated the creative design of ethnographic studies that find new ways to investigate both human and environmental factors.

More recent perspectives of development have attempted to capture its complex, ever changing nature. Bronfenbrenner (1979) outlined an approach that viewed development in a set of widening contexts, and urged us to interpret changes in a child's behavior in the light of both the immediate and distant social and physical environments in which the child lived. Sameroff (1982, 1990) proposed a transactional model that analyzed development in terms of reciprocal interactions between children and their caregivers, with the child both influencing and being influenced by the environment. On the one hand, these theories have encouraged us to see development as resulting from the integration of a kaleidoscopic combination of factors within and outside the child; on the other hand, they have offered little in the way of new perspectives for examining the process of developmental change as it occurs in the child's own view.

One integrated, dynamic view of development that allows us to study the process itself is the salient responses model (Lewis & Starr, 1979). In this view, development can be understood by examining eight attributes of change, or salient responses, that every child experiences and exhibits in his or her individual process of development. The salient responses include "quantity, quality, speed of acquisition, utilization, affective tone, generalizability, organizational properties, and intention in the use of information" (p. 657). The appeal of this model lies in the fact that it is without the limitations inherent in a set of discrete domains and it provides a standard (but *not* standardized) means of understanding a child's development by professionals from a variety of disciplines, who usually bring their own theoretical propositions, often different from their peers, to their common tasks. Moreover, the salient responses are not bound by time, setting, milestones, or domains. They encompass both biological and environmental considerations, and they cannot be labelled as maturational, constructivist, or behavioral. This model, along with other integrated views of development, has both implicitly and explicitly provided an impetus for much of the qualitative assessment and observation of children's development that has taken place recently in early childhood education and early intervention programs.

A RECONCEPTUALIZATION OF
DEVELOPMENTALLY APPROPRIATE PRACTICE

A holistic, integrated, dynamic, transactional view of development nec-essarily has significant implications for DAP. First, our understanding of the basic tenets of age appropriateness and individual appropriateness must expand to include considerations of family and social contexts. Sec-ond, the notion of individual appropriateness must be based upon care-ful analysis of the particular actions, cognitions, and emotions that the child demonstrates during routine natural activities. And, finally, changes in the specific features of the child's actual behavior, rather than the expected form or outcome, must be identified and examined if develop-mental progress is to be determined.

Perhaps an example will help to clarify these points. An educator was observed attempting to teach a 4-year-old boy to engage in direct motor imitation using a baby rattle and a rag doll. Despite a variety of prompts, repeated trials, and the promise of edible reinforcers, the child made no effort to imitate the desired shaking action. Then, after the edu-cator asked the child to imitate dialing a toy telephone with similar lack of effect she concluded that the child was not "ready" for the learning task. Shortly afterward, she allowed the child to return to free play, whereupon he began dialing the telephone, a toy to which he had had no previous access. What are we to make of this incident? If we analyze it from the perspective of developmental stages and domains and mile-stones, we can only conclude that he did not demonstrate an age-related sensorimotor skill observed in younger children and may be exhibiting a motor or cognitive delay. If we examine the incident from an integrated perspective of development, however, quite a different picture emerges. Let us first ask a series of questions:

- Did the child lack the motor skills to engage in shaking the doll or rattle?   ·
- Did he lack the cognitive skills to understand the concept of imitation?
- Did he lack familiarity with the rattle and doll as objects of play, but not the telephone?
- Did he refuse to imitate with objects he devalued as related to babies or girls?
- Did he resist performing when commanded by others?
- Did he demonstrate the more advanced skill of deferred imitation but not immediate imitation?

To answer these questions, we must engage the child in additional interactions in which we closely observe his behavior upon modification of the setting, materials, and activity so that we can come to understand his individual response patterns as well as the specific features of the environment in which they occur.

If, in this case, we apply the salient responses model we learn that, in fact, the child easily learns to imitate shaking with a novel yet more age-appropriate object such as a tambourine (speed of acquisition), he prefers to imitate the actions of peers or familiar adults (affective tone), he displays precise imitation of complex skills such as dialing a telephone (quantity and quality), he readily imitates actions in other settings at school and at home (generalizability), and he incorporates deferred imitation of social skills like a handshake into natural play routines with stuffed animals (organization and intent). None of these findings suggest the presence of a developmental delay; in fact, given this particular child's history of frequent hospitalizations, isolation from other children, and restrictions on physical activity due to congenital heart disease, they could suggest that he is an exceptionally capable individual!

Effective programs in early childhood education and intervention must be based on a clearly articulated perspective of child growth and change from which the program can derive its developmentally appropriate practice with respect to philosophy, model, outcomes, implementation practices, and evaluation procedures. Without these theoretical underpinnings, it is difficult (if not impossible) to coordinate the various aspects of program delivery or to measure the accomplishment of program goals. As noted earlier, recent research has indicated that many programs use a practical if eclectic approach based on "what works" rather than a conceptual approach that "makes sense" because staff lack adequate preparation in theories of development (Bricker, 1988; Miller, 1991). This atheoretical bias on the part of program developers and service providers has clouded data interpretation used to evaluate program efficiency and effectiveness.

In the field of early intervention, many recent proposals for programmatic change suggest that practitioners are beginning to adopt a more integrated and dynamic view of development. New approaches to measurement of child behavior and performance, including naturalistic assessment (Barnett, Macmann, & Carey, 1992; Linehan, Brady, & Hwang, 1991), arena assessment (Connor, Williamson, & Siepp, 1978; Linder, 1990; McCune, Kalmanson, Fleck, Glazewski, & Sillari, 1990; Wolery & Dyk, 1984), and judgment-based assessment (Bailey, 1987; Dunst & Trivette, 1987) reflect a growing interest in obtaining a comprehensive, multiperspective picture of the child in relation to the variety of natural settings in which she or he interacts. Innovations such as activity-based intervention (Bricker & Woods-Cripe, 1992; Lowenthal, 1992), emphasis on natural routines of caregiving and social interactions as contexts for learning (Noonan & McCormick, 1992), and provisions for child-initiated learning (Bricker & Veltman, 1990) reveal increasing recognition of the ways in which skills from many domains are easily and naturally learned together in instructional activities involving exploration, social interaction, or play. Even current practices in the area of program evaluation such as goal attainment scaling and growth modeling (Hauser-Cram, 1990), and qualitative methodology such as interviews and participant observation (Stainback & Stainback, 1990), suggest new ways of measuring developmental changes that take into account the complexity and contexts of development.

TOWARD A RECONCEPTUALIZATION OF THEORY AND PRACTICE

It is clear that there can be no significant advances in the field of early childhood education and intervention unless and until we adopt a reconceptualization of development and allow it to reshape our programs and practices. The concept of DAP will be insufficient to stimulate such innovation if it is not founded upon an integrated theory of development. Bruner (1983), posits three questions that will help shape our understanding of the process of development:

1. By what means do growing human beings represent their experience of the world?

2. In what ways do growing human beings organize for future use the experiences they have encountered?
3. How do growing human beings use this organization to increase their mastery of the environment?

In Bruner's view (Bruner, Olver, & Greenfield, 1966), development occurs as the child reexperiences activities through different modes of engagement: initially in the enactive mode by physical manipulation of the environment; then in the iconic mode through use of two-dimensional representations; and, finally in the symbolic mode through formation of mental images and language concepts. In our view, the Lewis and Starr model of salient responses (1979) offers a promising framework for studying the specific behavioral changes that occur during developmental transformations.

Our efforts to answer Bruner's questions through research and reflection will force us to move away from relying upon developmental domains, milestones, and stages as the basic concepts for organizing our knowledge about human development, and to advance toward a more integrated, dynamic, and transactional perspective of child development. As songwriter Jimmy Buffet put it, if we make "changes in attitude" by focusing on different characteristics and processes and using different research designs and methods, we will soon make "changes in latitude" that will allow us to see children and their development in a new, clear light. Such a new perspective will allow us to create genuine developmentally appropriate practice to foster the optimum developmental progress for each and every child.

REFERENCES

Bailey, D. B. (1987). Collaborative goal setting with families: Resolving differences in values and priorities for services. *Topics in Early Childhood Special Education, 7* (2), 59–71.

Barnett, D. W., Macmann, G. M., & Carey, K. T. (1992). Early intervention and the assessment of developmental skills: Challenges and directions. *Topics in Early Childhood Special Education, 12* (1), 21–43.

Berkeley, T. R., & Ludlow, B. L. (1992). Developmental domains: The Mother of all interventions; or, the subterranean early development blues. *Topics in Early Childhood Special Education, 11* (4), 13–21.

Berkeley, T. R., & Ludlow, B. L. (1989). Toward a reconceptualization of the developmental model. *Topics in Early Childhood Special Education, 9* (3), 51–66.

Biringuier, J-C. (1980). *Conversations with Piaget,* (B. M. Gault, Trans.). Chicago: University of Chicago Press.

Bredekamp, S. (1987). *Developmentally appropriate practice in early childhood programs serving children from birth through age 8.* Washington, DC: National Association for the Education of Young Children.

Bricker, D. (1988). Commentary: The future of early childhood special education. *Journal of the Division for Early Childhood, 12* (2), 276–278.

Bricker, D., & Veltman, M. (1990). Early intervention programs: Child-focused approaches. In S. J. Meisels & J. P. Shonkoff (Eds.), *Handbook of early childhood intervention* (pp. 373–399). Cambridge, England: Cambridge University Press.

Bricker, D. D., & Woods-Cripe, J. J. (1992). *An activity-based approach to early intervention.* Baltimore: Paul H. Brookes.

Bronfenbrenner, U. (1979). *The ecology of human development: Experiments by nature and design.* Cambridge, MA: Harvard University Press.

Bronfenbrenner, U. (1992). NCCIP: Achievement and challenge: Remarks upon receiving the Dolly Madison Award. *Zero to Three, 12* (3), 32–33.

Bruner, J. S. (1983). *In search of mind: Essays in autobiography.* New York: Harper/Colophon.

Bruner, J. S., Olver, R., & Greenfield, P. (1966). *Studies in cognitive growth: A collaboration at the Center for Cognitive Studies.* New York: John Wiley and Sons.

Bryant, D. M., Clifford, R. M., & Peisner, E. S. (1991). Best practices for beginners: Developmental appropriateness in kindergarten. *American Educational Research Journal, 28* (4), 783–303.

Carta, J. J., Schwartz, I. S., Atwater, J. B., & McConnell, S. R. (1991). Developmentally appropriate practice: Appraising its usefulness for young children with disabilities. *Topics in Early Childhood Special Education, 11*(1), 1–10.

Connor, F. P., Williamson, G. G., & Siepp, J. M. (1978). *Program guide for infants and toddlers with neuromotor and developmental disabilities.* New York: Teachers College Press.

Deiner, P. L. (1993). *Resources for teaching children with diverse abilities.* Fort Worth, TX: Harcourt Brace Jovanovich.

DeVries, R., & Kohlberg, L. (1990). *Constructivist early education: Overview and comparison with other programs.* Washington, DC: National Association for the Education of Young Children.

Dunst, C. J., & Trivette, C. M. (1987). Enabling and empowering families: Conceptual and intervention issues. *School Psychology Review, 16* (4), 327–342.

Elkind, D. (1990). Developmentally appropriate practice: Philosophical and practical implications. *Phi Delta Kappan, 72* (2), 113–117.

Feldman, D. (1980). *Beyond universals in cognitive development.* Norwood, NJ: Ablex.

Frank, I. (1986). Psychology as a science: Resolving the idiographic-nomothetic controversy. In J. Valsiner (Ed.), *The individual subject and scientific psychology* (pp. 23–33). New York: Plenum Press.

Hauser-Cram, P. (1990). Designing meaningful evaluations of early intervention services. In S. J. Meisels & J. P. Shonkoff (Eds.), *Handbook of early childhood intervention* (pp. 583–602). Cambridge, England: Cambridge University Press.

Haywood, H. C., & Switzky, H. N. (1986). The malleability of intelligence: Cognitive processes as a function of polygenic-experiential interaction. *School Psychology Review, 15* (3), 245–255.

Holdgrafer, G., & Dunst, C. J. (1986). Communicative competence: From research to practice. *Topics in Early Childhood Special Education, 6* (3), 1–22.

Jensen, M. R. (1990). Change models and some evidence for phases and their plasticity in cognitive structures. *International Journal of Cognitive Education and Mediated Learning, 1* (1), 5–16.

Klein, N. K., & Campbell, P. (1990). Preparing personnel to serve at-risk and disabled infants, toddlers, and preschoolers. In S. J. Meisels & J. P. Shonkoff (Eds.), *Handbook of early childhood intervention* (pp. 679–699). Cambridge, England: Cambridge University Press.

Lewis, M., & Starr, M. (1979). Developmental continuity. In J. D. Ofsoksy (Ed.), *Handbook of infant development* (pp. 635–670). New York: John Wiley and Sons.

Linder, T. (1990). *Transdisciplinary play-based assessment: A functional approach to working with young children.* Baltimore: Paul H. Brookes.

Linehan, S. A., Brady, M. P., & Hwang, Chi-en. (1991). Ecological versus developmental assessment: Influences on instructional expectations. *Journal of the Association for Persons with Severe Handicaps, 16* (3), 146–153.

Lowenthal, B. (1992). Functional and developmental models: A winning early intervention combination. *Infant-Toddler Intervention, 2* (3), 161–168.

Mallory, B. L. (1992). Is it always appropriate to be developmental? Convergent models for early intervention practice. *Topics in early childhood special education, 11*(4), 1–12.

Meisels, S. J. (1992). Early intervention: A matter of context. *Zero to Three, 12* (3), 1–6.

McCune, L., Kalmanson, B., Fleck, M. B., Glazewski, B., & Sillari, J. (1990). An interdisciplinary model of infant assessment. In S. J. Meisels & J. P. Shonkoff (Eds.), *Handbook of early childhood intervention* (pp. 219–245). Cambridge, England: Cambridge University Press.

Miller, P. S. (1991). Linking theory to intervention practices with preschoolers and their families: Building program integrity. *Journal of Early Intervention, 15* (4), 315–325.

Noonan, M. J., & McCormick, L. (1992). A naturalistic curriculum model for early intervention. *Infant-Toddler Intervention, 2* (3), 147–160.

Norris, J. A. (1991). Providing developmentally appropriate practice to infants and young children with handicaps. *Topics in Early Childhood Special Education, 11* (1), 21–35.

Odom, S., & McEvoy, M. A. (1990). Mainstreaming at the preschool level: Potential barriers and tasks for the field. *Topics in Early Childhood Special Education, 10* (2), 48–61.

Sameroff, A. J. (1982). The environmental context of developmental disabilities. In D. Bricker (Ed.), *Intervention with at-risk and handicapped infants: From research to application* (pp. 141–152). Baltimore: University Park Press.

Sameroff, A. J. (1990). Neo-environmental perspectives on developmental theory. In R. M. Hodapp, J. A. Burack, & E. Zigler (Eds.), *Issues in the developmen-*

tal approach to mental retardation (pp. 93–136). Cambridge, England: Cambridge University Press.

Schickendanz, J. A., Hansen, K., & Forsyth, P. D. (1990). *Understanding children.* Mountain View, CA: Mayfield.

Shonkoff, J. P. (1992). Early intervention research: Asking and answering meaningful questions. *Zero to Three, 12* (3), 7–9.

Sroufe, L. A. (1979). The coherence of individual development. *American Psychologist, 34* (8), 834–841.

Stainback, W., & Stainback, S. (1990). *Understanding qualitative research.* Reston, VA: Council for Exceptional Children.

Wolery, M., & Dyk, L. (1984). Arena assessment: Description and preliminary social validity data. *Journal of the Association for Persons with Severe Handicaps, 9* (3), 231–235.

Yonemura, M. V. (1986). *A teacher at work: Professional development and the early childhood educator.* New York: Teachers College Press.

Zigler, E. F. (1990). Foreword. In S. J. Meisels & J. P. Shonkoff (Eds.), *Handbook of early childhood intervention* (pp. ix–xiv). Cambridge, England: Cambridge University Press.

6

. . . . . .

Understanding Development in a Cultural Context

The Challenge for Teachers

BARBARA T. BOWMAN AND FRANCES M. STOTT

Over the past half-century, research and theory in child development have provided an increasingly comprehensive knowledge base regarding the sequence and negotiation of developmental accomplishments of young children and the environmental supports needed to stimulate and sustain these. The National Association for the Education of Young Children has led a movement to tie early childhood teaching practices to this developmental framework under the rubric developmentally appropriate practices (DAP). DAP focuses teachers' attention on the interdependence of development and the teaching environment—both human and material—as a guide for educating children.

Making child development a linchpin for practice is a major contribution to early childhood pedagogy. Key developmental principles have provided a useful guide for practice. These include such ideas as: (1) children actively construct their own intelligence; (2) there are individual differences in the pace and styles of children's development; and (3) all domains of development (emotional, social, physical, and cognitive) are important and interrelate in determining behavior. These principles, however, often have been seen as having only one cultural representation. Schools and centers have ignored the fact that there are different cultural interpretations of development and, therefore, different "appropriate" educational practices. This chapter proposes a conceptual framework for thinking about the relationship of culture and development and for using such a framework in classrooms for young children.

DEVELOPMENT AND CULTURE

There is a significant body of theory and research outlining the patterns of development of children. The infant is viewed as coming into the world with biologically prepared propensities to be active and with organized capacities for self-regulation. In addition, there are multiple ways of developing functions to reach species-important goals (Bertalanffy, 1968). For example, congenitally blind children, congenitally deaf children, and those with cerebral palsy go through infancy with different sensorimotor experiences yet, as Sameroff (1981) has pointed out, all of these children typically develop object permanence, representational intelligence, and self-awareness in early childhood. Further, there is a strong tendency for developmental functions to self-right, or get back on a developmental pathway, after deficit or perturbation (Sameroff & Chandler, 1975).

Developmental accomplishments thought to transcend cultural differences include such tasks as establishing mutually satisfying social relationships, organizing and integrating perceptions, learning language, developing category systems, thinking, imagining, and creating. Since children's growth and development are reasonably orderly, developmental achievements are learned in a similar fashion by all children and occur in predictable sequences.

Children also mature according to an individual blueprint. Each child is born with a unique genetic structure that moderates when and how rules of development are activated and expressed. For instance, some children are bundles of pain while teething, and others scarcely seem to feel the intrusion. Some children's thrust for autonomy is mild and episodic, while others stand full-square shouting their need to "do it alone." Some girls reach sexual adulthood as early as age 9, others as late as age 15. Individual difference in development are to be expected, and the younger the child, the greater the normal variation. This is itself a rule of development.

Developmental milestones, however, take on their *meaning* only in the context of social life. The meaning of behavior is determined by the values and expectations of members of a culture as passed from one generation to the next. Children, therefore, learn to balance their needs and wishes with the constraints and freedoms of the social world in which they live, to express their developmental predispositions in ways that are consistent with their family's and culture's practices.

Super and Harkness (1982), for example, note that culture influences communication and affect, which are universally human, by organizing, practicing, and regulating their elements of expression. Smiling, which appears universally around three months of age, generates parental recognition and response across cultures. Nevertheless, the method of response to affective behaviors is reflective of what is considered culturally appropriate behavior. Thus in Uganda, where personal skills are a powerful means to gaining status and material resources, infants are encouraged to smile. In contrast, Japanese seek quiet, contented babies, therefore preferring to soothe and lull them gently in response to affective behaviors (Caudill and Frost, 1973).

Viewing development in its cultural context complicates the ways in which we attempt to understand or assess children. Thus, for example, while all infants may cry in hunger (a rule of development), when a particular infant screams his agony, we do not immediately know if this is a child who feels more pain or has less tolerance for hunger pangs (individual variation in development) or an infant who has learned from interaction with caregivers to be more vigorous in stating his biological needs. Further, we do not know if his screams will be met with solicitousness because of the caregivers' personal inclinations or because of their views regarding appropriate child rearing.

At one level, cultural differences in behavior are simply different ways of arriving at human ends: Children may whimper or scream their hunger, or have temper tantrums or passively resist in the struggle for autonomy, or wound one another with blows or with words, or play with blocks or dolls. All represent cultural variations on normal developmental accomplishments. At another level, however, what is learned is of far deeper significance. How children learn to organize their environment, which language they learn to speak, how they occupy their leisure time—all have significance for the kinds of problems they will solve and the strategies they will use to do so. The languages children speak offer different opportunities and constraints for the expression of ideas. How children learn to display anger affects the nature of the social order. Whether they play with blocks instead of dolls may lead to a different understanding of geometry. As children grow and develop, the ideas of the social world in which they live penetrate their age/stage and individual characteristics to shape their development.

Cultural factors play an important role in determining how and what children learn (Rogoff, Gauvain, & Ellis, 1984). They interface with age/stage potential, personal characteristics, and experience—giving them direction and substance. Culture is important, therefore, to any discussion of DAP since it deeply affects the teaching/learning process. Cultural differences can lead teachers to misunderstand children, to misassess their developmental competence, and to plan incorrectly for their educational achievement.

TEACHERS' SOURCES OF KNOWLEDGE

Advocates of DAP have focused teachers' attention on two powerful sources of knowledge about children: first, formal knowledge that encompasses theories of child development; and second, teachers' own personal experiences of making sense of the world. Each source of knowledge, by failing to include culture as a critical component, has compromised practice.

Theories of Development Revisited

Developmental theories focus on change over time. They seek to provide a description of development and to offer a set of general principles or rules for change in the course of development. Theories are helpful in that they organize and give *meaning* to facts and they guide further observation and research. But theories are not value free. Theorists are, after all, themselves products of a particular culture—therefore inferences about observations are necessarily colored. As Kuhn (1970) states, "An apparently arbitrary element, compounded of personal and historical accident, is always a formative ingredient of the beliefs espoused by a given scientific community at a given time" (p. 4). Like culture, theories provide a prism through which we ascribe meaning to behavior; they can only arise from the autobiography of the theorist. Two aspects of traditional developmental theory are suspect because of their ethnocentric bias: the notion that principles of development are universal in their application and that intelligence is independent of culture.

UNIVERSALITY OF DEVELOPMENT. An example of a developmental theory criticized for its assumptions of universality is attachment theory, as described by Bowlby (1969). Attachment is the pattern of behaviors whose purpose is to seek proximity with someone more capable, especially when frightened, fatigued, or ill; the felt experience is of security. The theory provides an explanation for observed behaviors in infants— particularly beginning around 8 months when separation and stranger anxiety are occurring. Bowlby maintained that attachment serves the biological function of protection from predators and other dangers and as such is characteristic of all humans. Thus, mother-care is biologically based and conforms to a species prototype.

However, the universality of mother-only care has been questioned. Tronick, Morelli, and Winn (1987) argue that natural evolutionary relationships are but one of many factors that shape caretaking practices and that the theory described by Bowlby for mother-only care (and stranger fear) is only one of a variety of viable models. They coined the phrase *continuous care and contact model* for Bowlby's attachment formulation. When the mother is primarily responsible for providing the infant with relatively continuous care (constant contact and frequent nursing bouts), the relationship between the dyad will develop differently than in multiple caregiving models. They describe a second model, *the caretaker-child strategy* model, that conceptualizes human development as a process shaped by behavioral exchanges occurring between children and caregivers. These exchanges are affected by a variety of factors including evolved capacities and motivations, cultural beliefs and practices, residence patterns, and situational factors. The caretaking practices of the Efe (Pygmy), who inhabit a section of Zaire, are an example of a multiple caretaking model. Among the Efe many adults and older children perform caretaking functions. This results in a quality of the relationship between children and their biological mothers, and with other members of the community, that is very different from that found in mother-only care models.

We join with Hinde (1983) in concluding that there is no universally optimum caretaking strategy, only ones that better deal with the factors to which caretaking must adapt. One implication of the caretaker-child strategy is that when cultural practices begin to change, community members may have to pay a cost for new strategies. For instance, Tronick (1989) suggests that such changes may be a source of anxiety, as may happen when parents who come from a continuous care and contact model place their infants in a group day care setting. Since the unconscious and conscious cultural messages call for mother-only care, any departure creates anxiety and perhaps guilt for doing it differently. Thus cultural change often stimulates considerable angst, requiring more than one generation to stabilize.

CULTURE AS A FACTOR IN INTELLIGENCE. One of the most influential theories with respect to DAP has been that of Piaget (1952, 1962), which has emphasized the universality of sequences in development and learning characteristics of children. Piaget's theory drew our attention to the organization of thought rather than to specific pieces of knowledge and to stagelike changes in development rather than to a gradual accumulation of knowledge. It has been of enormous importance to the practice of early childhood education by pointing out that children are active learners who construct their own intelligence, and by noting the similarities in how and what children learn across cultures.

However, aspects of Piaget's theory are increasingly being called into question—especially the idea that children's cognition develops in invariant sequence, and his emphasis on a particular form of cognition, that of logical-mathematical. The newer focus requires a reconsideration of what motivates individual development and what the meaning is of development.

One example of another theory of intelligence is that of Howard Gardner (1983) who posits multiple intelligences. Instead of seeing all children as constructing their own logical-mathematical thinking, as Piaget did, or thinking that only two kinds of intelligence are really important—verbal and logical-mathematical—as I.Q. tests and most schools assume, Gardner suggests that the brain has developed several discretely different kinds of intelligence to respond to different kinds of information from the environment. Gardner proposes that in addition to verbal and mathematical intelligence, there are at least five others: spatial, musical, bodily-kinesthetic, interpersonal, and intrapersonal. Gardner's theory thus proposes different ends that intelligence can be directed toward.

Piaget's logical-mathematical thinking is a possible end-state of development, but that end is determined by Western culture that values technology. If we define intelligence as Howard Gardner (1992) does, as "the ability to solve a problem or fashion a product that is valued in at least one culture or community," we might dare to imagine that a dancer, athlete, or musician is the most intellectually advanced member of a culture.

In placing emphasis on a particular kind of knowledge—logical-mathematical and verbal knowledge—schools have been misled in their assessment of children's development. Children whose intelligence fits this way of knowing because of individual talent or cultural emphasis, are judged positively, while those less individually able or less culturally invested are perceived as having something "wrong" with them. Thus, poor achievement on standardized tests is viewed as indicative of developmental deviance and/or psychopathology. The goal of measurement—to discover what makes an individual distinctive and valuable—is lost to one particular form of achievement.

The Relationship Between Development and Culture

Rather than seeing intelligence as a property of a person or his or her brain, or as constructed by a developing child alone, it can be seen as co-constructed, or as a dialectic between a person and his or her community or culture (including the determination of what end-states are valued). Thus the importance of the sociohistorical context assumes the foreground in discussions of children's learning (Cole & Bruner, 1972; Vygotsky, 1978). The ability to form and value social contracts begins in the first infant/caregiver relationships and continues throughout life as humans live together. The relationship that evolves as caregivers respond to the dependent infant lays the basis for social ties. Children learn from and through identification with the people who care for them and are emotionally important to them. Emotional and social ties bind children first to their primary caregivers and then to others of their group, providing the impetus to think, feel, and behave like them.

It is from social interaction that children not only learn how to behave, but build the basis for their behavior into their definitions of themselves. Erikson (1950) pointed out that it would be a mistake to assume "that a sense of identity is achieved primarily though the individual's complete surrender to given social roles and through his indefinite adaptation to the demands of social change" (p. 368). Instead, children strive to integrate the cultural roles ordained by family and community with their own individual needs, abilities, and wishes.

Patterns of interactions guide the developing child, but they are not straightjackets that bind the social participant in all situations to a narrow range of responses. Each child makes behavior selections from a pool of possible responses depending upon personal capabilities and inclinations and an understanding of what the situation (context) requires. Because a child chooses a particular response in a given situation does not mean that he or she is incapable of another, only that the response given is the one most consistent with his or her own capabilities and interests and the requirements of the situation as he or she understands it.

In every human endeavor, culture influences the behavior of individuals, and individuals sustain their culture. Children learn to construe the meaning of experience through their interactions with other people, and because they construe meanings in similar ways, members of groups enact their common culture. Thus, culture and individual development are mutually embedded; both are essential to understanding what people mean by what they do (Rogoff, Gauvain, & Ellis, 1984).

The interface between culture and development leads to two questions: First, are all childrearing environments equally good for helping children reach their developmental potential? The answer is no. There is clear evidence that in all cultures some early environments result in children failing to thrive physically, emotionally, socially, and cognitively. But, except for severe deprivation of basic needs, it is difficult to describe the characteristics of such environments since effects are buffered by social support systems, personal resiliency and vulnerability, and the meaning people attribute to the kind of care and education they provide for children. In order to determine the adequacy of a childrearing environment, the entire relationship of the child to his or her environment must be assessed.

The second question is, are all cultural accomplishments valid in all contexts? The answer is also no. Behavior that prepares children well for one setting may place them at risk in another (Bowman, in press). LeVine (1980) suggests that every method of childrearing has benefits and costs. Furthermore, when changes are introduced in the environment, strategies that worked in the past may no longer be adaptive. Parental behavior, when directed to vital short-term goals, potentially may interfere with a child's long-term development. For example, being carried for protection until 18 months may assure survival, but limit the child's emotional and cognitive development.

The belief that there is only one valid behavioral manifestation of developmental adequacy creates an impediment to understanding young children and teaching them. By equating child developmental competence with particular forms of behavior, teachers misread the meaning of children's behavior and are led toward practices that compromise learning potential. The behavior that indicates a developmental accomplishment may be context specific and difficult to assess outside of that particular learning setting. Recognizing the richness and complexity of various cultural permutations of normal development requires a new orientation for teachers. They must look for developmental equivalence as they seek to understand competence across culture-specific tasks.

A culturally responsive view of the relationship between children and their social world is not one in which they are seen as unfolding according to preordained developmental stages with minor concessions to socializing practices and individual variations in rate and style of learning. If learning is inherently social and co-constructed, then teacher and child play equally active roles, and motivation to learn resides neither in the child nor the adult, but rather is tied to the relationship. The new metaphor for development is a dialectic between a "pre-wired" but permeable child struggling to confirm what he or she thinks is known and a social world that assists and ascribes meaning to experience.

Personal Experience Examined

Teachers are not solely dependant upon professional knowledge to guide their interactions with children (Bowman, 1989a; Freud, 1963; Jersild, 1967; Jones, 1987). Understanding comes from inner-perceived as well as outer-conceived experience, and teachers subject formal knowledge about children to the "meaning-making" of their own experience. While the subjective understanding of the experience of others is essential to social living, it is particularly important for teachers of young children. Young children are generally unable to say how they think and feel and why they behave as they do and, therefore, are more dependant upon teacher empathy than older children and adults (Bowman, 1989a). To supplement teacher understanding of children, Anna Freud (1963) wrote, "We have to rely upon the capacity of the normal adult to remember things" (p. 22). When teachers are sensitive to their inner selves, when they are willing to draw on their own past, when they easily remember how they have thought and felt, they are in a better position to understand children. Few teachers need more than a gentle nudge to be reminded of "shame" (perhaps of wet pants), "fear" (the dark), "joy" (rolling down a hill), or "excitement" (racing through sprinklers). Children's experience evokes "inner meaning" in teachers because they connect it with feelings and thoughts from their own past. Because they have access to their own memories, they can make sense of the behavior of young children and develop interpretive connections between their acts of teaching and the meaning their behavior will have for children.

While projecting parts of our own psyche onto children can create a familiarity that allows greater empathy and closeness, it can also be troublesome. If, for example, we project negative aspects of ourselves, we will fear or disdain in others what we most reject in ourselves. Thus projection in its extreme form can create a prejudice of others. It is critical to find some balance between identifying, or finding sameness, and being able to pull back and notice and respect differences.

It is also important to note that while great psychological similarities exist among the peoples of the world (Whiting, 1977), there are, as has been discussed, very different cultural meanings that can be attributed to very similar behaviors, ideas, or perceptions. Intuitive knowledge about the world of childhood is shaped by cultural experiences of our own. Having experienced it, teachers know the feeling of shame, but what causes shame is learned from others. Similarly, feelings of joy, excitement, dread, and pleasure are a part of universal experience; however, the causes and forms of expression for these emotions are embedded in social meanings.

Teachers, like all of us, make generalizations about other people, ideas, and events on the basis of their personal constructions of reality, even though their "reality" may be quite different from someone else's. Teachers who do not integrate new perspectives of people and events can become victims of their own naive and culture-bound conceptions. Considerable research documents the difficulty that teachers have incorporating new visions of reality when these conflict with their own personal beliefs and experience (Ball, 1989). When confronted with dis-

crepancies, teachers cling to their own "meaning- making" theories, forcing evidence to the contrary to fit their old beliefs (Ball, 1989). Thus,
behavior that does not fit preconceived notions is "doctored" to conform
to their sense-making hypotheses (Cazden, 1991; Jipson, 1991). Meier
(1992) wrote, "We pile new theories on top of old conceptions rooted in
childhood experience, language, and symbols, and they are absorbed in
some odd commonsensical way" (p. 597). When adults and children do
not share common experiences, if they do not hold common beliefs
about the meaning of experience, they are apt to misunderstand culturally encoded interchanges (Bowman, 1989b). Thus teachers fail to appre-
ciate real similarities and differences between their understanding of the
world and that of the children they teach.

Personal knowledge is a two-edged sword: because teachers can
connect with their own feelings and memories of their childhood, teachers can draw on a reservoir of emotions and thoughts to inform their
understanding of the world of children. But teachers are misled when
they use only their own experiences as the hallmarks for the experiences
of others, when they fail to recognize the differences between themselves and others. Teachers always run the risk of having their own personal issues evoked by particular children, but when teachers and children do not share cultural experiences, the markers for development are
even more difficult to apply.

REFLECTIVE PRACTICE

How can teachers stay open to children from different cultures and still recognize the invariant rules that govern child development? How can teachers
use their own experience to help them understand other people without
assuming everyone is just like themselves? Making developmental practices
responsive to cultural differences presents a significant challenge for train-
ers of teachers and teachers themselves, requiring them to adopt role definitions, curriculum, and teaching practices that may challenge rather than
reflect the values and theories of the wider society and their own.

Culturally sensitive and developmentally appropriate practice must
begin in training institutions. While there is some consensus on the contents of the field of child development, it is important to recognize DAP
in the context of Western culture and its goals. It is also important to present more than one developmental theory, recognizing the contributions
and limitations of each. Study of development and psychopathology
must focus on the interplay of culture, temperament, individual experience, and change over time (Cohler, Stott, & Musick, in press). Thus the

process of integrating information and placing emphasis on contextual factors can begin, as teachers formulate their understanding of the theories of development as they operate for each child, from each family, and from each community.

Equally, if not more important than placing formal knowledge in perspective, training institutions must help teachers begin the process of reflection—not only about the act of teaching and the nature of the contexts in which teaching and learning take place, but about themselves. Teachers need to consider how what they do affects children and why, and how what children do affects them. They must accept and reject ideas on the basis of thoughtful inquiry and not just on the basis of superficial opinion, private belief, or standard practices. Teachers need to recognize that teaching is a complex, professional activity requiring constant effort on their part.

There are a number of models for thoughtful inquiry or teacher reflection that can help teachers come to understand their own practice better (Bowman, 1989a; Jones, 1987; Manley-Scsimir & Wasserman, 1989; Schön, 1983). These reflective strategies focus on a process for reorganizing how teachers think about teaching, for integrating new information without distorting it to serve old theories, and for generating and checking explanations for their own and children's behavior.

Teachers need time to reflect on themselves with the same intensity and vigor that is given to the study of others. Teachers' beliefs and behaviors are deeply rooted in their own past experiences. In order to accommodate to new ideas, new values, and new practices, teachers must restructure their own personal knowledge systems and clarify realities obscured by their personal blind spots. Unless teachers are encouraged to restructure and reorganize their personal as well as their developmental and pedagogical knowledge, they "may be able to recite more modern ideas, but their understanding will remain paper-thin" (Meier, 1992, p. 597).

Schools and centers also need to encourage reflection, although currently few programs leave sufficient time to do so. There is little institutional emphasis on teachers reflecting about their goals and objectives, about their teaching strategies, or their children's progress. Neither self-study—using diaries, case studies, or anecdotal records—nor collaborative reflection—using staff meetings, case consultation, and supervisory feedback and problem solving conferences—is valued highly by most schools and centers. Yet, such techniques help teachers "check out" for themselves and with their colleagues, supervisors, and experts the meaning of their own behavior and that of the children and families with whom they work.

There are no standard strategies to direct cross-cultural professional practice. Teachers of young children must rely on their own ability to make sense of what is happening to children using child development information, personal knowledge, and cultural sensitivity as the grist for their "meaning-making" mill. The following guidelines are based on Florio-Ruane's (1987) questions for those seeking to pass behavior through a cultural filter:

1. What is the "context" (interpersonal, personal, physical, and material) of the settings where interactions are occurring? Teachers will want to know how children's lives are usually organized in the other settings in which they live and how these compare with school. Similarities and differences in developmental accomplishments across culture are difficult to see.

2. What do specific actions mean to teachers, to children, and to parents? Teachers will need to find ways to test the meaning others have attributed to their behavior since different behaviors can have similar meanings and similar behaviors can have different meanings.

3. How do teachers, children, and families interpret each other both as individuals and as members of social systems? What are the perceptions of each group about the other that form a backdrop against which interactions are made meaningful? Teachers may want to have cultural informants who are able to see and interpret honestly the perceptions of families and communities with differing ways of organizing social life and perceiving the social world, informants who can see beyond stylistic differences to the meanings behaviors are meant to convey. Teachers should also include collaborative judgments of colleagues from different groups since the implicit nature of culture makes it as hard to see in ourselves as in others.

A particularly poignant and painful experience for a child is that of being expected to conform to the mainstream expectations of a school while experiencing very different expectations from the home (Rodriquez, 1983). Both addressing the expectations of the new culture and supporting and respecting the family is a profound challenge for teachers. If teachers devalue culturally different children, they may force an ominous cultural choice: Identify with family and friends and reject school culture, or reject family and friends in favor of school and face emotional/social displacement. The result is that many young children opt for family and friends and become unwilling participants in school culture. Cultural conflict forces them into a defensive posture to avoid the possible contention that they really are inferior. These defensive postures include avoidance of opportunity, withholding of effort, and self-segregation (Steele, 1989). Projects such as the Kamahameha Elementary Education Program (Au & Kawakami, 1991) have demonstrated that when children are not required to renounce their cultural heritage, school achievement improves markedly.

CONCLUSION

To ignore cultural expression is to misunderstand the nature of development. Child development principles operate in a tangle of ontological, personal, and social meanings. Although theories of development do not have the same applicability to all people, and teachers and children often come from different backgrounds, our message is neither to abandon formal knowledge nor call for sameness of background. Rather the challenge is to recognize the importance of educating teachers to place development in a cultural context.

Culturally sensitive practices will require structural changes in how teachers are presented with, understand, and use the knowledge systems available to them. Child development constructs must place increased emphasis on the contextual factors in children's learning. Personal histories must be consciously reexamined and informed by new experiences, new ways of looking at people. The task of teachers is to try to grasp the parallels between themselves and others, while still appreciating the fundamental differences in each group's and each person's perceptions of the world.

Educating all children will require the will and commitment to understand and respond to cultural difference. To the extent that teachers know and understand how children's past experiences have been organized and explained, they are better able to fashion new ones for them. When teachers plan experiences that connect them to their children through understanding and respect, they can "make meaning" together.

REFERENCES

Au, K. H., & Kawakami, A. J. (1991). Culture and ownership. *Childhood Education, 67* (5), 280–284.

Ball, D. (1989). *Breaking with experience in learning to teach mathematics.* (Issue Paper 88). East Lansing, MI: National Center for Research on Teaching.

Bertalanffy, L. von. (1968). *General system theory: Foundation, development, applications.* New York: Braziller.

Bowlby, J. (1969). *Attachment and loss: Vol. I: Attachment.* New York: Basic.

Bowman, B. (1989a). Self-reflection as an element of professionalism. *Teachers College Record, 90* (3), 444–451.

Bowman, B. (1989b). Culturally sensitive inquiry. In J. Garbarino & F. Stott (Eds.), *What children can tell us* (pp. 92–107). San Francisco: Jossey Bass.

Bowman, B. (in press). Research review: Early childhood education. In L. Darling-Hammond (Ed.), *Review of research in education* (Vol. 19). Washington, DC: American Educational Research Association.

Caudill, W., & Frost, L. A. (1973). A comparison of maternal care and infant behavior in Japanese-American, American and Japanese families. In W. Lebra (Ed.), *Youth socialization and mental health: Vol. 3. Mental health research in Asia and the Pacific.* Honolulu: University Press of Hawaii.

Cazden, C. (1991). Contemporary issues and future directions: Active learners and active teachers. In J. Flood, J. Jensen, D. Lapp, & J. Aquire (Eds.), *Handbook of research on teaching the English language arts* (pp. 418–422). New York: MacMillan.

Cohler, B. J., Stott, F. M., & Musick, J. (in press). Adversity, vulnerability and resilience: Cultural and developmental perspectives. In D. C. Cicchetti & D. J. Cohen (Eds.), *Manual of developmental psychopathology* (Vol. 2). New York: John Wiley and Sons.

Cole, M., & Bruner, J. S. (1972). Cultural differences and inferences about psychological processes. *American Psychologist, 26,* 867–876.

Entwhistle, D., & Alexander, K. (1989). Children's transition into full-time schooling: Black/white comparisons. *Early education and development, 1* (2), 85–104.

Erikson, E. (1950). *Childhood and Society.* New York: Norton.

Florio-Ruane, S. (1987). Sociolinguistics for educational researchers. *American Educational Research Journal, 24* (2), 185–197.

Freud, A. (1963). *Psychoanalysis for teachers and parents.* Boston: Beacon Press.

Gardner, H. (1983). *Frames of mind.* New York: Basic Books.

Gardner, H. (1992). *The art in the mind of the child.* Paper presented at Erikson Institute Conference, Literature, the Child, and Child Development, Chicago.

Hinde, R. A. (1983). *Biological bases of the mother-child relationship.* Manuscript. Medical Research Council Unit on the Development and Integration of Behavior, Madingley, Cambridge.

Jersild, A. (1967). *When teachers face themselves.* New York: Bureau of Publications, Teachers College.

Jipson, J. (1991). Extending the discourse on developmental appropriateness: A developmental perspective. *Early Education and Development, 2*(2), 95–108.

Jones, E. (1987). *Teaching adults: An active learning approach.* Washington, DC: National Association for the Education of Young Children.

Kuhn, T. S. (1970). *The structure of scientific revolutions.* Chicago: University of Chicago Press.

LeVine, R. A. (1980). A cross-cultural perspective on parenting. In M. D. Fantini

& R. Cardenas (Eds.), *Parenting in a multicultural society* (pp. 17–26). New York: Longman.

LeVine, R. A. (1988). Human parental care: Universal goals, cultural strategies, individual behavior. In R. LeVine, P. Miller, & M. West (Eds.), *Parental behavior in diverse societies* (pp. 3–11). San Francisco: Jossey-Bass.

LeVine, R. A., & Miller, P. M. (1990). Commentary. *Human Development, 33,* 73–80.

Manley-Scsimir, M., & Wasserman, S. (1989). The teacher as decision-maker. *Childhood Education, 65*(5), 288–294.

Meier, D. (1992). Reinventing Teaching. *Teachers College Record, 93* (4), 594–609.

Phillips, D., McCartney, K., Scarr, S., & Howes, C. (1987). Reflective Review of Infant Day Care Research: A Cause for Concern. *Zero to Three, 7*(3), 18–21.

Piaget, J. (1952). *The origins of intelligence in children*. New York: International Universities Press.

Piaget, J. (1962). *Play, dreams and imitation in childhood*. New York: Norton.

Rodriguez, R. (1983). *The hunger of memory: The education of Richard Rodriguez*. New York: Bantam Books.

Rogoff, B., Gauvain, M., & Ellis, S. (1984). Development viewed in its cultural context. In M. H. Bornstein and M. E. Lamb (Eds.), *Developmental psychology*. Hillsdale, NJ: Erlbaum.

Sameroff, A. J. (1981). Psychological needs of the mother in early mother-infant interaction. In G. Avery (Ed.)., *Neonatology* (2nd ed.) (pp. 303–321). Philadelphia: Lippincott.

Sameroff, A. J. & Chandler, M. J. (1975). Reproductive risk and the continuum of caretaking casualty. In F. D. Horowitz, M. Hetheington, S. Scarr-Salapatek, and G. Sigel (Eds.), *Review of child development research* (Vol. 4) (pp. 187–244). Chicago: University of Chicago Press.

Schön, D. A. (1983). *The reflective practitioner: How professionals think in action*. New York: Basic Books.

Steele, S. (1989). Being black and feeling blue. *American Scholar, 58* (4), 497–508.

Super, C., & Harkness, S. (1982). The development of affect in infancy and early childhood. In D. Wagner & H. Stevenson (Eds.), *Cultural perspectives on child development,* (pp. 1–19). San Francisco: W.H. Freeman.

Tronick, E. Z. (1989). Conference Discussion: New Research and Policy Perspectives, Harvard University.

Tronick, E. Z., Morelli, G. A., & Winn, S. (1987). Multiple caretaking of Efe (Pygmy) infants. *American Anthropologist, 89,* 96–106.

Vygotsky. L. S. (1978). *Mind in Society*. Cambridge, MS: Harvard University Press.

Whiting, J. (1977). A model for psychocultural research. In P. Leiderman, S. Tulkin, & A. Rosenfeld (Eds.), *Culture and infancy,* (pp. 87–109). Norwood, NJ: Ablex.

PART III

Home and School Negotiations

. . . . . .

Moving beyond a critique of child development theory, the third section of this volume details some of the challenges associated with establishing productive and constructive home/school relations for parents and teachers of young children who represent cultural or developmental minorities. In chapter 7, Carol Brunson Phillips points out some of the many incongruities that African-American children experience as they travel between their home and school settings, and raises troublesome questions about what "cultural transmission" means to children and families from diverse ethnic or racial contexts. She considers the implications of these questions for our definitions of "appropriateness" in educational practice, and identifies several competing strategies for enabling the African-American child to cope with the conflicts associated with being on the margins of mainstream American society. She concludes her chapter by advocating for an explicit acknowledgement of the sociopolitical reality of American society, and the use of teaching strategies that foster children's abilities to "make it" in both worlds—everyday family and community settings as well as the larger racist society.

In chapter 8, Leslie Williams begins by identifying the underlying values embedded in current definitions of DAP, and in particular notes the salience of the individual, the importance of independent behavior, and the critical role played by language within the "deep structures of DAP." She then makes good use of extensive ethnographic literature on Native-American cultures to illustrate the incongruities between this minority culture's emphasis on group interdependence and America's mainstream value system. She concludes her chapter—and this section—by noting the *inappropriateness* associated with blanket applications of DAP guidelines without consideration of the risks involved for children and families with different value systems, and urges more thoughtful negotiations between teachers and communities in the determination of educational goals and practices.

The final chapter in this section illustrates many of the points raised in the previous two chapters. Douglas Powell continues the discussion regarding the role of parents in determining the nature of their children's early educational experiences. This chapter raises questions about the balance of power between early childhood professionals and parents who send their children off to school. Powell depicts the role of the parent as reflected in the NAEYC guidelines from two perspectives—that of consumer, and that of a contributor to the child's educational experiences. In his discussion of the parent as consumer, he suggests that a major purpose of developmentally appropriate practice guidelines as currently articulated is to influence parents' views regarding high quality early childhood education. However, Powell notes the relative inability of this effort to influence parental preferences among culturally diverse populations, which he attributes, at least partially, to the difficulty of separating parental decisions regarding early childhood programs from the broader context of parenting beliefs and practices. The role of cultural beliefs and values is further examined in the discussion of the challenges of establishing responsive partnerships between families and early childhood programs.

7

• • • • • •

The Movement of African-American Children Through Sociocultural Contexts

A Case of Conflict Resolution

CAROL BRUNSON PHILLIPS

> i dont wanna write
> in english or spanish
> i wanna sing
>
> *Ntozake Shange (1975)*

The task of a society to prepare its children to take their place in the world of adults involves, in its broadest sense, the transmission of culture. Although the process of cultural transmission takes place as the child interacts with the total social environment, in contemporary American society we regard families and schools as being primarily responsible for seeing that preparation for adulthood takes place.

The culture transmission process of the family generally is called enculturation, and refers to those aspects of childrearing that go beyond meeting children's physical needs in order to sustain life. Enculturation focuses upon the things that families do to enable children to know and understand society's shared ideas about values, attitudes, beliefs, and behaviors. This participation in an "idea system" gives children the power to influence their environment and have an impact on the world. For instance, as children come to know the ideas that govern speech and language in a society, they gain the power to communicate. As children come to know the ideas about how meaning is given to events in a society, they gain the power to interact with people and things. As children come to know the ideas about how experiences are organized in a society, they gain the power to define their world.

The consequences of enculturation are compelling, and society does not leave the responsibility of culture transmission solely to the family. The institution of school, too, is charged with the task (though in school the culture transmission process is called "education"). Continuing their family initiated preparation for adulthood, through their experiences in school, children are expected to become progressively more adept at exerting power over their reality. The consequence of this process in children is what we call "development."

What challenge does this concept of development pose when it comes to the African-American child? What practices can be called "appropriate" when the school experiences of these children are characterized by low academic achievement, high drop-out rates, illiteracy, and alienation, and suggest a process rendering them powerless? What does preparation for adulthood require from school and families, when the world for which the child is being prepared is one where black people are oppressed and without the resources needed to secure adequate health care, housing, education, and employment? What are the conflicts/struggles to be resolved between African-American families, striving to give to their children the power to influence their world, and American schools, representing an idea system that endorses their inferior status?

These are the issues with which this chapter is concerned. The central question to be explored is, how can families and schools appropriately define development for African-American children and provide a context in their early school years that guarantees and insures growth? The discussion will first examine the limitations of current thinking about the problems of African-American children in school. We will then propose an alternative model to examine the sociocultural context of the child. Finally, we will examine the interaction between the child and the school and propose some parameters for moving toward a transformation of those interactions.

VIEWS OF AFRICAN-AMERICAN CHILDREN AND SCHOOL COMPETENCY

Much literature has been devoted to understanding why African-American children fail to develop in the school environment. Three predominant explanations have been offered: hereditary, environmental deficiency, and cultural difference. In the hereditary view, development proceeds in a fashion thought to be primarily influenced by a biologically inherited plan. Human genes, internal to the organism, are believed to have the main influencing effect over many human traits, including intelligence. The gene pool of the African-American child is believed to be less than adequate for certain higher intellectual functions (Jensen, 1969). In this view, therefore, the question of African-American children and school competency is one of biologically inherited capability—a cause internal to the child.

The environmental deficiency view regards the activity of the environment external to the organism as the primary influence in development. For the African-American child, the organization of family life is seen as interfering with the child's development, acting against "normal" developmental trends, and thus limiting the child's capacity to benefit from education (Moynihan, 1965). In this view therefore, failure in school is explained by cognitive deficiencies, lack·of motivation, or low self-esteem, arising out of the socialization process.

The third explanation, the cultural difference view, is also grounded in the assumption that the active environment has primacy. In this view however, every child is socialized into cultural modes of behavior that express a full range of developmental competencies, but that reflect culturally specific values. It is argued that the African-American child experiences unique and legitimate cognitive, linguistic, and interpersonal styles of behavior within the family, that differ from the styles demanded by the school (Baratz & Baratz, 1970). Thus school failure is explained by the cultural behavioral styles that the child brings into the school setting.

Although each explanation advances a different prescription to address the problems of African-American children in school, all three share a view of development that isolates the organism from the context in which he or she operates. All treat behavior as if it were the consequence of a particular condition in the environment or a particular disposition of the individual—as something that "happens" to the person outside the situation in which he or she is found. Therefore, these explanations depend for their analyses upon a view of children outside the context of the schools and communities in which they interact.

The reality for African-American as well as all children, however, is that the experiences they have in school do not arise *because* of a particular genetic, social, or cultural disposition; rather, the processes operating to insure or to countervail against their competency are a consequence of an interaction between a particular organism and a particular setting.

To assert that human behavior is a product of the interaction between the growing human organism and its environment is a commonplace proposition in social science. One would thus expect psychology to give substantial, if not equal, emphasis to both person and environment, with special attention to the interaction between the two. According to Bronfenbrenner (1979) however, psychological literature contains a rich array of data dealing with the qualities of the person and behavioral tendencies of the individual, yet when it comes to the environment,

> The existing concepts are limited to a few crude and undifferentiated categories that do little more than locate people in terms of their social address—the setting from which they come. . . . Moreover, the data in . . . studies consist to an overwhelming degree of information not about the settings from which the persons come but about the characteristics of the person themselves, that is, how people from diverse contexts differ from one another.
>
> As a result, the interpretations of environmental effects are often couched in what [Kurt] Lewin called class-theoretical terms; thus observed differences in children from one or another setting (for example, lower class versus middle class . . .) are "explained" simply as attributes of the setting in question. Even when the environment is described, it is in terms of a static structure that makes no allowance for the evolving processes of interaction through which the behaviors of the participants in the system are instigated, sustained, and developed. (p. 17)

What is needed in order to understand the development of African-American children is an interactional perspective, where the child is viewed as an active agent in interaction with an active environment. Such a model addresses the problem of the child and school competency by asking: What are the interactions between the forces that produce the child and the forces that produce the school, that enhance or mitigate against success? By posing the question in this way, one is required to take a full view of the contexts through which the child moves and to take into account the systems interacting to produce "the consequence" about which we are concerned.

The Interactive Approach

The Fanon Center Model, which was developed at the Fanon Research and Development Center (in the name of Frantz Fanon), located at the Charles R. Drew Postgraduate Medical School in Los Angeles, addresses the interactions of human beings at the center of a particular sociopolitical order (King, 1980). In this model four elements—physical, historical, economic, and social—interact with each other producing a particular sociopolitical order, and within the individual, producing a particular psychological reality.

The model has several key principles:

1. All elements in the universe are formed as a product of continuous interaction with other elements in the universe.
2. The interaction between the elements is governed by the nature of the interacting parties.
3. The interaction between elements is reciprocal.
4. Change takes place through a dialectical process where the qualitative nature of the interacting parties is changed.

According to these principles, at any point in time and space, the development of human activity is determined by dialectical interaction between the set of elements constituting the individual and the set of elements constituting the sociopolitical space. Individuals interiorize the relations they find in the space; at the same time order in the space evolves out of the action of individuals. In other words, the individual is formed as a consequence of the order, and the order is formed as a consequence of the individual (for a fuller explanation, see King, 1981).

In this model any examination of the child's growth and development in school would have to take into account the interaction between the sociopolitical order of the school and of the child. The model predicts that the source of growth/change is in the interaction between the two rather than in the person or in the environment. To illustrate: The sociopolitical reality of the school includes the physical reality of the plant with certain types of furniture and without others, stocked with specific supplies and equipment. Its historical reality generates an organization according to traditions and values that competition is good, that quiet concentration is necessary for learning, that literacy is an important goal and that objectively relating to objects is a valid way to acquire knowledge. The economic reality is reflected in the amount of resources present as well as the type of preparation in the curriculum for the students to develop marketable skills. (Basic math is taught in the third grade, algebra in the ninth, etc.). The social reality rests with the roles, attitudes, expectations, and needs of the teachers and administrators, the children and parents who spend time there.

The child enters as a psychological entity with a biobehavioral and sociocultural repertoire of behaviors that are the consequences of early life experiences within family and community. The child speaks a particular language, is dressed in a particular way, and is accustomed to a certain response to his or her behaviors.

The child moves through (i.e., interacts with) the school setting, an active entity in an active environment. The child expects verbal instruction about what to do and waits to receive it. The teacher expects the child to sit still and listen to directions. The child understands and speaks standard English and uses a formal style of speech when talking to adults. The teacher asks, "What did you do over the weekend?" and expects a story told in standard English. The child needs something and asks the teacher for help. The teacher has the materials stored and expects to distribute them when it's time for the children to work.

Our child "grows" and demonstrates school competency because these interactions are growth-producing—not because of a particular school, or a particular teacher, or because of the child. In the interactions, the child is allowed to represent her particular psychological disposition to engage the environment and have an impact on the environment. In turn, the teacher reciprocates by validating the child's representation and moving with the child through the growth process.

An illustration of school failure from the same interactional perspective would be characterized by different circumstances. Sara Michaels (1980) describes such a situation in her study of morning sharing time in a first grade classroom. The children were assembled on the rug, and the teacher asked, "O.K., who has something to share?" The children raised their hands and were called upon one at a time to come before the class to talk. The teacher was actively involved in each turn, holding her arm around the child as he or she talked, helping the other children stay quiet and listen, and freely interjecting questions and reactions to the child or the group at large. Her interactions picked up on the child's topic and expanded it through her questions and comments, which generally stimulated more elaborate, focused talk on the same subject. However, a different interaction occurred in some cases:

> Some . . . children . . . were far more likely to use a "topic-chaining" style, that is, loosely structured talk which moved fluidly from topic to topic, dealing primarily with accounts of personal relations. . . . The topic-chaining style was generally characterized by an absence of lexicalized-markers other than "and" between topics. While topic shifts were signalled prosodically (with accent on a syllable), this kind of discourse was difficult to follow thematically, for those who, like the teacher, expected narrative to focus on a single topic. These sharing turns have the impression of having no beginning, middle or end, and hence no point at all. (p. 6)

The teacher, having difficulty discerning the topic of discourse and predicting where the talk was going, often mistimed questions, stopping children mid-clause. Moreover, the questions were often thematically inappropriate and seemed to throw children off-balance, interrupting their train of thought. These children often reverted to simple one word responses to the teacher's questions. In cases where the children continued to talk, these turns were often cut short by the teacher.

The children in this instance do not demonstrate school competency because their attempts to represent themselves in the interaction do not engage the environment in a reciprocal validating process (which Michaels attributes to a mismatch between the teacher's and child's expressive styles). The children's power is cut off and their development circumscribed. The outcome—underdevelopment—is a product of the interaction.

Focused thus on the interactions in the school as the locus for development, let us explore how we can facilitate the exercise of power by the African-American child. In order to better understand the frequently misinterpreted "cultural" dimension of what these children bring to their school interactions, the discussion will focus on the historical dimension of their sociopolitical context.

THE HISTORICAL REALITY OF THE CHILD

The African-American child is enculturated in a context whose historical values and traditions are a special admixture of a continued African world operating in a cultural milieu primarily defined by the philosophical assumptions and underpinnings of the Anglo-American community (Nobles, 1985). This perspective on African-American culture, though much debated, is not at all new and is reflected in early 20th century writings of Melville Herskovitzs (1966). In a 1930 essay, he asks:

> What do Africans do that the inhabitants of the Negro quarter of New York City also do? May we find perhaps on close examination that there are some subtle elements left of what was ancestrally possessed? May not some remnant, if present, consist of some slight intonation, some quirk of pronunciation, some temperamental predisposition? And if we do find these, may we ascertain the extent to which they are increasingly present as we find Negroes removed from white influence? That such factors are to be discovered is quite possible and this fact is something to be reckoned with in all studies of the Negro. (p. 6)

Pursuing these questions, Herskovitzs conducted extensive studies of Africans and African Americans and believed that Africans everywhere (United States, Caribbean, and South America) had retained Africanisms even though the degree of purity varied widely with locality, socioeconomic class, and religious affiliation. He argued that the enculturative process is carried on in the household and transmits to the child what members of the household have learned in their earliest years, as modified by their later experiences. The learned behavior passed on includes motor behavior and skills, linguistic modes, food patterns, and the attitudes, goals, and anxieties of the older generation. Thus the enculturative process makes for continuity and for change.

Some contemporary features of African-American family life growing out of this historical reality are described by Nobles (1985, 1987), who observes that:

1. The family is composed of individual households which interrelate and have an impact on the social dynamics within an individual household.
2. In periods of crisis and celebration one sees more authentic expressions of the African deep structure.
3. The family performs social and psychological functions, such as interpreting events for each other.
4. The family is a living force that expands and diminishes as times change.
5. The family is child-centered.

As families interact, children experience a particular organization of relationships. Through these they learn strategies to secure gratifying (growth-producing and powerful) interactions with their world. For instance, one striking feature found in many descriptions of African-American children is their person orientation (Hale, 1986). In her study of black families in a Georgia town, Young (1970) described in great detail the interpersonal environment of the child, calling the baby's environment "almost wholly human":

> Being held is an active relationship between holder and baby, a highly personal experience. Most mothers hold babies with relaxed posture, usually cradling the baby on one arm or in the lap. As she cradles him, the mother's free hand wipes, pets, pokes, investigates, and her eyes explore the baby's face and body. Newborn and very young babies are often laid in the groove between the legs as the mother sits with the baby's feet toward the mother. In either position mother and baby look into each other's faces and the mother's hands caress the baby. She talks to it, expressing in her manner pride and amusement and enjoyment in it. When not being held young babies are laid on a bed, usually lying on their backs, and children and adults lean over the young baby and talk to it. Babies old enough to turn over and pull themselves along are laid on a folded blanket on the floor, where the little children are likely to join them, leaning over or on top of them and testing the baby's responses. (pp. 202–203)

Young stresses the deep level of interpersonal involvement between mother and child through playfulness, deep eye contact, physical contact, and attentiveness. This great stimulation of the baby's responsiveness to people is contrasted with limited explorations of the inanimate environment.

> Few objects are given to babies or allowed them when they do get hold of them. Plastic toys are almost the only objects ever seen in the hands of a prewalker. . . . Babies reaching to feel objects or surfaces are often redirected to feeling the holder's face, or the game of rubbing faces is begun as a substitute. . . . The personal is thus often substituted for the impersonal. (p. 207)

Another frequently described feature of African-American life growing out of a particular historical reality is the language. Smitherman (1977) views the language of the community as a reflection of black America's linguistic cultural African heritage and the conditions of servitude, oppression, and life in America. Smitherman argues that the "residue of the African world view" persists in the many facets of the oral tradition that places a high value on the spoken word. "Afro-America's emphasis on orality and belief in the power of the rap has produced a style and idiom totally unlike that of whites, while paradoxically employing White English words" (p. 79). What results are verbal performances exhibited in the narration of myths, folktales, "lying," and black sermons; telling jokes; street corner/barber shop/beauty shop talk; signifying; capping; and other verbal arts. It is not speech for the sake of speech, but rather a "functional dynamic that is simultaneously a mechanism for learning about life and the world and a vehicle for achieving group approval and recognition" (p. 80).

Smith (1977) also describes features of the language of the African-American community that represent the linguistic continuation of the African Hamito-Bantu tradition in black America. He argues that the nature of the childrearing strategies of the continuously isolated African-American people are responsible for the fact that these patterns may be observed among children and adults in the community. The consistency with which language structures appear in the descriptions of African-American child rearing make it one of the most obvious characteristics of the enculturation process. In fact, whether the linguistic patterns of the African-American child are described as Black English, Negro Nonstandard Dialect, or Ebonics, which was defined by Williams (1975), as "the linguistic and paralinguistic features which on a concentric continuum represent the communicative competence of the West African, Caribbean and United States slave descendent of African origin," most writers agree that African-American children learn a specific mode of communication characterized by predictable and rule-governed patterns of structure and use, that can be distinguished from the language of the Euro-American community (Smith, 1977).

What these and other writers have observed are value-based behaviors that formed as a consequence of a particular historical reality—one that continues to evolve as it is shaped by the participants, and one that continues to exert its influence as it shapes its participants. While these just described are but a few, they serve to illustrate the point in essence that *an African-American psychological disposition (i.e., behavioral style) is both nurtured by and required for successful interactions among family and community.* The intent here is not to suggest that all African-American behavior is the same. Rather these descriptions delineate core cultural concepts in the anthropological tradition (Kluckhohn & Strodtbeck, 1961) and presume that individual children and families are embedded to varying degrees in the core African-American culture (see Phillips, 1992, 1988). Thus it is the style that the children raised in these settings are likely to possess when they enter school. Where schools and school personnel are grounded in the same historical reality, the child's sociocultural repertoire of behaviors is likely to engage the environment, and the teacher to reciprocate and validate the child's representations.

The Historical Reality of the School

That the traditions and values reflected in schools grow out of a different historical tradition, however, is well documented in educational literature (Roberts & Akinsanya, 1976). American educational practices emerge from traditions that are of European ancestry and world view. This European view of reality suggests that man and his universe are separate entities, man and nature are adversaries, and the survival of the fittest is the highest goal. European thought has subsequently been concerned with fixing things in time and space, with individuality, atomism, and mechanism.

This world view is believed to be reflected in a wide variety of school characteristics including standardization, conformity, atomistic information, deductive logic, abstraction, linear/analytic knowledge (Hilliard, 1976), scientific explanations for everything, future-time orientation, working to get ahead, efficient use of time, climbing the ladder of success, competition, striving to win, individuality, and saving for the future (Shade, 1989). Teachers and other school personnel are likely to be proficient with these characteristics and best prepared for successful (growth enhancing) interactions with children from the same tradition.

For African-American children, this school orientation contributes to a dual dilemma. At one level it represents discontinuity with that of their family and community and thus poses the task of learning to operate by a different set of behavioral rules, much like the difficulty an individual faces when moving to a foreign country. And indeed, mastering this task has importance well beyond the school setting, for the characteristics of the sociopolitical reality of the school are not unique to that institution but are part and parcel of the traditions and values of the wider society. Thus they reflect the skills, knowledge, and patterns of behavior necessary for productive and powerful roles as adults. Yet, the total context of African-American children is somewhat more complex, for they do not "move in" at the school. (Nor will they necessarily move "into" the wider society as adults.) When the dismissal bell rings at the end of the day, they return home to a community that is without power and productivity in the wider society. Under these circumstances, the children's developmental task of securing the reciprocal and reinforcing interactions that will foster power over their reality involves the added dimension of resolving the contradictions inherent in operating in two arenas, each with distinct traditions and behavioral rules—one defined by the school and the other defined by the family and community in which they continue to interact. Viewed in this way, African-American children are engaged in a conflict resolution process, facing at times opposing demands and opposite expectations.

TOWARD A NEW RESOLUTION

Since the development of African-American children is not often viewed by educational research as a conflict resolution process, not much is known about the psychological dynamics of it. What has been observed, however, are the outcomes—how these children appear to operate in school during the first few years.

From the perspective of the school, there are several outcomes. One is evidenced by the children who resist the attempts by the school toward acculturation and who simply continue to operate in the African-American style in any setting through which they move. These children may, for instance, consistently use Ebonics and an African-American learning style (Hale, 1988). They may well be regarded by the school as "uneducable" because they continue to fail in meeting the challenge of school demands. A second outcome is found when children capitulate to the school demands and abandon the African-American style altogether in any setting through which they move. These children, for instance, use a general dialect of standard English and an analytic learning style. They are regarded by the school as "successful," though from the standpoint of the community they fail to exercise power in interactions and thus are subject to stress in that setting. A third outcome is children who operate in both styles, each in the appropriate setting. These children switch language styles and behavioral styles and develop the capability for powerful interactions both in school and in their families and community. They thus have the potential for transforming relationships both within and between the settings.

Although oversimplified and generalized in its description, something akin to this third outcome appears to be an operational strategy that is adaptive within the sociopolitical context. This strategy permits children to experience continuity in growth-producing interactions as they move through the two contexts of school and family-community. Insofar as the exercise of power by our children is an outcome in which we as parents and teachers are interested, then our interactions with children should support this strategy. The question becomes, how can we as adults mediate the experiences of African-American children so that they become more proficient at exercising power over their reality?

Empowering the Child

Foremost among considerations in protecting the cultural/developmental integrity of children is insuring them the power to represent themselves in the school setting and to transform the interactions that take place there. This empowerment process demands that teachers go beyond the typical multicultural approaches where black images are brought into the classroom for a display and black heroes and holidays are celebrated. In the day-to-day interactions, children must be permitted to act upon their environment and to use their expressive styles to solve the problems and meet the challenges of school.

Creating power-nurturing interactional climates requires teachers to acquire a refined understanding of the cultural styles of behavior of African-American children. It has been suggested, for instance, by Boykin (1978) that the movement climate in the classroom should be examined. He believes that African-American children possess great "psychological/behavioral verve" which is a kind of behavioral vibrancy evidenced by their engagement in high energy level activities and their affinity for stimulus change. He suggests that they may learn faster with techniques that incorporate movement into the learning process and be more responsive to variety in teaching and learning formats. Shade (1989) also identifies some dimensions of classroom climate that she has found foster reading proficiency among African-American children. She cites several factors that create good teacher-student rapport, including warmth, verbal interplay during instruction, rhythmic styles of speech, and distinctive intonation patterns.

Whether through inservice training or outside sources, teachers must maintain access to information and expertise about African-American children. Community resources can be found among local college and university faculty, social service agency staff, clinicians in private practice, and the leadership and membership of community organizations. Parents and family members of the children themselves are also a source of such information, whether as formal speakers or organized into discussion groups by teachers themselves.

Helpful as well, is the educational and psychological literature. Although African-American culture has been the center of attention for many social scientists, a good deal of the literature suffers from inaccuracies and caution should be exercised about which information one chooses to use. Two major journals devoted to study of the African-American child and family are the *Journal of Negro Education,* and the *Journal of Black Psychology.* Both provide articles as well as references to further useful reading and sources of information.

Creating a climate for transformed interactions between African-American children and the school environment also requires teachers to examine their perspective on their roles as "teacher" within the present sociopolitical order. Since the vocation of an educator requires the manipulation and distribution of information and knowledge, it must be recognized that this too is an interaction that takes place in a particular social and political ecosystem, where economic oppression and social inequality are factors. These factors influence a teacher's information about and responses to cultural diversity, and they must be understood in relation to that information.

This process is particularly important in early childhood education because traditionally teachers of young children are taught that their role—to enhance cognitive-social-emotional development in young children—is a politically neutral one. Paulo Friere (1974) states, however, that no educational process is neutral; it either functions to facilitate the integration of the younger generation into the logic of the present system and bring about conformity to it, or it becomes the "practice of freedom," the means by which women and men deal critically and creatively in the transformation of their world. Professional responsibility then encompasses an examination of attitudes and a continuously evolving consciousness about the sociopolitical order and the role that institutions play in perpetuating the oppression of certain segments of the population. Writers like Carter G. Woodsen (1972), Albert Memmi (1965), William Ryan (1971), and Antonia Darder (1991) help us understand that education is socialization and that there is no such thing as a value free school. Teachers must consider their own actions and values as an integral part of how they understand particular children and their "needs." It is just as important that teachers know how to observe and comprehend social situations at work in the interest of social aims, as to understand the values held by different people.

Fostering a Conscious Awareness of the Conflicts

A second category of strategies for helping children resolve conflict includes those that foster a conscious understanding of the nature of the opposing demands. The process of clarifying the presumed confusion over differing behavioral expectations is often aided by helping children to develop an appreciation for context-situated behaviors. In the same way that we tell children that one whispers in the library and yells on the playground, *without devaluing either whispering or yelling as a human act,* we must address the conflicts that they face in reconciling home/community experiences and school experiences.

Holt (1981) after extensive research on the language of African-American children developed an educational linguistic approach for the Los Angeles Unified Schools as a curriculum model designed for kindergarten through third grade classrooms. The project both fosters psycholinguistic transfer (the child's ability to coordinate Ebonics and standard English codes so that no loss of cognition occurs) and sociolinguistic transfer (the child's ability to coordinate his home and community cultural experiences with experiences in the classroom). Smooth coordination between Ebonics and standard English is enhanced by teachers who manipulate language usage within its appropriate context. The program has developed a means by which the social context of language usage is brought to life by incorporating "outer city" language in the "inner city" of the classroom. The classroom is organized into a naturalistic social setting that includes both the social cues of the child's community as well as those of the school and mainstream society. In this way, standard English language skills are acquired in the same way the Ebonics language skills were first acquired—through community exchanges. For instance, dictation and pupil stories are repeated or written in the pupil's own idiolect, and comparative discussions take place. In this way, the pupil sees that an identifiable experience can be expressed in two different combinations of symbols. Pupils are taught to perceive their language as different, and a conscious awareness is fostered of the differences between Ebonics and standard English forms.

Application of this principle of raising contradictions is certainly not exhausted by this one example, and the potential for the development of new ones is limitless. The best future prospects rest with teachers in action, who, using their powers of observation, seize opportunities as they arise to help children understand their dual powers.

The same opportunity is present for parents at home to articulate to children the nature of the opposing demands between school and community. Children will often ask parents whether something was "right" or "wrong." The central thrust from parents must be to comment on how certain situations may call for certain behaviors and others call for different behaviors, as a way of socializing children to understand the reasons for the contradictory nature of the African-American sociopolitical reality.

Richardson (1981) explored the strategies used by African-American mothers in preparing their children to operate in a racist society where society's expectations for the children are the opposite of those of their families. Several childrearing practices were identified:

1. Emphasis on the child's need to develop a sense of self and group esteem and identity, where the family took full charge of providing positive black images in order to counteract the negative stereotypes prevalent in the broader society and articulated for children where these come from.
2. Conscious and repeated emphasis on the beauty, value, and worth of the child and comparisons between African-American and Euro-American peoples.
3. Identification and explanation of current racism experiences through discussions of family experiences and/or the identification of racism in public institutions, the media, or individuals. The thrust here was on helping children clarify, define, and assimilate accurate information about confusing encounters and help them view themselves separately from how they may be viewed by others.
4. Valuation of achievement, success, and happiness and corresponding support for "making it" in two worlds, by being pragmatic in their assessment of their social realities with regard to housing, education, economics, and politics, and exposing their children to strategies that blacks have historically utilized in "playing the game" or "getting over."

What these suggest is the need for parents to embed the child in the African-American experience, to continue to articulate the traditional value system and give it substance in everyday family and community interactions, and to refuse to give over to the school the full responsibility for the child's preparation for adulthood.

MEETING THE CHALLENGE

The final test of the effectiveness of one's efforts to transform interactions with African-American children lies not within the measurement of how much information was shared among adults, nor how much rhetoric was engaged in, nor how much reading was accomplished. The effectiveness can only be judged by the degree to which the home and school interactions change, the degree to which the power of children is enhanced, and the degree to which children are able to solve the problems and meet the challenges of their sociopolitical context.

What we have argued in essence, is that to achieve this will require a shift in perspective, both for advocates of a "developmentally appropriate" approach and a multicultural approach. For insofar as the definition of "developmentally appropriate" has two dimensions—age appropriateness and individual appropriateness (Bredekamp, 1987)—the consideration given a third dimension of development is minimized: cultural appropriateness. And insofar as multicultural education concentrates itself on artifacts or values implicit *in* children or *in* school settings, it risks inadequate consideration to creating culturally consistent contexts where the interactions produce growth.

Humanistic education has already made the promise that African-American children grow and develop in the school setting. In the face of a society where inequality and oppression are often fostered by the very institutions that espouse freedom and democracy, fulfilling this promise is a difficult task, and yet a debt we owe to those we teach.

REFERENCES

Baratz, J., & Baratz, S. (1970). Early childhood intervention: The social science base of institutional racism. *Harvard Educational Review, 40,* 29–50.

Bredekamp, S. (Ed.). (1987). *Developmentally appropriate practice in early childhood programs serving children birth through age 8.* Washington, DC: National Association for the Education of Young Children.

Boykin, W. (1978). Psychological/behavioral verve in academic/task performance: Pretheoretical considerations. *Journal of Negro Education, 47,* 343–354.

Bronfenbrenner, U. (1979). *The ecology of human development.* Cambridge, MA: Harvard University Press.

Darder, A. (1991). *Culture and power in the classroom.* New York: Bergin & Garvey.

Friere, P. (1974). *The pedagogy of the oppressed.* New York: Seabury Press.

Hale, J. (1986). Cultural influences on learning styles of Afro-American children. In Lee Morris (Ed.), *Extracting learning styles from social/cultural diversity* (pp. 7–27). Oklahoma: Southwest Teacher Corps Network.

Hale, J. (1988). *Black children: Their roots, culture, and learning styles*. Baltimore: Johns Hopkins University Press.

Herskovitzs, M. (1966). *The new world Negro: Selected papers in Afro-American studies*. Bloomington: Indiana University Press.

Hilliard, A. G. (1976). *Alternatives to I.Q. testing: An approach to the identification of gifted "minority" children*. Final Report. Sacramento, CA: State Department of Education.

Holt, H. (1981). *Language, cognition, and social attitudes in public education: A sociolinguistic and psycholinguistic analysis of kindergarten–third grade pupils*. Unpublished doctoral dissertation, Claremont Graduate School, Claremont, CA.

Jensen, A. (1969). Environment, heredity and intelligence. *Harvard Educational Review, 39,* 1–123.

King, L. (1980). Models of meaning in mental health: Model eight—The transformation of the oppressed. *Fanon Center Journal, 1,* 29–50.

King, L. (1981, November). *Theory and practice: The link between research and action in black child development*. Paper presented at the meeting of the National Black Child Development Institute, Washington, DC.

Kluckholn, F., & Strodtbeck, F. (1961). *Variations in value orientations*. New York: Row, Peterson.

Memmi, A. (1965). *The colonizer and the colonized*. Boston: Beacon Press.

Michaels, S. (1980, March). *Sharing time: An oral presentation for literacy*. Paper presented at the Ethnography in Education Research Forum, University of Pennsylvania, Philadelphia.

Moynihan, D. (1965). *The Negro family: The case for national action*. Washington, DC: United States Department of Labor.

Nobles, W. (1985). *Africanity and the black family: The development of a theoretical model*. Oakland, CA: Institute for the Advanced Study of Black Family Life and Culture.

Nobles, W. (1987). *African American families: issues, Insights and directions*. Oakland, CA: Institute for the Advanced Study of Black Family Life and Culture.

Phillips, C. (1992). Culture: A process that empowers. *Infant/toddler caregiving: A guide to culturally sensitive care* (pp. 2–10). Sausalito, CA: Far West Laboratory for Educational Research and Development.

Phillips, C. (1988). Nurturing diversity for today's children and tomorrow's leaders. *Young Children, 43,* (2), 42–47.

Richardson, B. (1981). *Racism and childrearing: A study of black mothers*. Unpublished doctoral dissertation, Claremont Graduate School, Claremont, CA.

Roberts, J., & Akinsanya, S. (1976). *Schooling in a cultural context*. New York: David McKay.

Ryan, W. (1971). *Blaming the victim*. New York: Pantheon.

Shade, B. (Ed.). (1989). *Culture, style and the educative process*. Springfield, IL: Charles C. Thomas.

Shange, N. (1975). *For colored girls who have considered suicide when the rainbow is enuf.* New York: Macmillan.

Smith, E. (1977). *The historical development of Ebonics: An examination and analysis of three linguistic views and ideological perspectives.* (Paper No. 38). California State University at Fullerton, Department of Linguistics.

Smitherman, G. (1977). *Talkin' and testifyin': The language of black America.* Boston: Houghton Mifflin.

Williams, R. (Ed.). (1975). *Ebonics: The true language of black folks.* St. Louis, MO: Institute of Black Studies.

Woodsen, C. (1972). *The miseducation of the Negro.* New York: Associated Publishers. (Originally published in 1933.)

Young, V. (1970). Family and childhood in a southern Negro community. *American Anthropologist, 72,* 269–288.

8

• • • • • •

Developmentally Appropriate Practice and Cultural Values

A Case in Point

LESLIE R. WILLIAMS

Values underlie any form of educational practice. This tenet is commonly understood by those who have considered the content of education, and the dynamics of teaching and learning (Spodek, 1991). There are those who would argue that the act of teaching is most essentially the actualization of a value system, and that "value-free" practice is an impossibility (Ayers, 1989; Kessler & Swadener, 1992; Schultz, 1988; Tobin, Wu, & Davidson, 1989).

A corollary of this tenet is that values also must underlie any guidelines intended to establish or improve practice. When, for example, a professional association takes a stand regarding excellence in education, the resulting document will embody the values of its writers or, in the larger sense, the values of the culture(s) that influenced those writers. This chapter examines what possible effects these circumstances may have on the current articulation of developmentally appropriate practice (DAP) in the United States in relation to one example of variation—traditional values affecting teaching and learning behaviors still retained in some Native-American (American Indian)[1] communities.

THE CULTURAL CHALLENGE

As pointed out in the introduction to this volume, the National Association for the Education of Young Children (NAEYC), the largest professional organization representing early childhood education in this country, has spent a great deal of time and energy over the past decade to define DAP. The guidelines resulting from that effort (Bredekamp, 1987) have been widely disseminated and are used as a basis for granting accreditation to schools or other early childhood centers located across the country that wish such validation.

Increasingly, recognition of the cultural plurality of the United States has begun to call into question the suitability of using such universal guidelines without first examining them in the light of possible cultural variation (Jipson, 1990). At the annual meeting of NAEYC in New Orleans in November, 1992, several major sessions were devoted to the issue of cultural diversity in relation to DAP; and this chapter is written in the spirit of continuing the dialogue through analysis of a specific instance of consonance or clash.

Given that developmentally appropriate practice has largely been defined through the published guidelines, the question to be examined here is how the values underlying that definition intersect with those underlying the childrearing and educational practices of the hundreds of Native-American communities attempting to apply the guidelines. Are the values represented in DAP so fundamental that they transcend differences? Or might they significantly conflict with deep-seated community values, and thus become a potential source of tension in some early childhood programs?

THE VALUE SET OF
DEVELOPMENTALLY APPROPRIATE PRACTICE

For the purposes of this initial exploration, values are defined as principles, standards, or qualities considered to be desirable or worthwhile.[2] Values stem from the underlying belief systems held by individuals or communities. While values themselves are not immediately visible, they shape individual behavior and group custom by setting expectations for performance within any realm of human endeavor.

What values, then, might be seen to be embedded in DAP? NAEYC's document on DAP defines "developmental appropriateness" as having two dimensions—age appropriateness and individual appropriateness. The former assumes that human physical, social, emotional, and cognitive development proceed through successive stages involving qualitatively different capacities at different points of time. As the child matures, earlier stages become subsumed into those that follow until an integrated and coordinated psychomotoric system is developed, high levels of social and emotional elaboration and stability are achieved, and the capacity for formal logic and hypothetical thought is fully developed.

The latter dimension assumes the uniqueness of persons, with personality and (possibly innate) learning style, among the factors that define individuality. Family backgrounds and cumulative experience (including, as Greenberg [1992] elucidates, children's cultural, religious, and socioeconomic experience, and experience with being parented) are also considered to be interactive with innate characteristics. Such interactions create unique configurations that must be acknowledged and utilized in order for teaching to be effective in the long term.

The guidelines themselves are divided into sections that address curriculum, adult-child interaction, relations between the home and program (or school), and developmental evaluation of children, with awareness of differential applications across the 8-year age span. Taken as a whole, the directives in these areas can be seen to be child-centered, experiential/constructive, interactive, and family-oriented.

The Child-Centered Perspective

The child is seen as the primary source of curriculum. It is through observation of emerging physical, social, emotional, and cognitive capabilities in children's natural activity at home and/or in early childhood settings that teachers can discover the content and form of activities to foster children's growth across developmental domains. Adults are expected to respond quickly and directly to children's "needs, desires, and messages" (Bredekamp, 1987, p. 9). Part of that response is to provide many opportunities for and encouragement of verbal communication both between adults and children, and among children themselves. It is considered important for children to seek and receive answers to their questions, and to receive direct indications of appreciation of their accomplishments from the significant adults in their lives.

Adults are considered to be responsible for reducing or eliminating undue stress in children's lives. They are also expected to encourage the growth of self-esteem in children and facilitate their development of self-control. These aims may be at least partly achieved through a home-school partnership, where information about the child is exchanged between parents and teachers.

As with curriculum, assessment procedures should regard observation of the child as the first source of relevant information. Measures used are expected to take into account the variabilities stemming from gender, culture, and socioeconomic class, as well as from age. Preestablished norms for performance on a measure are considered to be far less important than the particularities of a child's performance in the matter of assessing the child's present accomplishments or future potential.

Experiential/Constructive Orientations

Children are understood to be active constructors of their own knowledge. Mental activity is enhanced by wide experience with people, materials, and events, through which children form concepts and develop perceptions. Children's skills also are refined through repeated experience. Curriculum is therefore expected to provide multiple opportunities for children's direct and concrete engagement. This view of children's learning places the locus of control of the process within children themselves. Adults are not the pivotal factors in the process. They can provide a conducive setting, but it is the children's inner structures that impel them to learn.

Interactive Priorities

The key to construction of knowledge is interaction. In the guidelines it is clear that interaction must occur between children and all the dimensions of their environment. The interaction between children and materials and among children themselves may sometimes be enhanced by direct adult involvement, but may often be better served by the adult's preparing the environment or monitoring the situation without directly intervening. Again the locus of control stays largely with the children in such practices.

Home-school relations are expected to be interactive as well. That is, the earlier model of one-way communication from the teacher to the parent is replaced by a vision of information exchange in the service of fostering the child's growth. Even assessment procedures are expected to facilitate direct interaction of the child with concrete materials, communicative interaction between child and assessor, and exchange between assessors and parents.

Family Emphasis

The frequent reference to parents in the above summary reveals the guidelines' family-orientation. An assumption that the parent knows the child well, and that the parent's knowledge is crucial to planning a meaningful educational program for the child, threads its way through all the guidelines. Similarly, the acknowledgement of the family as a setting for formative interactions is clear, although "family" often appears to be equated directly with "parents" (thus narrowing family's definition). It is within the family that children first experience the personal exchanges that trigger the internal structures of their development.

ASSUMPTIONS UNDERLYING
DEVELOPMENTALLY APPROPRIATE PRACTICE

The prominence of the individual in the guidelines is striking. There appears to be an assumption that the highest good in child care and education lies in the perfection of individual capability across domains of development. The family, and the group(s) to which the family may belong are seen as a very important backdrop to that individual progress, rather than as the primary consideration in decision making. The value of the individual is thus raised over that of the group.

Another pronounced feature of the guidelines is the value accorded to independence in the construction/acquisition of knowledge. Practitioners are urged not to impose their own visions on the children, but to encourage exploratory behavior. For example, children's own creations, uninfluenced by teacher models, are the ultimate aim of artistic and constructive activities, and child initiation is to take precedence over adult direction for the better part of the working day.

A third prominent tendency lies in the valuing of overt expression of language. Language development is seen to occur through the children's direct practice and the exercise of as many opportunities as possible to integrate language throughout the day. Child-talk is valued in what would appear to be virtually all situations.

CULTURAL TENDENCIES AND DISPOSITIONS IN
NATIVE-AMERICAN COMMUNITIES

The underlying assumptions described above stand in interesting contrast to tendencies and dispositions nurtured in many Native-American communities. Little Soldier (1992) and Paul (1992a, 1992b), among others, have pointed out childrearing and traditional educational practices that could be seen as having different implications for the definition and implementation of "developmental appropriateness" in the care and education of young children.

While both authors emphasize that there is variation in belief and practice among the American Indian nations, they also feel that there are belief systems that are widely shared. The following reflections are, therefore, presented with the understanding that they may not hold true for all Native-American groups, or for all individuals within a particular group, but that they are prominent enough to be recognizable by many American Indian people.

The Group as Center

The development of the individual is not seen to be as worthy of attention as is the relationship of that individual to the group. The growth of any one person is seen as integrally tied with the health and integrity of the group as a whole. Thus, the focus is not so much on the internal dynamic as on relationship of the self to others—and others can include human beings, other beings (including spiritual entities), and the external, material world. The highlighting of relationship may sometimes mean the subsuming of self for the good and the enhancement of others.

This understanding may take many forms in a child's behavior or in the overt expectations of teachers. Little Soldier speaks of some Indian children's high sensitivity to direct forms of personal criticism and to anything that might be interpreted as ridicule. Direction of individual attention, even in the form of praise, may be intensely embarrassing to some Indian children. In contrast, group activity and cooperative effort may be favorably received; group accomplishment (as in a team victory in sports) may be an acceptable way for an individual to experience approval. Some Native-American teachers may find the fostering of individual accomplishment in children distasteful for the same reasons and may promote group awareness as an alternative.

Interdependence and Knowledge

In some Native-American cultures, development across domains is considered to proceed through observation of a model/mentor (usually a respected adult) who could be viewed as a keeper (guardian) of knowledge. Thus, knowledge is understood to be not so much individually constructed as socially constructed. The process is still an active one, but it requires a very different type of engagement. What is truly worthwhile knowledge is usually passed on from the older person to the younger one through a process of modeling and imitation in concrete situations of application.

In educational situations, therefore, child initiation may be less important than the child's ability to observe carefully and to follow a model in carrying out a particular task or assignment. Practice on one's own then follows. Resourcefulness is valued within that framework of learning, with awareness of and respect for what has gone before. Activity is respected in relationship to the group's knowledge. Rather than independence, interdependence is emphasized.

Zimiles (1991) suggests that cultures may have variation in children's emotional readiness for schooling especially regarding teacher/community expectations of independence as a proper goal of activity, and of acquired patterns of intellectual functioning. Zimiles cites Gardner's (1983) and Gardner and Hatch's (1989) work on a theory of multiple intelligences as particularly helpful in understanding these phenomena. Perewardy (1993) also draws upon Gardner in his examination of a successful example of Indian education, again highlighting both social and cognitive interdependence as salient features of knowledge construction among American Indian peoples.

Interactive Rule Structures

Many Native-American communities have highly elaborate oral traditions. Language and its elegant use clearly have places of great importance within such a tradition and children are expected to develop complete command of it. At the same time, though, Little Soldier (1992) points out that silence is comfortable in many traditional Indian cultures. Paul (1992a, 1992b) emphasizes that in the storytelling traditions of many groups, the older people speak, while the children are expected to listen. Rather than creating many opportunities for the children to speak, adults may make many opportunities for the children to listen.

At the same time, as Philips (1974/1983) points out in her now classic study of the communicative patterns on the Warm Springs Indian Reservation, signs of attention to speakers may be different from those given by non-Indian listeners. Especially when the conversation is among peers, or when the person speaking is not viewed as the authority, lack of gaze exchange, nodding, or verbal signaling among Indian participants may indicate a distinctive communicative rule structure significantly at variance with non-Indian expectations. When one speaks, and what one speaks about, may be defined differently than in Eurocentric cultures.

Both Paul and Philips note that speaking and listening are often engaged in within the context of other activity, such as doing routine tasks, making something, or following a particular procedure. Following too closely on the words of another or interrupting another's speech can be considered rude in some circumstances. If listeners wait and watch closely, their questions will be answered without disrespect to others.

However, as Paul points out, in many other circumstances, children's behavior (including their talkativeness) is viewed leniently in terms of some non-Indian standards. Part of the cultural training involves development of discernment as to when speech is appropriate. Thus communicative competence is developed through practice in defined circumstances, not at every available opportunity.

Importance of the Extended Family

The context for development is still the family, but family is much more broadly defined than in the DAP guidelines. Paul emphasizes the importance of the extended family in many American Indian communities and notes that the individual responsible for overseeing a child's education may not be the child's biological parent. Exchanges of information between teachers and family members may therefore need to take place within the context of these multiple associations.

It would seem that the model presented by the teacher might influence the manner in which such exchanges occur. If the teacher is seen as someone who is not mentoring the children in traditional ways, that is, presenting models for the children to follow in the execution of particular activities, there may be some reluctance on the part of the family to share information. An atmosphere of exchange must be built through demonstration to the family of the utility of the information in the teaching process.

UNDERLYING EXPECTATIONS IN NATIVE-AMERICAN COMMUNITIES

The value systems found to the present day in some American Indian communities emphasize the well being of the group as part of the responsibility of the individual. From a very young age, children learn that they should contribute toward a group effort, rather than seek individual recognition. There are exceptions to this rule. For example, in concepts of bravery held by groups such as the Lakota, individuals might "count coup"[3] by pitting the self against highly dangerous or seemingly insurmountable odds (Neihardt, 1961; Sandoz, 1961). However, the overall orientation appears to be more toward group action, not only in the regulation of social behavior, but in the tacit understanding of how learning best proceeds.

Interdependence, rather than independence, is the natural outcome of such a world view. Acceptance of a relationship of one to the whole has far-reaching ramifications for the ways children might respond to teaching/learning situations. Some children might be more comfortable in observing models or finished products before beginning their own efforts, than they would be in unstructured exploration. They might expect adult authority to assume overt forms through direction and the setting of clear standards. And, they might be reluctant to display verbal facility in a situation where they might feel themselves being judged by peers.

Speech and language proficiency thus might take somewhat different forms than those implicitly envisioned by the DAP guidelines. Therefore, children's silence cannot be interpreted as lack of ability. In another situation, the children may show themselves to be powerful speakers indeed. The rules for display of one's knowledge may simply be different.

THE CONTINUING DIALOGUE

It would seem that applying the DAP guidelines in programs of child care and early education without awareness of possible differences in value systems poses some risks to teachers and children. The analysis above indicates possible points of clash in expectations. An early childhood program designed to inflexibly reproduce the educational vision of the presently existing DAP guidelines could, in some circumstances, create an environment that stresses children rather than supports their growth and development. Native teachers raised with traditional values may find DAP runs contrary to their deepest dispositions and beliefs about what they think best for young children.

At the same time that there are points of potential conflict, there are also positive intersections between DAP and traditional values. The emphasis on activity as an appropriate avenue for learning, for example, is a common thread connecting the two perspectives. Visions of interaction with the people, materials, and events comprising a child's immediate environment also share some common elements.

The time seems to have come for a rethinking of the guidelines, with consideration of the negotiations possible in the setting of "standards." Creating the kind of flexibility that will enable local communities to become part of the guidelines' continuing construction may encourage a deepening attention to the needs of young children as it honors the part of teachers and family in the definition of worthwhile learning.

NOTES

[1] The designations "Native American" and "American Indian" have politically defined connotations. "Progressives" or "liberals" both inside and outside indigenous communities tend to use the term "Native American," while "moderates" or traditionally minded people tend to speak of "American Indians" or simply "Indians." Within group, people often refer to themselves by the name of their native nation, such as Lakota (Sioux) or Denaina (Nondalton/Stony River Athapaskan). In this chapter, the terms Native American, American Indian, and Indian will be used interchangeably to describe peo-

ple of indigenous origin in the United States.

[2]This definition is derived from those offered by *The American Heritage Dictionary of the English Language,* New College Edition. Boston: Houghton Mifflin Company, 1976.

[3]One traditionally "counted coup" by approaching the enemy in the thick of battle and striking an opposing warrior on the head and then leaving. The touch itself is what was important, not extent of injury to the person. This concept may be understood both literally and figuratively.

REFERENCES

Ayers, W. (1989). *The good preschool teacher*. New York: Teachers College Press.

Bredekamp, S. (Ed.). (1987). *Developmentally appropriate practice in early childhood programs serving children from birth through age eight.* Washington, DC: National Association for the Education of Young Children.

Gardner, H. (1983). *Frames of mind*. New York: Basic Books.

Gardner, H., & Hatch, T. (1989). Multiple intelligences go to school: Educational implications of the theory of multiple intelligences. *Educational Researcher, 18* (8), 4–10.

Greenberg, P. (1992). Why not academic preschool? II. Autocracy or democracy in the classroom? *Young Children, 47* (3), 54–63.

Jipson, J. (1990). *Developmentally appropriate practice: Limiting possibilities.* Paper presented at the annual meeting of the American Educational Research Association, Boston.

Kessler, S., & Swadener, B. B. (Ed.). (1992). *Reconceptualizing the early childhood curriculum.* New York: Teachers College Press.

Little Soldier, L. (1992). Working with Native American children. *Young Children, 47* (6), 15–21.

Neihardt, J. G. (1961). *Black Elk speaks: Being the life story of a holy man of the Oglala Sioux.* Lincoln, NB: University of Nebraska Press.

Paul, A. S. (1992a). Early childhood education in American Indian and Alaskan Native communities. In G. M. Charleston (Ed.), *Indian nations at risk: Solutions for the 1990s* (Chapter 9). Washington, DC: U.S. Department of Education.

Paul, A. S. (1992b). American Indian (Native American) influences. In L. R. Williams and D. P. Fromberg (Eds.), *Encyclopedia of Early Childhood Education* (pp. 11–13). New York: Garland Publishing.

Perewardy, C. (1993). *How to teach the Native student.* Paper presented at the annual meeting of the Association of Teacher Educators, Los Angeles.

Philips, S. U. (1974/1983). *The invisible culture: Communication in classroom and community on the Warm Springs Indian Reservation.* New York: Longman.

Sandoz. M. (1961). Crazy Horse: The strange man of the Oglalas. Lincoln, NB: University of Nebraska Press.

Schultz, S. B. (1988). *The hidden curriculum: Finding mechanisms of resistance and control in the preschool.* Unpublished doctoral dissertation, Teachers College, Columbia University.

Spodek, B. (1991). Early childhood curriculum and cultural definitions of knowledge. In B. Spodek and O. Saracho (Eds.), *Yearbook in early childhood education: Vol. 2. Issues in Early Childhood Curriculum* (pp. 1–20). New York: Teachers College Press.

Tobin, J. J., Wu, D. H. Y., & Davidson, D. H. (1989). *Preschoolers in three cultures: Japan, China and the United States.* New Haven, CT: Yale University Press.

Zimiles, H. (1991). Diversity and change in young children: Some educational implications. In B. Spodek & O. N. Saracho (Eds.), *Yearbook in early childhood education: Vol. 2. Issues in early childhood curriculum* (pp. 21–45). New York: Teachers College Press.

9

•••••

Parents, Pluralism, and the NAEYC Statement on Developmentally Appropriate Practice

Douglas R. Powell

A critical question facing the field of early childhood programs is the extent to which the dominant professional culture will control decisions about the appropriateness of programs providing early education and care. In the past decade, the largest professional organization representing early childhood educators has taken ambitious steps to establish and promote indicators of quality in early childhood programs. As noted in the introduction, the centerpiece of these efforts is the statement on developmentally appropriate practice (DAP) generated by the National Association for the Education of Young Children (NAEYC).

Attempts to exert influence on the nature of early childhood programs face the onerous circumstance of an open-market environment with minimal government control over a loosely organized set of autonomous and diverse providers of early education and care. Of necessity, parents have been cast as major players in strategies to ensure adherence to professional images of good settings for young children. Most plans aimed at improving the quality of early childhood programs envision parents as supporters of prevailing wisdom about what constitutes appropriate practices.

At issue is the inclusion of parent perspectives in decisions about the characteristics of a good setting for a young child. In a highly pluralistic society that places a premium on individual choice and parental authority, the accommodation of diversity is of paramount importance in initiatives aimed at increasing professional influence on the care and education of young children.

This chapter examines the roles of parents in professional efforts to improve the quality of early childhood programs through use of developmentally appropriate practices. It considers the contexts in which the DAP statement was developed, the feasibility of using parents as promoters of developmentally appropriate practice, and the provisions for enabling programs to accommodate diversity through the inclusion of parent perspectives.

CONTEXTS OF THE DAP STATEMENT

The DAP statement was developed in the context of a field that historically has (1) functioned in an environment of parent choice and expectations of close coordination between program and family, (2) embraced a healthy amount of pluralism, and (3) existed as a profession of marginal status. These factors are interrelated and each one is a direct or indirect target of the DAP statement.

As noted earlier, programs of early education and care operate under open-market conditions, with relatively little government oversight (Holloway & Fuller, 1992), and with images of parents as consumers (Mitchell, Cooperstein, & Larner, 1992). Due to societal stratification, the parent choice concept has been implemented to a greater extent by middle- and upper middle-class parents than by lower-income parents (e.g. Greenberg, 1989; Mitchell et al., 1992). Nonetheless, this is a field shaped partly by market forces involving parents' preferences and ideas about appropriate settings for young children.

A central part of the professional early childhood community's ethos is that continuity should exist between family and program. This perspective stems from the doctrine of parental rights—a core American value that places responsibility for determining the child's best interest first and foremost with parents—and a recognition that the education and care of young children are value-laden processes. The parental rights doctrine is the basis for laws that mandate parent involvement in decisions affecting the education of handicapped children. Continuity between family and early childhood program also has been assumed to result in positive benefits for children. Program-family discontinuities, which are of the greatest magnitude for children from low income and ethnic minority families, are thought to have negative effects on children's academic outcomes and socialization experiences (for a review, see Powell, 1989). Program-family connections, then, have been valued in early childhood program traditions. Especially when compared with other levels of education and types of human services, the early childhood education field has been a pioneer in working with parents (Powell, 1991).

Frequent two-way communication between home and school has long been viewed as an element of good practice toward achieving program-home continuity. Sometimes this strategy is accompanied by calls for prospective parent-users to become familiar with a program's philosophy and practices, with the aim of enabling the parents to select a program that is well matched to their family values.

There are two other strands of practice aimed at realizing program-family continuity, based on different ideas about the appropriate directionality or flow of influence in the parent-staff relationship (Fein, 1980; Powell, 1991). One strand focuses on mechanisms for strengthening program responsiveness to parental values. Examples of attempts to incorporate a family's values into early childhood program services include the mandated provisions for parent participation in key program decisions found in Head Start, the collective parent ownership of early childhood programs practiced in the cooperative nursery school movement, and the legal rights of parents in decisions about educational programs for children with special needs. Another distinct strand of practices employed in the name of program-family continuity emphasizes the role of the early childhood program in providing information and guidance on parenting. In one version of this strand, information is offered to parents on child development and activities to pursue with children. By doing this, it is hoped that the program's view of children and curriculum approaches will be reinforced and extended in the home (Powell & Stremmel, 1987).

These two strands are not mutually exclusive, although attempts to incorporate both with equal status in a program have proven difficult (e.g., Joffe, 1977); the strands represent different assumptions about the resourcefulness of parents. The parent-as-program-decision-maker has been a source of tension in the early childhood field, in part because it restricts professional autonomy. The parent education function has been less controversial, even though concerns have been voiced about the potentially paternalistic character of conventional parent education practices (e.g., Dunst & Trivette, 1988) and the problems of imposing the culture of the school on the culture of the family, especially with ethnic minority populations (Laosa, 1979).

One result of the early childhood profession's interest in program-home continuity is a high level of pluralism across programs. Groups representing different racial, cultural, and ethnic backgrounds as well as ideologies have managed to coexist within the early childhood field and sometimes within the same program. The field's pluralistic nature has been aided by the absence of huge bureaucracies and centralized control, resulting in a loose patchwork of highly autonomous programs, and by the absence of traditional credentials (e.g., baccalaureate degree) for gaining entrance to positions in the field, resulting in the employment of many workers who represent values indigenous to the community being served.

The field also has been pluralistic in the sense that no single view of the child has been thought to explain all developmental phenomena and, as a corollary, no single method of working with young children has been deemed to be superior to others. As a consequence, strikingly different program models have flourished, many leaving their mark on modal practices in the field. Until the 1980s, research evidence supported the idea that any well administered curriculum could contribute to positive child outcomes (e.g., Weikart, Epstein, Schweinhart, & Bond, 1978). Curriculum comparison studies were unable to identify one approach as better than another, although, as discussed later in this chapter, more recent evidence suggests that certain types of programs may have beneficial results (for a review, see Powell, 1987).

In many ways, the pluralistic nature of the early childhood field is a function of the field's marginal status in society. High-status professional groups are characterized by significant professional autonomy and detachment from the lay public. In prestigious professions such as medicine and law, it is the professional, not the client, who defines what is needed and how needs will be met. Professions are self-directing, with control over the production and application of knowledge to the services or work performed by members of the profession. Efforts are made to have exclusive jurisdiction over the services offered, and there is an element of trust within society granted to a professional body (Hughes, 1971).

What makes the early childhood field a weak profession is the lack of a "license and mandate" to deliver early education and care (Joffe, 1977; see also Hughes, 1971). The profession has no control over the nature of services and the persons who provide services. The absence of a "license and mandate" is the result of a more fundamental problem regarding the perceived lack of a distinctive data base or body of knowledge to serve as a foundation of the early childhood field. The work of caring for young children is familiar to almost everyone, especially the parent-client (Joffe, 1977).

NAEYC's policy statement on attributes of good early childhood programs is a bold beginning of a remedy for the field's weak status. The DAP statement may be seen as an effort to make claim to a distinctive body of knowledge for work with young children. To ensure this knowledge is put into practice, the DAP statement targets two aspects of the parental role: the parent as consumer in the selection of an early childhood program and the parent's contributions to the relationship with a program.

PARENT AS CONSUMER

From the perspective of the early childhood profession, the parent choice element of the early childhood field is problematic because, without constraints, parent choice can sanction early childhood settings and practices that run contrary to prevailing professional judgment. Thus, it is not surprising that a primary intent of the DAP statement is to have impact on parents' views of what constitutes a good early childhood program. In this sense, the DAP statement is a tool for reforming the early childhood field via parent choice. The plan is that informed parents will demand, use, and monitor programs practicing developmental appropriateness and, conversely, diminished parent use of poor quality programs will contribute to the demise of inappropriate early childhood settings.

Recommendations for reaching parents with the DAP information are included in the 1987 volume reporting the DAP statement, in a section titled "Informing Others About Developmentally Appropriate Practice" (Black & Puckett, 1987). The suggestions include talking to parents about how programs provide developmentally appropriate care and education, quoting from the DAP statement in newsletters to parents or in parent meetings, and using the Week of the Young Child and other public forums "to educate parents and the general public about appropriate teaching practices" (Black & Puckett, 1987, p. 86).

The DAP statement supports a child-centered approach to early education and care, and deems didactic or highly teacher-directed practices to be developmentally inappropriate. The merits of didactic versus non-didactic or child-centered strategies of working with young children long have been a contentious issue in early childhood education (e.g., Kohlberg & Mayer, 1972). Proponents of child-centered methods have argued that teacher-controlled instruction undermines children's intrinsic interest in learning, children's perceptions of competence, and children's willingness to take academic risks. It also has been argued that didactic teaching methods with young children foster dependence on adults' authority for defining what should be done on a task and how it should be evaluated (Stipek, 1992). Research evidence appearing in the 1980s (for a review, see Powell, 1987) and more recently (e.g., Daniels, 1992) suggests that child-centered approaches have beneficial results and didactic methods may be associated with negative outcomes.

What is the likelihood that parents will use basic ideas of the DAP statement to exert influence on early childhood programs through the selection and monitoring of early childhood options? The answer to this question rests with an understanding of existing parental beliefs about how best to work with young children, and of the process by which parents search for early childhood programs.

The DAP statement's endorsement of a child-centered approach provides a stark contrast with the images of appropriate settings for young children generally held by lowerincome and ethnic minority parents. For example, in a study of 161 parents of children enrolled in Los Angeles area early childhood programs, African-American, Latino, and Asian parents endorsed didactic approaches to early childhood education more than Caucasian parents. Latino parents endorsed didactic techniques more than the African-American and Asian parents. Also, parents in the three ethnic minority groups reported using significantly more formal teaching activities in the home than Caucasian parents. Parents' educational level was held constant throughout the analyses, suggesting that cultural background was the primary variable associated with attitudes toward formal instruction. Overall, higher levels of parents' formal education were associated with less didactic beliefs. However, among highly educated parents who had their children enrolled in didactic programs, beliefs in didactic approaches were similar to the didactic educational orientations of less educated parents (Milburn, 1992). These recent findings regarding ethnicity are consistent with Joffe's (1977) earlier discovery that African-American parents wanted an early childhood program that emphasized traditional academic content and didactic teaching methods.

The act of using strangers for child care was seen as an "audacious step" by white, working- and lower middle-class families in Zinnser's (1991) ethnographic study of first, second, and third generation descendents of mainly Italian immigrants. In this population, the strong, clear preference is for child care to be provided by family members or close friends. In Zinnser's discussions with family day care providers, it appeared that children were well fed, clean, and safe, but she heard no accounts of providers encouraging or even taking note of dramatic and imaginative play, fantasy, storytelling, or other expressive forms of activity. Children were neither encouraged to draw or paint freely, nor to dance or sing. No provider mentioned regular reading or book-centered activities. Yet the care provided by these sitters was within family traditions and community-accepted norms of childrearing practices.

Class differences in parents' childrearing orientations and ideas about appropriate educational environments have long been established in the literature (e.g. Hess, 1970). Years ago, Kohn (1977) argued that middle-class families value self-direction in children while lower-income families value child conformity to external demands. Research suggests that parents generally place their children in early childhood programs that match their educational beliefs, although there are instances of parents placing pressure on their children at home who intentionally select a less academic school as a way to temper the press of their home environment (Hirsh-Pasek, Hyson, & Rescorla, 1990).

Until the early 1980s, middle-class Caucasian parents' expectations of early childhood programs were thought to be similar to what professionals call a child-centered approach. In a mid-1970s study of Berkeley, California, early childhood programs, for example, Joffe (1977) found that middle-class Caucasian parents tended to view their child as a tourist who needed to be psychologically fit to leave home and venture into new territories at his or her own pace. The child was "not to be hurried from place to place, or event to event, against his will" in a guided tour-group fashion (Joffe, 1977, p. 69). Caucasian parents did not object to their child knowing basic academic skills such as reading and writing, but they did not want the teaching of these skills to begin too early. The most important dimension along which Caucasian parents assessed their children was the child's social capabilities, especially independence.

Middle-class parents' preferences appeared to change in the 1980s. As Sigel (1991) has observed, "Middle-class parents used to want preschool purely as a social experience for their children. Now they seem to want a head start to Harvard" (p. 87). Anecdotal reports indicate that in the 1980s rapidly growing numbers of middle- and upper middle-class parents wanted an academic-oriented program for their young children (Gallagher & Coche, 1987). This development appears to have been fueled by well-publicized reports showing American children to be lower in math and science knowledge than children in other countries, concerns about the implications of increased global competitiveness in business and industry, and a decrease in general public confidence in the efficacy and efficiency of American schools (Kagan & Zigler, 1987).

A recent study of 436 middle- and upper middle-class parents from intact, mostly Caucasian families (218 mothers, 218 fathers) found a tendency for parents to place greater emphasis on intellectual skills than on social-emotional skills as important school readiness attributes (Knudsen-Lindauer & Harris, 1989). In response to the question, "When a child goes to kindergarten the most important thing to know is . . . ," both mothers and fathers overall ranked the following three skills and abilities as the most important in a list of 13 items: listening, self-confidence, and following directions. Fathers ranked counting and reading significantly higher than did mothers. Both mothers and fathers ranked counting, writing, and reading significantly higher than did a group of kindergarten teachers. Being independent and curious were ranked significantly higher by teachers than by mothers and fathers.

The study also examined expectations of curriculum emphasis in kindergarten. Mothers, fathers, and teachers were in agreement that listening and confidence were the two most important developmental areas and skills to be emphasized. Teachers rated social skills as the third most important item. From another study, consider the voices of mothers who placed their children in early childhood programs emphasizing traditional academic content: "I didn't want them to be playing all the time." "I was looking for a preschool that was a little bit more than just two and a half hours of free play; something a little bit more structured, that would make use of this year" (Hyson, 1991, p. 32).

Leaders in the early childhood field responded assertively to the 1980s erosion of middle-class parent support for child-centered program philosophies. Parents were viewed as primary promoters of the movement toward academic preschool programs (Hyson, 1991) and as major contributors to escalating pressures on young children. Accordingly, the organized profession's response focused mostly on parents "pushing" their young children with drill and practice teaching methods at home, overinvolvement in extracurricular activities and lessons, and enrollment in academic-oriented early childhood programs that were thought to rob children of their childhood (Sigel, 1987). David Elkind, who served as the elected president of NAEYC, authored two books on the topic, *The Hurried Child* (1981) and *Miseducation: Preschoolers at Risk* (1987). Numerous national and regional conferences explored whether early academic training was a help or hindrance to young children. Research on the characteristics and consequences of academic-oriented early childhood classrooms was conducted (e.g., Burts, Hart, Charlesworth, & Kirk, 1990), and a special issue of the *Early Childhood Research Quarterly* (Vol. 2, No. 3, 1987) was devoted to the "hothousing" topic.

It is difficult to know whether the 1980s growth of middle-class parent interest in the use of traditional academic methods with young children persists on a widespread basis in the 1990s. Middle-class parents are likely to follow, or at least give the public appearance of following, the popular advice and recommendations of childrearing experts (Young, 1990). Interestingly, one group of researchers on parental pressuring of young children has speculated that upper middle-class mothers may have given "low-pressure" answers to the researchers' questions in an effort avoid a "pushy parent" label in light of media warnings about the dangers of pushing preschoolers (Hyson, Hirsh-Pasek, Rescorla, Cone, & Martell-Boinske, 1991).

One could argue that parents who hold beliefs at odds with the DAP statement are simply uninformed or misinformed about the features of good early childhood programs. This argument supports the idea of public education initiatives designed to tell parents and others about appropriate practices with young children. Yet the DAP statement is rooted most strongly in particular theoretical perspectives, not value-free science (Powell, in press), and thus ideological orientations are at hand.

Professional advice about the merits of distinctive approaches to early childhood education confronts a larger pattern of parenting. Parents' decisions about preschool cannot be separated from parenting beliefs, behaviors, and personality. Mothers with high expectations for formal academic work and adult instruction tend to enroll their preschool children in programs that emphasize teacher-directed learning, paper-and-pencil activities, and practice in school-related skills (Hyson, Hirsh-Pasek, & Rescorla, 1990). Moreover, middle- and upper middle-class mothers who believe strongly in early, formal academic instruction have been found to behave in a directive and controlling way with their preschool children, and to receive high ratings on anxiety, rigidity, and criticalness from interviewers (Hyson et al., 1991).

The fact that values are involved in parents' decisions about appropriate programs for young children does not negate the important role of consumer education in helping parents find quality early childhood programs. However, consumer education is not promotion nor is it an attempt to change the consumer's values or preferences nor is it to be used to influence behavior in a particular direction (Mitchell et al., 1992).

The prospect of the DAP statement having influence on early childhood programs via parent choice depends on more than parental agreement with and understanding of the DAP statement. It also hinges on an in-depth search process for high-quality programs and a degree of dissatisfaction with present options. The extant literature suggests that, generally, these conditions do not exist. In a critique of the contributions parental choice has made to improve the quality of child care, Holloway and Fuller (1992) concluded that parental choice of child care does not inevitably lead to high-quality care as defined by professionals. They cite available evidence indicating that parents are able to identify components of child care quality that most professionals would endorse, but tend to engage in a cursory investigation of child care options and generally are satisfied with their child care arrangements. Moreover, the limited purchasing power of lower-income parents places serious restraints on their range of available program options.

In sum, the content of the DAP statement must be considered in relation to class and race, and available evidence indicates many lower-income and ethnic minority parents prefer didactic programs for their young children that probably are not compatible with the DAP statement. Furthermore, parental readiness to actively use the DAP messages through in-depth searches and dissatisfaction with present options do not seem to exist on a widespread basis.

PROGRAM-PARENT RELATIONS

In keeping with early childhood program traditions, the DAP statement emphasizes program-family continuity and consistency for the child. Parent-staff communication is the primary mechanism through which "mutual understanding and guidance" and "mutual problem solving about concerns regarding (child) behavior and growth" are to occur (Bredekamp, 1987, p. 12). Parents are encouraged to observe and participate in the program, and teachers are charged with responsibility for establishing and maintaining frequent contact with families. The DAP statement for toddlers calls for parents and staff to talk daily about the child's activities, and appropriate practice with 4- and 5-year-olds calls for "communicating regularly" with parents (p. 57). Inappropriate practice includes infrequent parent-staff communication (e.g., at conferences only) and staff avoidance of "controversial issues rather than resolving them with parents" (p. 38).

The DAP statement also incorporates the two previously described sets of strategies in managing relations with parents, one aimed at educating and supporting parents for their childrearing roles, and another focused on mechanisms for ensuring program responsiveness to parental values and preferences. The role of staff as parent educators is clear in the DAP statement. Teachers are to "share child development knowledge, insights, and resources as part of regular communication and conferences with family members" (Bredekamp, 1987, p. 12). An example of appropriate practice with parents of toddlers is to help parents anticipate the child's next areas of development and "prepare them to support the child" (p. 38). An inappropriate practice example is to "fail to provide parents with information or insights to help them do what is best for their child" (p. 38). In a less obvious way, the DAP statement is a substantive guide on how parents should accommodate young children's needs at home. Presumably the DAP statement's lists of appropriate and inappropriate practices with young children apply to school and to home.

With regard to program responsiveness to parental values and preferences, the DAP statement incorporates elements of the field's tradition of placing parents in program decision-making roles. The DAP statement indicates "parents have both the right and the responsibility to share in decisions about their children's care and education," and the parent-staff relationship is described as a "partnership" (Bredekamp, 1987, p. 12). The list of inappropriate practice includes examples of staff feeling in competition with parents of toddlers, and parents viewing "teachers as experts" and feeling isolated from their children's experiences. Further, teachers are to "promote mutual respect by recognizing and acknowledging different points of view to help minimize confusion for children" (p. 12).

At the same time, the DAP statement can be interpreted as ambivalent about the importance and role of parents' contributions to decisions covering the nature of the child's experiences in a program. The call for parents to share in decisions about their children's care and education is a one-sentence recommendation, and the report offers no concrete examples of how this practice is to be implemented or specifically how teachers show respect for parents' alternative points of view. Items in the lists of "appropriate" and "inappropriate" practices do not include examples of parents as contributors to decisions other than as communicators with teachers. The most informative statement on this point is found in the interpretation of criteria for high quality early childhood programs included in the accreditation criteria and procedures of the National Academy of Early Childhood Programs (1991). The interpretation states that "staff do not capitulate to parents' demands, but they should demonstrate respect for parents as the principal influence in their child's life" (p. 27).

Missing in the DAP statement is endorsement of the practice of including parents in the formal decision-making structures of a program. There is a wealth of many years of experience with this approach in the cooperative nursery school movement and more recently in Head Start, where acknowledgement of parent perspectives is mandated through votes on the local policy council, and in programs for children with special needs.

The ability of program staff to engage in perspective-taking—an important step in the development of a partnership with parents—presumably is enhanced through specialized preparation in topics dealing with parenting, parent development, and family life. The DAP statement indicates that early childhood teachers should have college level preparation in early childhood education/child development, but does not mention content focused on parents. However, the program accreditation criteria include the provision of regular training opportunities for staff to improve skills in working with families, including communication and relations with families.

The DAP policy statement leans toward, but does not fully embrace, a conventional paradigm of professional helping in its portrayal of how program staff should relate to parents. Among other things, this paradigm submits that professionals carry out their work without interference from lay persons. Professionals are seen as resourceful, and the flow of influence is one way, from professional to client. This is in contrast with a collaborative relationship in which both parents and staff have equal status in defining the nature of a situation, goals of the work, the problem-solving process, and the evaluation of its success (Tyler, Pargament, & Gatz, 1983). There has been movement toward a true collaborative relationship with parents of disabled children (Szanton, 1991); and Almy (1986) called for use of this model in relations between researchers and practitioners in early childhood education.

The DAP statement's descriptions of staff providing parents with child development information and guidance also imply an expert mode of relating to parents. The resourcefulness of parents as providers of child-rearing information and advice is not acknowledged. Given research findings on the informal support networks that can form among parents using a program (Joffe, 1977; Powell, 1989), one possible appropriate practice is for programs to facilitate the development of supportive interpersonal ties among parents in the program. With this strategy, knowledge about children and child rearing flows from parents as well as staff.

Movement toward a conventional model of professional helping in the DAP statement is consistent with the statement's specification of good program experiences for young children. The document would have an odd asymmetrical character if it advanced a mechanism of parent-program interactions that enabled parents to significantly modify the recommended practices of the DAP statement. For program directors and teachers facing parental pressures for their programs to provide traditional academic content and pedagogy, the DAP statement provides a professional mandate or rationale for staff to "hold the line" against unwanted external meddling with child-centered programs. Staff can now point to an authority larger than their own judgment as the source of their methods. The value of children's free play and other core elements of child-centered approaches now has official sanction from the largest and primary professional group of early childhood educators in the United States.

While indications of a conventional model of professional helping are evident in the report, there also is ambivalence. The DAP statement calls for "joint planning" between teacher and parent (Bredekamp, 1987, p. 12), for instance, but does not offer suggestions on how this might proceed.

The DAP statement envisions parent-clients who are supportive of a particular program philosophy and therefore are likely to make few or no demands on staff for program changes or alterations. The accreditation criteria are clear about the need for information about program philosophy and goals to be shared with a program's new and prospective users. This enables parents to make "an informed decision about the best possible arrangement for their child" (National Academy of Early Childhood Programs, 1991, p. 26).

In sum, the DAP statement seems to reflect a profession in an understandable quandary about how to accommodate parents. It is clearer in specifying how program staff should help parents with their child-rearing role than in specifying how parents should contribute to the nature of program experiences for children. The statement stops short of characterizing the meaning of, and identifying needed support systems for, the role of parents as contributors to decisions about their child's care and education. Hence, it avoids the controversial matter of parents having influence on early childhood programs.

CONCLUSIONS

The NAEYC policy statement on developmentally appropriate practice is an impressive effort to increase the profession's influence on early childhood programs by targeting factors that have contributed to the profession's marginal status. The statement addresses the field's fundamental problem, the perceived absence of a distinctive knowledge base, by setting forth a series of recommended practices in early childhood programs. Whether the present or a modified DAP statement will be supported in the future by professional consensus and research data remains to be seen. Clearly it is desirable to encourage practices that are supported by collective professional judgment and credible research findings. Widespread adoption of the DAP statement's recommendations hinges on numerous and complicated factors, including societal willingness to provide sufficient resources for high quality early childhood programs.

Parents cannot be ignored in strategies to alter the settings in which early education and care occur. Open market conditions involving parent choice, minimal government standards, and scores of autonomous and loosely organized settings make the field of early childhood programs difficult to penetrate. Accordingly, the DAP statement envisions parents in lead roles as promoters and monitors of developmentally appropriate practice in early childhood settings.

While there has been limited experience with uses of the DAP statement, it is unlikely parents will prove to be effective agents for extensively promoting the profession's ideas about quality in early childhood programs. Certainly there are, and will continue to be, instances in which parental influence supports program quality as defined by the DAP statement. But as this chapter has demonstrated, the child-centered approach inherent in the DAP statement runs contrary to the didactic program preferences of many lower-income, ethnic minority parents, and some middle- and upper middle-class parents. What is more, parents' early childhood program preferences are connected to parenting practices and beliefs, and thus efforts to change parents' ideas about good program settings indirectly address deeply rooted patterns of individual behavior and thinking. Further, as Holloway and Fuller (1992) have shown, several conditions necessary for effective employment of parent choice—dissatisfaction with current arrangement and a norm of in-depth investigations of options—generally have not existed in the child care market.

The DAP statement challenges the pluralistic character of the early childhood field by recommending practices that some populations are unlikely to value, and by recommending relatively modest, and at times ambiguous, mechanisms for ensuring program responsiveness to parental values and preferences, even within the parameters of quality as defined by the DAP statement. As described in this chapter, the DAP statement leans toward the use of a conventional model of professional helping in its descriptions of appropriate parent-staff relations, and is unclear about the balance of power in the parent-staff partnership. Moreover, the statement can be interpreted as ambivalent about the merits of parents' contributions to decisions about the education and care of their children.

Clarity on the essential characteristics of a program-family partnership is central to improving the inclusiveness of the DAP statement for accommodating diversity in early childhood programs. Needed are clear statements about equality in the parent-provider relationship, the importance of joint decision-making in matters affecting child and program, and mutual support that includes trust and celebrations of each other's contributions to children's development (Swap, 1993). Inclusiveness requires genuine collaborations that transcend limited partnerships involving "we-they" approaches to the parent-program relationship.

Substantively, it is essential to maintain responsive partnerships between families and early childhood programs as a means of supporting the healthy development of children, families, and the program. Politically, it is imperative that practitioners in the early childhood field maintain close ties with parents as advocates for expanding resources for early childhood programs. A rethinking of the model of professionalism embodied in the DAP statement may prove to be a seminal key to advances in the quality of the nation's early childhood environments.

ACKNOWLEDGMENTS

Portions of this chapter were presented at the A. L. Mailman Family Foundation symposium, *The Shifting Contexts of Parent Choice in Early Childhood Education,* June 1992.

REFERENCES

Almy, M. (1986). The past, present, and future for the early childhood education researcher. *Early Childhood Research Quarterly, 1,* 1–13.

Black, J. K., & Puckett, M. B. (1987). Informing others about developmentally appropriate practice. In S. Bredekamp (Ed.), *Developmentally appropriate practice in early childhood programs serving children from birth through age 8* (pp. 83–87). Washington, DC: National Association for the Education of Young Children.

Bredekamp, S. (Ed.) (1987). *Developmentally appropriate practice in early childhood programs serving children from birth through age 8.* Washington, DC: National Association for the Education of Young Children.

Burts, D. C., Hart, C. H., Charlesworth, R., & Kirk, L. (1990). A comparison of frequencies of stress behaviors observed in kindergarten children in classrooms within developmentally appropriate versus developmentally inappropriate instructional practices. *Early Childhood Research Quarterly, 5,* 407–423.

Daniels, D. (1992, April). *Didactic versus child-centered program effects on children's achievement, perceived competence, and emotions.* Paper presented at the annual meeting of the American Educational Research Association, San Francisco.

Dunst, C. J., & Trivette, C. M. (1988). A family systems model of early intervention with handicapped and developmentally at-risk children. In D. R. Powell (Ed.), *Parent education as early childhood intervention* (pp. 131–179). Norwood, NJ: Ablex.

Elkind, D. (1981). *The hurried child.* Reading, MA: Addison-Wesley.

Elkind, D. (1987). *Miseducation: Preschoolers at risk.* New York: Knopf.

Fein, G. (1980). The informed parent. In S. Kilmer (Ed.), *Advances in early education and day care* (Vol. 1, pp. 155–185). Greenwich, CT: JAI Press.

Gallagher, J. M., & Coche, J. (1987). Hothousing: The clinical and educational concerns over pressuring young children. *Early Childhood Research Quarterly, 2,* 203–210.

Greenberg, P. (1989). Parents as partners in young children's development and education. *Young Children, 44,* 61–75.

Hess, R. D. (1970). Social class and ethnic influences on socialization. In *Carmichael's manual of child psychology* (Vol. 2). New York: John Wiley and Sons.

Hirsh-Pasek, K., Hyson, M. C., & Rescorla, L. (1990). Academic environments in preschool: Do they pressure or challenge young children. *Early Education and Development, 1,* 401–423.

Holloway, S. D., & Fuller, B. (1992). The great child-care experiment: What are the lessons for school improvement? *Educational Researcher, 21,* 12–19.

Hughes, E. C. (1971). *The sociological eye: Selected papers on work, self, and the study of society* (Vol. 2). Chicago: Aldine.

Hyson, M. C. (1991). Building the hothouse: How mothers construct academic environments. In L. Rescorla, M. C. Hyson, & K. Hirsh-Pasek (Eds.), *New directions for child development: Vol. 53. Academic instruction in early child-*

hood: Challenge or pressure? (pp. 31–37). San Francisco, CA: Jossey-Bass, Inc.

Hyson, M. C., Hirsh-Pasek, K., & Rescorla, L. (1990). The classroom practices inventory: An observation instrument based on NAEYC's guidelines for developmentally appropriate practices for 4 and 5 year old children. *Early Childhood Research Quarterly, 5,* 475–494.

Hyson, M. C., Hirsh-Pasek, K., Rescorla, L., Cone, J., & Martell-Boinske, L. (1991). Ingredients of parental "pressure" in early childhood. *Journal of Applied Developmental Psychology, 12,* 347–365.

Joffe, C. (1977). *Friendly intruders: Childcare professionals and family life.* Berkeley, CA: University of California Press.

Kagan, S. L., & Zigler, E. F. (1987). Preface. In S. L. Kagan & E. F. Zigler (Eds.), *Early schooling: The national debate* (pp. xiii–xviii). New Haven, CT: Yale University Press.

Knudsen-Lindauer, S. L., & Harris, K. (1989). Priorities for kindergarten curricula: Views of parents and teachers. *Journal of Research in Childhood Education, 4,* 51–61.

Kohlberg, L., & Mayer, R. (1972). Development as an aim of education. *Harvard Educational Review, 42,* 449–496.

Kohn, M. L. (1977). *Class and conformity: A study in values.* Chicago: University of Chicago Press.

Laosa, L. (1979). Social competence in childhood: Toward a developmental, socioculturally relativistic paradigm. In M. W. Kent & J. E. Rolf (Eds.), *Primary prevention of psychopathology: Vol. 3. Social competence in children.* Hanover, NH: University Press of New England.

Milburn, S. (1992, April). *Parents' beliefs and behaviors related to teaching basic skills to young children.* Paper presented at the annual meeting of the American Educational Research Association, San Francisco, CA.

Mitchell, A. (1992). Consumers and child care: An annotated bibliography. New York: National Center for Children in Poverty, Columbia University.

Mitchell, A., Cooperstein, E., & Larner, M. (1992). *Child care choices, consumer education, and low-income families.* New York: National Center for Children in Poverty, Columbia University.

National Academy of Early Childhood Programs (1991). *Accreditation criteria and procedures* (revised edition). Washington, DC: Author

Powell, D. R. (1987). Comparing preschool curricula and practices: The state of research. In S. L. Kagan & E. F. Zigler (Eds.), *Early schooling: The national debate* (pp. 190–211). New Haven, CT: Yale University Press.

Powell, D. R. (1989). *Families and early childhood programs.* Washington, DC: National Association for the Education of Young Children.

Powell, D. R. (1991). Parents and programs: Early childhood as a pioneer in parent involvement and support. In S. L. Kagan (Ed.), *The care and education of America's young children: Obstacles and opportunities.* Ninetieth yearbook of the National Society for the Study of Education (pp. 91–109). Chicago: National Society for the Study of Education.

Powell, D. R. (in press). A differentiated analysis of research-practice linkages in early childhood programs. *Journal of Applied Developmental Psychology.*

Powell, D. R., & Stremmel, A. J. (1987). Managing relations with parents: Research notes on the teacher's role. In D. L. Peters & S. Kontos (Eds.), *Continuity and discontinuity of experience in child care* (pp. 115–127). Norwood, NJ: Ablex.

Sigel, I. E. (1987). Does hothousing rob children of their childhood? *Early Childhood Research Quarterly, 2,* 211–225.

Sigel, I. E. (1991). Preschool education: For whom and why? In L. Rescorla, M. C. Hyson, & K. Hirsh-Pasek (Eds.), *New directions for child development: Vol. 53. Academic instruction in early childhood: Challenge or pressure?* (pp. 83–91). San Francisco, CA: Jossey-Bass, Inc.

Stipek, D. (1992). *Differentiating early childhood education programs.* Paper presented at the annual meeting of the American Educational Research Association, San Francisco, CA.

Swap, S. M. (1993). *Developing home-school partnerships: From concepts to practice.* New York: Teachers College Press.

Szanton, E. (1991). Services for children with special needs: Partnerships from the beginning between parents and practitioners. In D. G. Unger & D. R. Powell (Eds.), *Families as nurturing systems* (pp. 87–97). New York: Haworth Press.

Tyler, F. B., Pargament, K. I., & Gatz, M. (1983). The resource collaborator role: A model for interactions involving psychologists. *American Psychologist, 38,* 388–398.

Weikart, D. P., Epstein, A. S., Schweinhart, L. J., & Bond, J. T. (1978). *The Ypsilanti Preschool Curriculum Demonstration Project: Preschool years and longitudinal results.* Ypsilanti, MI: High/Scope Press.

Young, K. T. (1990). American conceptions of infant development from 1955 to 1984: What the experts are telling parents. *Child Development, 61,* 17–28.

Zinnser, C. (1991). *Raised in East Urban: Child care changes in a working class community.* New York: Teachers College Press.

PART IV

Early Educational Practices

Problems and Promises

• • • • • •

The four chapters in this culminating section of the volume are intended to illustrate some of the practical implications of the historical, theoretical, and sociocultural issues raised up to this point. Of particular interest to the writers in these chapters is the role the classroom teacher plays in selecting appropriate instructional approaches, assessing children's learnings and capacities over time, and fostering particular competencies judged to be important for academic success.

In chapter 10, Atwater and her colleagues point out the shortcomings of the NAEYC guidelines with respect to children with developmental disabilities, and suggest ways to incorporate more direct intervention approaches necessary for such children into an expanded model of developmentally appropriate practices. They raise fundamental questions about the limits of traditional early childhood practices, which assume a high degree of self-directed learning, for young children who are not able to independently perceive, explore, or construct their own environments. The authors argue that some approaches associated with special education models can become a part of a more inclusive definition of appropriate practice. The aim of this methodological integration is to establish a basis for an expanded conceptualization and application of practices that can support children with diverse learning characteristics and needs.

In chapter 11, Meisels reminds us of the difficulties of conducting valid and reliable assessments with young children, especially those whose cultural or developmental histories do not coincide with the models assumed in standardized and norm-referenced instruments. Given the multiple factors associated with developmental risk and delay, multiple lenses are required if we are to gather information that is educationally useful. Thus, Meisels calls for "developmentally appropriate assessment." He cautions us regarding the difficulties of this task, and emphasizes the limits on the uses of assessment for making long-term predictions about

183

development. In his deliberate use of the term *measurement* in this chapter, Meisels calls our attention to the dilemma of making objective that which is inherently human, and therefore subjective.

While Meisels' focus is primarily on the technical problems inherent in measurement, Bloch et al., in chapter 12, examine the subjective nature of teachers' perceptions of children's competencies. They report on a major study of teacher-based assessments in primary schools that has focused on the extent to which such assessments are influenced by judgments about what is most salient and appropriate in children's school performance. By conducting ethnographic studies in three different elementary schools with varying demographic characteristics, Bloch and her colleagues are able to demonstrate the influence of local contextual variables on the assessment process. Their findings reveal the power of teachers' attitudes when confronted with children who do not belong to the core culture. The crucial theme that emerges from these ethnographies is that teachers' good intentions are sufficient neither to compensate for a lack of knowledge about children's backgrounds nor to override prevailing norms based on the majority culture.

In the final chapter, Genishi et al. offer a more optimistic view of the capacity of schools and teachers to respond to cultural and linguistic differences. In their examination of the development of language and literacy among diverse immigrant children (e.g., Russian, Haitian, Chicano), these authors illustrate ways to capitalize on the richness of children's lives, rather than pathologizing or suppressing differences. Vignettes from Fassler's observations of an ESL kindergarten, and Dyson's work in a primary school serving African-American children, illustrate the problems as well as promises that can be realized when diversities are not treated as liabilities. This chapter has implications for the continuing debates over bilingual, bicultural educational policies, and contributes to our knowledge about language, reading, and writing development in young children.

The themes that emerge in this section reiterate those found throughout the book. Drawing on their own extensive research and experience, all of the authors have demanded that we pay attention to the difficulty and importance of designing early childhood education programs that are developmentally and culturally appropriate. As we stated in the Introduction, this volume articulates dilemmas more than solutions, but the process of defining these dilemmas challenges us to take the first step toward the design of inclusive early education practices. A past history of "regressing to the mean" has blinded us to the interesting and challenging realities that exist in the lives of children who live on the margins of mainstream America. The chapters in this volume are intended to contribute to the effort to achieve the aims of equitable, effective, and accessible early childhood education for all.

10

· · · · · ·

Blending Developmentally Appropriate Practice and Early Childhood Special Education

*Redefining Best Practice
to Meet the Needs of All Children*

JANE B. ATWATER, JUDITH J. CARTA, ILENE S. SCHWARTZ,
AND SCOTT R. MCCONNELL

Since the passage of Public Law 94-142 (the Education for All Handicapped Children Act) in 1975, the mission of integrating children with disabilities into least restrictive educational environments has evolved into the more far-reaching mission of creating inclusive educational environments that effectively serve children of diverse abilities and needs (Salisbury, 1991). This shift in focus presents significant challenges and opportunities for early childhood professionals, for it requires more than just a cooperative relationship between the fields of early childhood education (ECE) and early childhood special education (ECSE). Truly inclusive educational environments will require an unprecedented collaborative effort to establish coherent, comprehensive sets of goals and standards to guide the development of programs that serve and benefit all young children.

The challenge of this task is reflected in the professional debate that has arisen from the attempt to apply the standard of developmentally appropriate practice (DAP) (Bredekamp, 1987) across the broad range of programming for young children. Although the DAP guidelines were intended as "one index of quality" (Bredekamp, 1991, p. 202), the standard of developmental appropriateness has been adopted widely as the hallmark of best practice for typically developing children in early childhood programs and has been proposed as being equally beneficial for children with disabilities (e.g., Mahoney, Robinson, & Powell, 1992).

Nonetheless, the expanding influence of the DAP guidelines has generated questions about their applicability across children with diverse backgrounds, abilities, and needs (e.g., Carta, Schwartz, Atwater, & McConnell, 1991; Jipson, 1991; Wolery, Strain, & Bailey, 1992). Among ECSE professionals, a primary concern has been that developmental appropriateness as a programming standard be balanced with other considerations, such as effectiveness and efficiency, that are fundamental to best practice in early childhood special education.

A premise of this chapter is that the DAP guidelines, in themselves, are not sufficient as a guide for planning and evaluating effective programs for young children with special needs, but that they do provide an excellent base for incorporating intervention components with demonstrated efficacy into the context of inclusive educational environments (Wolery et al., 1992). Our purpose is to offer a framework for expanding the concept and application of developmentally appropriate practice to accommodate effective intervention for children with diverse learning needs. To accomplish this, we will review the common goals and assumptions of DAP and ECSE, describe distinctive features of ECSE that are vital to support the inclusion of children with special needs, and suggest strategies for blending DAP and ECSE to develop a set of best practices that meet the needs of all young children.

CONCEPTUAL INTEGRATION OF ECSE AND DAP

Common Goals and Assumptions

Many fundamental principles of early childhood assessment and teaching practice are identified as easily with DAP as they are with ECSE. In fact, most indicators of ECSE best practice are mentioned in the original DAP guidelines (Bredekamp, 1987). While the principles may not be emphasized to the same extent or articulated with equal precision in the two approaches, it is important to understand the emphasis placed on these principles by both perspectives.

INDIVIDUALIZATION. The necessity for individualizing education is a fundamental principle of special education and is a legal mandate of Public Law 94-142 (1975). Thus, the notion that children with special needs require individualized programming is inherent in ECSE practice. Assessment information that is linked to curriculum provides the basis for documenting a child's skills and for determining the educational objectives óf the child's individualized program (Bricker & Veltman, 1990). Similarly, the general early childhood literature reflects a conviction that children should be treated as individuals (Charlesworth, 1985, 1989; Doremus, 1986), and the DAP guidelines advocate individual appropriateness in early childhood curricula (Bredekamp, 1987, 1991). No specific direction is provided in the DAP document, however, for ensuring that programs meet the needs of all children. In fact, a common perspective on individualization from the traditional early childhood perspective is that "children should be treated as individuals and guided to bloom in their own good time" (Charlesworth, 1989, p. 11). Some children, however, need more than a rich and stimulating early childhood environment to reach their full potential, and inclusive programs must be prepared to address the specific needs of those children. All professionals working with young children must be vigilant in ascertaining whether the content they teach, as well as the strategies they employ, meet the needs of, and continue to be appropriate for, the children in their programs.

DEEMPHASIS OF STANDARDIZED ASSESSMENT. A recent theme in both the ECSE and DAP literatures is the inadequacy of traditional standardized assessment to represent a child's skills, outcomes, and potential for growth. The DAP guidelines note that "scores derived from psychometric tests should never be used as the sole criteria for recommending enrolling or retention in a program or placement in special or remedial classes" (Bredekamp, 1987, p. 13). This point was made recently in even plainer language in the ECSE literature: "Early intelligence testing must be indicted, tried, and convicted for malpractice. The use of such tests for young children with developmental delays and disabilities must be abandoned" (Neisworth & Bagnato, 1992, p. 1). The view of assessment shared by both DAP and ECSE is that traditional testing approaches place too much weight on a very limited sample of a child's behavior (Morado, 1987; Neisworth & Bagnato, 1992). Both perspectives underscore the point that testing must be broader in scope and must be conducted in more natural contexts than is typical with standardized measures (Barnett, Macmann, & Carey, 1992; Peck, McCaig, & Sapp, 1988).

CURRICULUM-LINKED ASSESSMENT. If the purpose of assessment is to inform intervention and teaching, then the most functional measures are those that integrate assessment with curricula. Curriculum-linked instruments provide information about children's performance on items that typically would be taught within a program and, thus, have clear utility for planning and monitoring a program's impact. The importance of the match between assessment and curriculum was underscored recently in the NAEYC (National Association for the Education of Young Children) guidelines on curriculum and assessment: "Assessment is congruent and relevant to the goals, objectives, and content of the program. Assessment results in benefits to the child such as needed adjustments in the curriculum or more individualized instruction and improvements in the program" (NAEYC & NAECS/SDE, 1991, p. 32). This curriculum-embedded approach to assessment has long been a hallmark of ECSE and is exemplified in such instruments as the Early Learning Accomplishment Profile (ELAP) (Glover, Preminger, & Sanford, 1978) and the Hawaii Early Learning Profile (HELP) (Foruno et al., 1979).

CHILD-INITIATED ACTIVITIES. A key construct of the DAP guidelines is the critical importance of infusing the early childhood curriculum with child-initiated activities. For example, the guidelines point out that, "Much of young children's learning takes place when they direct their own play activities. . . . Such learning should not be inhibited by adult-established concepts of completion, achievement, and failure" (Bredekamp, 1987, p. 3).

Advancing a somewhat different argument, ECSE researchers have suggested that activities a child initiates and continues probably have the most appeal to the child and thus require the least external support and extrinsic motivation (Bricker & Woods-Cripe, 1992). This principle was validated in Hart and Risley's studies of language intervention for preschoolers from disadvantaged environments (1968, 1975). During naturally occurring social interactions, teachers responded to children's interests by modeling compound sentences. This child-focused strategy led to increases in children's language goals during their interactions with the teacher, and also during their social exchanges with peers. "Taking the child's lead" to promote language has become a cornerstone of milieu language intervention (Kaiser, Hendrickson, & Alpert, 1991; Warren & Bambara, 1989) as well as many other naturalistic approaches to teaching language (e.g., Rice, 1986; Snyder-McLean, Solomonson, McLean, & Sack, 1984).

ACTIVE CHILD ENGAGEMENT. The focus on child-initiated activities, included in both the DAP and ECSE perspectives, reflects a shared appreciation of the critical role that a young child's level of engagement plays in learning. This basic tenet crosses many theories of learning and development and, thus, is equally at home in the theories of Dewey, Piaget, Bijou, and Baer. It is not surprising then, that the importance of facilitating children's active engagement within early childhood programs is stated explicitly in the DAP guidelines (Bredekamp, 1987; NAEYC & NAECS/SDE, 1991) and is also a key principle of effective ECSE practices

(Carta, Atwater, Schwartz, & Miller, 1990; Jones & Warren, 1991; McWilliam & Bailey, 1992). A critical distinction in the ECSE focus on engagement is the recognition that, for young children with disabilities, active engagement does not always occur spontaneously. Therefore, a goal of early intervention is to arrange the environment to promote active engagement but, when needed, to assist the child in becoming actively engaged in learning and exploration.

SOCIAL INTERACTION. The development of social competence is an important focus in the education of young children with and without disabilities (Guralnick, 1990; Hartup, 1983; Odom, McConnell, & McEvoy, 1992; Vygotsky, 1978). The developmental literature firmly establishes that young children expand not only their social competence, but also their language and cognitive skills, through their increasingly complex interactions with peers (Gottman, 1983; Guralnick, 1981; Murray, 1972). Not surprisingly, then, the importance of social interaction in early educational programs is shared by both DAP and ECSE. Most preschools provide many opportunities for children to learn through social interaction; but, as with engagement, ECSE practice recognizes that simply providing opportunities and arranging classroom environments to promote social interaction may not, for some children, be sufficient to promote peer interaction. Some children require specialized intervention to enhance their social competence (McEvoy, Odom, & McConnell, 1992). Many social skills interventions exist that can be implemented by regular early childhood personnel and that are compatible with the spirit of the DAP guidelines (Odom et al., 1992).

CULTURAL DIVERSITY. The literatures of both ECSE and DAP reflect an emerging recognition of the importance of cultural diversity in our society and its implications for early childhood programs (Bredekamp, 1987; Derman-Sparks & A. B. C. Task Force, 1989; Lynch & Hanson, 1992; Vincent, Salisbury, Strain, McCormick, & Tessier, 1990). In particular, there is broad agreement that cultural appropriateness should be a prime concern in the assessment of young children and that program activities should emphasize the integrity of all cultures and celebrate the individual differences among children. Most recently, the field of ECSE has adopted an expanded notion of cultural sensitivity, especially as it pertains to involvement with families (e.g., Lynch & Hanson, 1992). As part of this effort, early interventionists are focusing on skills and information that will help them to understand and accommodate families' values and world views. Such competencies are essential for professionals who work with young children and their families in our increasingly diverse society (Hanson & Lynch, 1992).

Distinctive Features of ECSE

Despite the commonalities that we have described, the field of early childhood special education does emphasize certain standards of practice that have not been addressed directly in the NAEYC guidelines and that may appear to conflict with specific recommendations for developmentally appropriate practice. Three of those standards are highlighted in this section. We believe that these distinctive features of ECSE do not represent irreconcilable points of division with DAP, for all are directly related to the unifying principle of individualization. Rather, we believe that these features would complement and enrich developmentally appropriate practice, by enabling early childhood programs to serve children with diverse needs and abilities effectively.

FLEXIBILITY IN INSTRUCTIONAL STRATEGIES. The emphasis on individualization in ECSE dictates that programs offer a range of services that vary in intensity based on the needs of the children and families they serve (e.g., Beckman, Robinson, Jackson, & Rosenberg, 1988; Bricker, 1989; Peterson, 1987; Wolery et al., 1992). This principle acknowledges that young children and their families present a wide range of needs that must be addressed through a wide range of programming options. Some children, at times, need relatively structured instruction to achieve important goals—instruction designed to ameliorate primary disabilities, to prevent the development of secondary disabilities, or to facilitate their access and adaptation to less formal learning opportunities. For example, many children, in the absence of direct intervention, will show significant delays in their development of critical "keystone skills" (i.e., those abilities, such as initiating play with objects or other people, that make a number of important, more complex behaviors, possible) (Wolery, 1991). Without such skills, the child's ability to engage and learn from the environment is severely constrained. However, once the skills are learned, child-initiated, child-directed activities become a true option.

Although DAP guidelines stress individual appropriateness, their strong emphasis on child-centered, relatively unstructured programming sometimes has led to the assumption that more structured, adult-directed programming is never appropriate. It is important to note, however, that Bredekamp (1991) has cautioned that the drafters of the DAP position statements did not intend to suggest that child-centered activities be used exclusively. Similarly, although ECSE practice sometimes has been characterized as being predominantly teacher-directed (Mahoney et al., 1992), ECSE standards emphasize the importance of child-directed activities, incorporate a wide variety of nonintrusive, child-driven strategies, and assert that highly directive intervention strategies should not be used until less intrusive procedures have proven to be ineffective or unacceptable for a given child (e.g., Strain et al., 1992; Wolery & Brookfield-Norman, 1988).

CRITERION OF THE NEXT ENVIRONMENT. An important aspect of individualized programming is the explicit consideration of skills that will be required in the child's future environments, including home, school, and community settings (Carta et al., 1990; Fowler, Schwartz & Atwater, 1991; Salisbury & Vincent, 1990). From the DAP perspective, this practice, especially as it applies to school environments, sometimes has been interpreted as an inappropriate downward shifting of academic standards from elementary grades to the preschool and kindergarten levels. From the ECSE perspective, however, preparation for the next environment directly serves the goal of facilitating a child's progress through a natural succession of inclusive educational environments. Because we, as interventionists, want children to flourish in those environments, we place importance on preparing the children and the environments in advance. Children with special needs often have problems with major educational transitions (e.g., from home-based intervention to preschool, from preschool to kindergarten and first grade), because they have not had sufficient opportunities to learn and practice skills that will be expected in the future environment (Carta, Sainato & Greenwood, 1988). Moreover, when children begin at a disadvantage relative to their classmates, they have a greater likelihood of falling farther behind as time goes by. To counteract such declines, an accumulating body of evidence indicates that intervention at the preschool and kindergarten levels can be effective in helping a child to make that major transition successfully (e.g., Carta, Atwater & Schwartz, 1992). In turn, the child's transition should be facilitated by supportive, inclusive practices in the receiving environment.

OUTCOMES-BASED ASSESSMENT AND MONITORING. The mandated principle of individualization also requires that ECSE programs focus on specified individual goals, or outcomes, and document the program's effectiveness in assisting the child and family to achieve those outcomes (e.g., Bagnato & Neisworth, 1991; Bailey & Wolery, 1992). These requirements carry two key implications that may appear to diverge from developmentally appropriate practice, but may simply reflect the distinctive missions of ECSE and ECE. The first implication relates to the issue of whether early childhood programs should attempt to accelerate children's development. The DAP guidelines, designed initially for typically developing children, were based on the assumption that children would do well without specific strategies to advance their development (Bredekamp, 1987). In contrast, ECSE was founded on the assumption that interventionists can act to enhance the development of young children with disabilities and are bound, ethically and professionally, to develop effective strategies for accomplishing that goal (Shonkoff & Meisels, 1990; Smith & Strain, 1988). Second, because interventionists have a responsibility to enhance children's developmental outcomes, they must be accountable to individual children and families to demonstrate that programs actually are benefiting them as planned. This requires that ECSE providers frequently assess the program's effectiveness in terms of the child's progress toward identified goals and, when needed, refine or adjust the program to strengthen its effectiveness (Bagnato & Neisworth, 1991; Wolery et al., 1992). Furthermore, ECSE professionals have a responsibility to the general population of young children with special needs to demonstrate that early intervention programs are efficient, beneficial, and necessary (Carta & Greenwood, 1989; Guralnick, 1991). As Guralnick observed, our ability to act as advocates for continued funding of early childhood services may rest on our ability to demonstrate that we are doing our jobs effectively.

Obviously, the areas of overlap between ECSE and DAP are substantial, sharing emphases on the individual child; on expanded, valid assessment strategies; on activities that foster children's initiation, engagement, and social interaction—and underscoring all of these with an emerging recognition of rich cultural diversity. ECSE and DAP proponents have much common ground for a constructive dialogue on the components of appropriate practice for all children. From the ECSE perspective, best practice also requires the provision of diverse instructional strategies, including programming focused explicitly on educational transitions, as well as systematic efforts to promote and document beneficial outcomes. On the surface, these standards appear to introduce points of divergence from some statements about developmentally appropriate practice; however, it seems likely that apparent differences arise from the distinctive histories and missions of the two perspectives. The original NAEYC guidelines were developed to bring early childhood education in line with the typical developmental progression, not to dictate programming for children with special needs. Thus, the guidelines simply did not address many matters of concern to early childhood special educators. Efforts to incorporate standards of best practice in ECSE within the framework of developmentally appropriate practice hold promise for promoting educational environments that effectively address the needs of all young children (Carta, Atwater, Schwartz & McConnell, in press; Mallory, 1992; Wolery et al., 1992).

INTEGRATION OF DAP AND ECSE IN PRACTICE

Intervention Strategies

Because of its explicit focus on individualization, the ECSE literature includes many strategies to facilitate the engagement of children with diverse abilities in typical early childhood activities. These strategies allow teachers to provide individually focused intervention, as needed, within the context of classroom activities that all children can share, and thus, are especially pertinent to the task of integrating DAP and ECSE in practice. In this section, we briefly describe three such strategies as examples of those that currently are available to practitioners.

EMBEDDING INTERVENTIONS IN CLASSROOM ACTIVITIES AND ROUTINES. Activity-based intervention, as described by Bricker and Cripe (1992), embeds individualized programming within the context of typical classroom routines and play activities. A teacher might arrange for instructional opportunities during daily routines (e.g., embedding opportunities for language during arrival or snack times) or might arrange opportunities for children to practice particular skills during otherwise child-structured play (e.g., asking one child with a language deficit to describe materials to classmates during an art activity, providing constructive play materials for children with pincer grasp goals). To the extent possible, activity-based intervention employs the natural structure and consequences of the activity, rather than teacher-delivered prompts and feedback, to encourage children's appropriate engagement. The teacher selects and organizes activities to increase the likelihood that all children will have an opportunity to learn and practice desired behaviors successfully, and to permit children's own successes within the activity to reinforce their developing skills.

One example of activity-based intervention to promote inclusion is Project EPIC (Ecobehavioral Programming for Individual Children), developed to assist teachers in planning activities that will foster engagement for all children in their classrooms, while targeting the specific needs of children with disabilities (McConnell & Spicuzza, 1992). EPIC combines instruction on isolated skills with programming embedded in multiple daily classroom activities. Using a computer-based system, the teacher not only develops individualized educational plans for children with disabilities, but also tracks goals for typically developing children. To facilitate activity-based programming, EPIC provides recommendations for selecting, adapting, and monitoring play activities that foster optimal engagement and benefit for all children involved.

ARRANGING THE ECOLOGY TO PROMOTE ACTIVE ENGAGEMENT. Children's participation, or active engagement, in classroom activities is a necessary condition for successful intervention. Indeed, recent research suggests that child engagement in classroom activities is one of the best single behavioral correlates of developmental status for children with and without disabilities (McConnell, Priest, & Peterson, 1992; McWilliam, Trivette, & Dunst, 1985). In turn, specific features of the classroom ecology, such as activity structure, materials, and group size, are associated with differences in the level of children's engagement (Carta et al., 1988, 1991). These findings testify to the importance of arranging the environment to make participation possible, and likely, for *all* children in the classroom.

As an example, to support children's engagement, play materials must be selected and arranged not only to be appropriate and accessible to all children, but also to promote the participation of individual children at their current levels of motor, cognitive, and linguistic development. To participate in a painting activity, for instance, a child with motor impairments might require an adaptive chair and brushes, while a child with typical motor skills might require brushes and paint cans at an easel. For a matching and sorting game, a teacher might select materials that differ in size, color, and complexity, so that both children with relatively high degrees of competence (e.g., categorization, numeration) *and* children developing basic skills (e.g., reach and grasp, color discrimination, size discrimination) can be actively engaged with appropriate materials in the same activity. The ultimate goal of such ecological arrangements should be to maintain each child's full inclusion in the activity (i.e., in proximity to peers, participating in similar ways to achieve similar results).

EMPLOYING "LEAST TO MOST INTRUSIVE" INTERVENTION STRATEGIES. The integration of DAP guidelines and ECSE practices will require strategies for determining children's individual needs for structured intervention, and for providing that structure as needed (but only as needed). The ECSE literature is replete with instructional techniques demonstrated to be effective in teaching specific skills and general competencies to a wide range of children with and without disabilities (e.g., Bailey & Wolery, 1992; Odom & Karnes, 1988). Some of these procedures, such as milieu language training (Warren & Kaiser, 1988) and environmental arrangements to promote social interaction (McEvoy et al., 1992), require little direct teaching. Other procedures, such as time-delay prompts for language and cognitive skills (Wolery & Brookfield-Norman, 1988) and peer-mediated strategies for social interaction (McEvoy et al., 1992), are effective when more structured intervention is required.

A relevant guiding principle in ECSE is that, when two or more procedures are likely to produce the same developmental outcome for an individual child, preference should be given to the intervention that is least intrusive, or most like that provided to children who are developing typically. Selection of the least intrusive, yet effective intervention may facilitate generalization of skills (Stokes & Baer, 1977), and also is consistent with the normalization goals of early childhood special education. The key is to select intervention procedures that are *effective* (i.e., procedures that maximize the likelihood that the child will acquire new skills and competencies), *efficient* (i.e., skills and competencies are acquired as quickly and easily as possible), and *minimally intrusive* (i.e., child participation in classroom activities and interaction with the teacher is as typical as possible).

By employing such strategies as activity-based interventions, supportive ecological arrangements, and "least to most intrusive" programming, teachers may begin to build a coordinated set of classroom services and practices that are, at the same time, "developmentally appropriate" and "individualized and outcomes-based." Children who need more structured intervention, regardless of their developmental status, will receive a continuum of services designed to address their needs. All children will be exposed to a wide spectrum of classroom experiences that permit flexibility and child-directed involvement. Pragmatically, then, teachers will have achieved integration of DAP guidelines and ECSE practices to benefit all enrolled children.

Professional Collaboration

To be successful, inclusive practices in early childhood programs must be supported by communication and collaboration across multiple disciplines and theoretical perspectives (Burton, Hains, Hanline, McLean, & McCormick, 1992; Odom & McEvoy, 1990). Although transdisciplinary collaboration has an established history in ECSE, extending that model to include early childhood providers may require flexibility, creativity, and persistence by all participants, especially in the face of social institutional policies that often impede such efforts (Smith & Rose, 1991). To promote and support inclusion effectively, collaborative efforts are important at several levels:

1. In professional organizations, to promote conceptual integration and communication among disciplines;
2. In preservice and inservice training, to prepare professionals who are committed to and proficient in collaboration and inclusion (Miller, 1992; Raver, 1991);
3. In communities, to advocate for inclusive early childhood programs.

However, the type of collaboration that will have the most immediate impact on current practice and on the quality of services received by young children is the ongoing collaboration of early childhood professionals. It is essential that professionals clarify the values and beliefs that drive their own teaching, work with colleagues from other disciplines to incorporate personal values into a program philosophy that addresses the needs of all children, and translate that philosophy into effective, inclusive instructional practices. As educators, we are driven by our values to provide inclusive and developmentally appropriate educational services to all young children. We must attend to the data, however, to determine those strategies that should be used within this developmentally appropriate framework to facilitate satisfactory outcomes for individual children.

Collaboration among professionals in national organizations, in teacher education programs, in communities, and in service to individual children sets the tone for coordinated services to children with and without disabilities. At this level of joint effort, collaboration will enable professionals to better understand the perspectives and approaches of their colleagues, to better communicate their own perspectives and approaches, and to begin to discuss—and implement—programs that integrate the perspectives, approaches, and competencies of multiple groups of professionals.

As shown by this chapter, and other contributions to this volume, the provision of truly inclusive early childhood programs presents numerous challenges, conceptually and practically. Yet, as with other challenging circumstances, the task also presents opportunities—opportunities to examine and refine our theoretical assumptions and to improve our services to young children and their families. Garbarino (1989) posed an interesting question, "What does it mean to approach children developmentally? It means that we recognize the child's changing capacities and that we recognize that a child has the capacity for change" (p. 30). Perhaps it also means that we acknowledge our own capacity to change and mature as a profession and to become more effective in the process.

REFERENCES

Bagnato, S. J., & Neisworth, J. T. (1991). *Assessment for early intervention: Best practices for professionals*. New York: Guilford Press.

Bailey, D. B., & Wolery, M. (1992). *Teaching infants and preschoolers with disabilities*. Columbus, OH: Macmillan.

Barnett, D. W., Macmann, G. M., & Carey, K. T. (1992). Early intervention and the assessment of developmental skills: Challenges and directions. *Topics in Early Childhood Special Education, 12* (1), 21–43.

Beckman, P. J., Robinson, C. C., Jackson, B., & Rosenberg, S. A. (1988). Translating developmental findings into teaching strategies for young handicapped children. *Journal of the Division for Early Childhood, 12,* 45–52.

Bredekamp, S. (Ed.). (1987). *Developmentally appropriate practice in early childhood programs serving children birth through age 8*. Washington, DC: National Association for the Education of Young Children.

Bredekamp, S (1991). Redeveloping early childhood education: A response to Kessler. *Early Childhood Research Quarterly, 6,* 199–209.

Bricker, D. D. (1989). *Early intervention for at risk and handicapped infants, toddlers, and preschool children*. Palo Alto, CA: Vort Corporation.

Bricker, D., & Woods-Cripe, J. J. (1992). *An activity-based approach to early intervention*. Baltimore, MD: Paul H. Brookes.

Bricker, D., & Veltman, M. (1990). Early intervention programs: Child-focused approaches. In S. J. Meisels & J. P. Shonkoff (Eds.), *Handbook of early childhood intervention* (pp. 373–399). New York: Cambridge University Press.

Burton, C. B., Hains, A. H., Hanline, M. F., McLean, M., & McCormick, K. (1992). Early childhood intervention and education: The urgency of professional unification. *Topics in Early Childhood Special Education, 11,* 53–69.

Carta, J. J., Atwater, J. B., & Schwartz, I. S. (1992, May). *Classroom survival skills interventions: Demonstration of short- and long-term effects*. Presented at the meeting of the Association for Behavior Analysis, San Francisco, CA.

Carta, J. J., Atwater, J. B., Schwartz, I. S., & McConnell, S. R. (in press). Developmentally appropriate practices and early childhood special education: A reaction to Johnson and McChesney Johnson. *Topics in Early Childhood Education*.

Carta, J. J., Atwater, J. B., Schwartz, I. S., & Miller, P. A. (1990). Application of ecobehavioral analysis to the study of transitions across early education. *Education and Treatment of Children, 13,* 298–311.

Carta, J. J., & Greenwood, C. R. (1989). Establishing the integrity of the independent variable in early intervention programs. *Early Education and Development, 1,* 127–140.

Carta, J. J., Sainato, D. M., & Greenwood, C. R. (1988). Advances in the ecological assessment of classroom instruction for young children with handicaps. In S. L. Odom & M. B. Karnes (Eds.), *Early intervention for infants and children with handicaps: An empirical base* (pp. 217–240). Baltimore, MD: Paul H. Brookes.

Carta, J. J., Schwartz, I. S., Atwater, J. B., & McConnell, S. R. (1991). Developmentally appropriate practice: Appraising its usefulness for young children with disabilities. *Topics in Early Childhood Special Education, 11,* 1–20.

Charlesworth, R. (1985). Readiness in early childhood education: Should we make them read or let them bloom? *Day Care and Early Education, 12,* 25–27.

Charlesworth, R. (1989). "Behind" before they start? Deciding how to deal with the risk of kindergarten "failure." *Young Children, 44,* 5–13.

Derman-Sparks, L., & the A.B.C. Task Force. (1989). *Anti-bias curriculum: Tools for empowering young children.* Washington, DC: National Association for the Education of Young Children.

Doremus, V. P. (1986). Forcing works for flowers, but not for children. *Educational Leadership, 44* (3), 32–35.

Education for All Handicapped Children Act of 1975, 20 U.S.C. 1401.

Foruno, S., O'Reilly, K. A., Hosaka, C. M., Inatsuka, T. T., Allman, T. L., & Zeisloft, B. (1979). *Hawaii early learning profile.* Palo Alto, CA: Vort Corporation.

Fowler, S. A., Schwartz, I., & Atwater, J. (1991). Perspectives on the transition from preschool to kindergarten for children with disabilities and their families. *Exceptional Children, 58,* 136–145.

Garbarino, J. (1989). Early intervention in cognitive development as a strategy for reducing poverty. In G. Miller (Ed.), *Giving children a chance: The case for more effective national policies* (pp. 23–36). Washington, DC: National Policy Press.

Glover, M. E., Preminger, J. L., & Sanford, A. R. (1978). *Early learning accomplishment profile.* Winston Salem, NC: Kaplan School Supply.

Gottman, J. M. (1983). How children become friends. *Monographs of the Society for Research in Child Development, 48* (Serial No. 201).

Guralnick, M. J. (1981). Peer influences on development of communicative competence. In P. Strain (Ed.), *The utilization of peers as behavior change agents* (pp. 31–68). New York: Plenum.

Guralnick, M. J. (1990). Social competence and early intervention. *Journal of Early Intervention, 14,* 3–14.

Guralnick, M. J. (1991). The next decade of research on the effectiveness of early intervention. *Exceptional Children, 58,* 174–183.

Hanson, M. J., & Lynch, E. W. (1992). Family diversity: Implications for policy and practice. *Topics in Early Childhood Special Education, 12,* 283–306.

Hart, B., & Risley, T. (1968). Establishing use of descriptive adjectives in the spontaneous speech of disadvantaged preschool children. *Journal of Applied Behavior Analysis, 1,* 109–112.

Hart, B., & Risley, T. (1975). Incidental teaching of language in the preschool. *Journal of Applied Behavior Analysis, 8,* 411–420.

Hartup, W. W. (1983). Peer relations. In M. Hetherington (Ed.), *Handbook of child psychology* (Vol. 4) (pp. 103–196). New York: John Wiley and Sons.

Jipson, J. (1991). Developmentally appropriate practice: Culture, curriculum, and connections. *Early Education and Development, 2,* 120–136.

Jones, H., & Warren, S. (1991). Enhancing engagement in early language teaching. *Teaching Exceptional Children, 23* (4), 48–50.

Kaiser, A., Hendrickson, J., & Alpert, C. (1991). Milieu language teaching: A second look. In R. Gable (Ed.), *Advances in mental retardation and developmental disabilities* (Vol. 4) (pp. 63–92). London: Jessica Kingsley.

Lynch, E. W., & Hanson, M. J. (1992). Steps in the right direction: Implications for interventionists. In E. W. Lynch & M. J. Hanson (Eds.), *Developing cross-cultural competence: A guide for working with young children and their families* (pp. 355–370). Baltimore: Paul H. Brookes.

Mahoney, G., Robinson, C., & Powell, A. (1992). Focusing on parent-child interaction: The bridge to developmentally appropriate practices. *Topics in Early Childhood Special Education, 12,* 105–120.

Mallory, B. (1992). Is it always appropriate to be developmental? Convergent models for early intervention practice. *Topics in Early Childhood Special Education, 11,* 1–12.

McConnell, S. R., Priest, J., & Peterson, C. (1992, May). *Development of a continuous progress measure for students in early childhood special education.* Paper presented at the meeting of the Association for Behavior Analysis, San Francisco, CA.

McConnell, S. R., & Spicuzza, R. (1992). *Ecobehavioral programming for individual children.* Minneapolis, MN: University of Minnesota.

McEvoy, M. A., Odom, S. L., & McConnell, S. R. (1992). Peer social competence intervention for young children with disabilities. In S. L. Odom, S. R. McConnell, & M. A. McEvoy (Eds.), *Social competence of young children with disabilities* (pp. 113–134). Baltimore, MD: Paul H. Brookes.

McWilliam, R. A., & Bailey, D. B. (1992). Promoting engagement and mastery. In D. B. Bailey & M. Wolery (Eds.), *Teaching infants and preschoolers with disabilities* (2nd ed.) (pp. 229–253). New York: Macmillan.

McWilliam, R. A., Trivette, C. M., & Dunst, C. J. (1985). Behavior engagement as a measure of the efficacy of early intervention. *Analysis and Intervention in Developmental Disabilities, 5,* 59–71.

Miller, P. S. (1992). Segregated programs of teacher education in early childhood: Immoral and inefficient practice. *Topics in Early Childhood Special Education, 11,* 39–52.

Morado, C. (1987, April). *Kindergarten alternatives for the child who is "not ready": Programs and policy issues.* Paper presented at the biennial meeting of the Society for Research in Child Development, Baltimore, MD.

Murray, F. (1972). The acquisition of conservation through social interaction. *Developmental Psychology, 6,* 1–6.

National Association for the Education of Young Children and the National Association of Early Childhood Specialists in State Departments of Education. (1991). Guidelines for appropriate curriculum content and assessment in programs serving children ages 3 through 8. *Young Children, 46* (3), 21–38.

Neisworth, J. J., & Bagnato, S. J. (1992). The case against intelligence tests in early intervention. *Topics in Early Childhood Special Education, 12* (1), 1–20.

Odom, S. L., & Karnes, M. B. (Eds.). (1988). *Early intervention for infants and children with handicaps: An empirical base.* Baltimore, MD: Paul H. Brookes.

Odom, S. L., McConnell, S. R., & McEvoy, M. A. (1992). Peer-related social competence and its significance for young children with disabilities. In S. L. Odom, S. R. McConnell, & M. A. McEvoy (Eds.), *Social competence of young children with disabilities* (pp. 3–37). Baltimore, MD: Paul H. Brookes.

Odom, S. L., & McEvoy, M. A. (1990). Mainstreaming at the preschool level: Potential barriers and tasks for the field. *Topics in Early Childhood Special Education, 10* (2), 48–61.

Peck, J., McCaig, G., & Sapp, M. E. (1988). *Kindergarten policies: What is best for children?* Washington, DC: National Association for the Education of Young Children.

Peterson, N. (1987). *Early intervention for handicapped and at-risk children.* Denver, CO: Love.

Raver, S. A. (1991). *Strategies for teaching at-risk and handicapped infants and toddlers: A transdisciplinary approach.* New York: Macmillan.

Rice, M. L. (1986). Mismatched premises of the communicative competence model and language intervention. In R. L. Schiefelbusch (Ed.), *Language competence: Assessment and intervention* (pp. 261–280). San Diego, CA: College Hill Press.

Salisbury, C. L. (1991). Mainstreaming during the early childhood years. *Exceptional Children, 58,* 146–155.

Salisbury, C. L., & Vincent, L. J. (1990). Criterion of the next environment and best practices: Mainstreaming and integration 10 years later. *Topics in Early Childhood Education, 10* (2), 78–89.

Shonkoff, J. P., & Meisels, S. J. (1990). Early intervention: The evolution of a concept. In S. J. Meisels & J. P. Shonkoff (Eds.), *Handbook of early childhood intervention* (pp. 3–31). New York: Cambridge University Press.

Smith, B. J., & Rose, D. F. (1991). *Identifying policy options for preschool mainstreaming.* Pittsburgh, PA: Allegheny-Singer Research Institute.

Smith, B. J., & Strain, P. S. (1988). Early childhood special education in the next decade: Implementing and expanding P. L. 99-457. *Topics in Early Childhood Special Education, 8,* 37–47.

Snyder-McLean, L., Solomonson, B., McLean, J., & Sack, S. (1984). Structuring joint action routines. *Seminars in Speech and Language, 5,* 213–228.

Stokes, T. F., & Baer, D. M. (1977). An implicit technology of generalization. *Journal of Applied Behavior Analysis, 10,* 349–367.

Strain, P. S., McConnell, S. R., Carta, J. J., Fowler, S. A., Neisworth, J. T., & Wolery, M. (1992). Behaviorism in early intervention. *Topics in Early Childhood Special Education, 12,* 121–141.

Vincent, L. J., Salisbury, C. L., Strain, P., McCormick, C., & Tessier, A. (1990). A behavioral-ecological approach to early intervention: Focus on cultural diversity. In S. J. Meisels & J. P. Shonkoff (Eds.), *Handbook of early childhood intervention* (pp. 173–195). New York: Cambridge University Press.

Vygotsky, L. S. (1978). *Mind in society: The development of higher psychological processes.* Cambridge, MA: Harvard University Press.

Warren, S., & Bambara, L. (1989). An experimental analysis of milieu language intervention: Teaching the action-object form. *Journal of Speech and Hear-*

ing Disorders, 54, 448–461.

Warren, S. F., & Kaiser, A. P. (1988). Research in early language intervention. In S. L. Odom & M. B. Karnes (Eds.), *Early intervention for infants and children with handicaps: An empirical base* (pp. 89–108). Baltimore, MD: Paul H. Brookes.

Wolery, M. (1991). Instruction in early childhood special education: "Seeing through a glass darkly . . . knowing in part". *Exceptional Children, 58,* 127–135.

Wolery, M., & Brookfield-Norman, J. (1988). (Pre)academic instruction for handicapped preschool children. In S. L. Odom & M. B. Karnes (Eds.), *Early intervention for infants and children with handicaps* (pp. 109–128).

Wolery, M., Strain, P. S., & Bailey, D. B. (1992). Reaching potentials of children with special needs. In S. Bredekamp & T. Rosegrant (Eds.), *Reaching potentials: Appropriate curriculum and assessment for young children* (Vol. 1) (pp. 92–111). Washington, D.C.: National Association for the Education of Young Children.

11

● ● ● ● ● ●

Designing Meaningful Measurements for Early Childhood

SAMUEL J. MEISELS

Measurement—the systematic assessment of various aspects of children's knowledge, skill, or personality—carries with it some of the most difficult questions that early childhood researchers, practitioners, and policymakers must face. For example, which features of a child's knowledge, skills, or personality can and should be measured? Can the rapidly changing characteristics of infants, toddlers, and preschoolers be measured reliably? How can we enhance the accuracy of the measurements that are conducted in early childhood? Are measurements in early childhood meaningful when conducted in isolation from the child's family and living conditions? Does information from early childhood assessments successfully predict long-term developmental status? These questions will be addressed in this chapter, which will focus on describing conceptual and practical criteria that should be met in order for meaningful measurements of various aspects of child growth and development that take place in the first 5 years of life.

Technically, measurement is a means of assessment and is not synonymous with it. It is a tool for answering specific questions, and it typically involves the collection of quantified representations of several aspects of children's knowledge, skill, achievement, or personality. Some guidelines, such as those concerning developmentally appropriate practice (Bredekamp, 1987), treat measurement and assessment as if they are identical. But assessment is a broader concept than measurement. It can be defined generically as the process of obtaining information for the purpose of making evaluative decisions; measurement is one of the ways that such information is collected and the appropriateness of a given measurement is closely associated with the type of decision that one wishes to make. For example, measurements can be performed in order to identify children who are likely to be members of high-risk groups (screening), confirm the presence and extent of a disability (diagnosis), determine appropriate remediation (program planning), ascertain a child's relative knowledge of specific skills and information (readiness tests), or demonstrate the extent of a child's previous accomplishments (achievement tests). When the information that is obtained for making these decisions is systematic, and when it is based on observable (and typically quantifiable) criteria, one is engaged in a measurement activity, regardless of whether one is performing an assessment of an individual child, studying the characteristics of a group of children, seeking to understand similarities and differences between groups of children across time, or even trying to ascertain the impact of intervention.

Numerous publications describe and critique formal measurement techniques that are used widely during the first five years of life (e.g., Bailey & Wolery, 1989; Dunst, 1986; Francis, Self, & Horowitz, 1987; Gibbs & Teti, 1989; Johnson, McGonigel, & Kaufmann, 1989; Korner et al., 1987; Krauss & Jacobs, 1980; Martin, 1986; Meisels, 1987, 1989a, 1989b; Meisels & Provence, 1989; Molfese, 1989; Stallman & Pearson, 1990; Vietze & Vaughan, 1988; Wachs & Sheehan, 1988). The instruments and procedures reviewed in these publications encompass a variety of measurement devices, such as screening tests, general developmental inventories, cognitive assessment devices, communication assessment instruments, motor assessment tools, social/emotional assessments, self-help assessment instruments, family assessment devices, reading readiness tests, and preschool rating scales.

Despite the diversity in focus, purpose, processes, and use of measurement in early childhood, there are a number of critical assumptions, guidelines, and cautions that should regulate measurement activities. To the extent that these assumptions, guidelines, and cautions are part of the process of making measurement decisions, the measurement activity is likely to be meaningful. "Developmentally appropriate measurements" have meaning when they provide us with sensitive and accurate information about children's characteristics, and when they do not mislead us into adopting theories of growth and development that are spurious, or convey information that might mislead or misdirect our research and practice. These assumptions, guidelines, and cautions will be discussed in the chapter, and a final section will focus on the problems of long-term predictions based on measurements in early childhood.

REPRESENTATIVENESS AND RELATEDNESS

From the outset it is essential to recognize that measurement—like all assessment—is primarily a sampling process. It consists of a "snapshot," or series of snapshots, of a child's knowledge, skills, abilities, or personality characteristics taken at a particular time, from a particular vantage point, and with a particular instrument or recording device. McCune and her colleagues (McCune, Kalmanson, Fleck, Glazewski, & Sillari, 1990) define early childhood assessment as sampling behavior in which specific tasks are presented and specific responses are observed "in order to determine the nature of [children's] underlying competencies and ways of organizing the world" (p. 220). Thus, test items and other forms of measurement in early childhood are intended to permit us to draw inferences about other tasks of the same or related class. For example, "when babies are asked to release a block into a cup, we hope to learn about their understanding of container and contained, about their motor control, and about how they relate to requests from an adult. From this perspective, the primary goals of assessment are to determine level of developmental accomplishment as well as the manner in which the child's organizing abilities appear to be operating at that time" (McCune et al., 1990, p. 220).

This inferential quality of measurements can also be described in terms of their "representativeness" (Cicchetti & Wagner, 1990). A measurement that is not representative will not be meaningful because "the microdevelopmental time of the testing session should be representative of the child's functioning in the macrodevelopmental time of the normal ontogenetic process" (Cicchetti & Wagner, 1990, p. 249). For example, the "Strange Situation" (Ainsworth, Blehar, Waters, & Wall, 1978) is intended to capture in about 20 minutes the history of the parent's caregiving across the first year of life. The HOME scale (Home Observation for Measurement of the Environment; Caldwell & Bradley, 1970) purports to provide sufficient information from a 20–30 minute observation of a child's living arrangements to draw conclusions about the conditions under which children are being reared. And the General Cognitive Index of the McCarthy Scales of Children's Abilities (McCarthy, 1972) is designed to capture a child's general intellectual functioning by reflecting multiple aspects of verbal, perceptual-motor, and quantitative performance. Meaningful measurements allow us to draw accurate inferences from limited data.

This is a particularly important feature of measurement, since the first half-decade of life is a period of such immense modification, growth, and development. This is a time when the human organism goes from being helpless to being independent; when language and communication evolve from isolated gestures, cries, facial expressions, and eye movements to complex syntactic, semantic, and gestural constructions; when movement is no longer largely reflex-driven and constrained, but becomes smooth, voluntary, and directed; when thought processes are transformed from sensory-motor constructions to concrete operational inventions; and when socio-emotional growth begins to move beyond egocentrism and dependence on the caregiver to expressions of ego-control, ego-resilience, and reaching out to others and their separate worlds. In evaluating the appropriateness or meaningfulness of a measurement, it is essential to specify which aspect of development is of particular concern. Moreover, the constructs and phenomena that are measured should have some relatedness to human growth and development.

It is not difficult to identify constructs upon which individuals will differ. The difficulty emerges when we try to measure a construct that is related to something else of either theoretical or practical importance. "The principle of relatedness enjoins us to describe a difference as a difference only if it makes a difference" (Cicchetti & Wagner, 1990, p. 249). Assessments that report differences in achievement without regard for such factors as whether the children have had prior experience with the type of response format being used, or whether the children are disadvantaged due to not speaking English as their first language, would not measure enduring or thoretically significant differences. Instead, a construct can be claimed to be related to a significant feature of development if it meets one or both of the following criteria. First, if the characteristic being measured (e.g., temperament) is predictive, that is, if a child maintains his or her relative position over time when that construct is measured, then, other things being equal, we have surely found a construct that is related to development in that particular area. An example of the first criterion might be secular changes associated with height, head circumference, or general morphology. However, since we can certainly imagine developmental change consisting of a sequence of epigenetic transformations in which predictions across stage boundaries or substantial periods of time would be difficult to make (cf. Piaget's stage theories of mental development), it is essential to have an alternative criterion for defining relatedness. Thus, the second criterion consists of showing that change can be monitored through use of the initial assessment as an anchor, or baseline that is strongly associated with subsequent assessments. In this way, we can indicate something of the relatedness of a construct to something else of theoretical or practical importance.

The second criterion is exemplified by mother-child interactions in the first 2 years of life that are strongly associated with such subsequent developmental indicators as language development, cognition, and socio-emotional functioning (Bee et al., 1982; Sameroff & Fiese, 1990). Apgar scores, which indicate a newborn's motoric, respiratory, cardiac, and reflex status, have little or no relationship to future development (O'Donnell & Oehler, 1989). Nevertheless, Apgar scores and other indicators of neonatal status can be used as markers of contemporaneous risk status. When associated with other risk factors by being incorporated into a formal "risk index," they begin to acquire more collective predictive and "anchoring" power for later measurements (Meisels & Wasik, 1990; Siegel, 1981).

ASSUMPTIONS ABOUT YOUNG CHILDREN'S DEVELOPMENT

Measurement does not occur in a vacuum. For measurement to be meaningful, it is essential that measurement decisions be informed by basic knowledge of how development transpires, and how children's growth in the first years of life is enhanced. This is not to say that every measurement of a developmental construct or characteristic must be a measurement of development in general. That would be an impossible task. Rather, all measurements should be designed with the purpose of representing or illuminating some aspect or construct of development. Similarly, not all measurements are theory driven, but they should all potentially reflect an understanding of how children grow and change.

Central to this task is the recognition that children's development is complex and is determined by multiple factors from the very beginning of life. Measurements in early childhood can focus on a child's status in a number of specific areas (e.g., language, mobility, cognition, the organization of experience, and psychosocial and affective development). Although these areas of development can be addressed separately, they are not necessarily independent. Rather, they are interdependent, and they interact in ways that at times appear to defy our ability to fully describe them (Emde, 1981). The interactive character of human developmental abilities is one of the reasons that it is so difficult to obtain reliable measures of specific developmental functions (e.g., language, motor, or perceptual development) in early childhood.

Related to this interactivity is the recognition that infants and young children are subject to biological and environmental influences that operate to support, facilitate, or impede development. Among these biologically and environmentally sensitive characteristics are the infant's "shared, species-specific biological heritage, the infant's unique genetic makeup, the conditions of intrauterine life, the health of the mother, and events during and immediately following labor and delivery" (Meisels & Provence, 1989, p. 11). Further, the child's environment is molded by the individual and collective capabilities of the child's caregivers and their ethnic and cultural background, and they in turn are affected by the child's biological characteristics, developmental progress, and presence or absence of disabling conditions, amidst a host of other factors (Garbarino, 1990; Sameroff & Fiese, 1990). Except in cases of significant injury to the central nervous system, the older the child, the greater the influence of the child's environment. Thus, interpretations of measurement data should consider both the child's biological status and the impact of environmental factors on that aspect of development. For example, when assessing general cognitive functioning of a 2-year-old, the measurement data that one obtains will be viewed differently if the child is premature, living in poverty, residing with only one parent, and was born with other medical complications, or if the child is the product of a healthy, full-term delivery living in an intact, secure, two-parent household.

An understanding of environmental factors is fundamental to creating meaningful measurement designs in early childhood. This is particularly the case for very young children and for those who are at-risk developmentally. Longitudinal research by Sameroff and his colleagues very clearly makes this point (Sameroff, Seifer, Barocas, Zax, & Greenspan, 1987). In their study of 215 families in Rochester, New York, they examined 10 variables thought likely to have a major impact on the development of children's competence at age 4. Among the variables they studied were maternal mental health, anxiety, education and occupation, family social support, and stressful life events. They found that the higher the number of risk factors, the lower the competence of the child. More than 50 percent of the variance in 4-year-olds' verbal IQ could be explained when the environmental context of the child was taken into account.

Similar findings were reported by Werner (1986) in her 18-year longitudinal study on the island of Kauai. She noted that the presence of four or more predictors of risk by age 2 years appeared to be a dividing line between children who developed serious learning and/or behavior problems by age 10 or 18 and those who were able to cope successfully with the developmental tasks of childhood and adolescence. The central point is that no single factor is always present or always absent when high levels of socio-emotional and intellectual incompetence are discovered by measurement activities. Thus, a mixed measurement strategy that incorporates a wide range of data seems to be called for.

Measurement procedures that ignore the environmental context of caregiving—that view the child in isolation—will not provide meaningful information. Children's skills, knowledge, and personality characteristics are determined by multiple factors and are supported, facilitated, or hampered by numerous biological, societal, and cultural influences. Among these cultural influences are access to multiple approaches to literacy, expectations regarding educational accomplishments, explicit and implicit connections to rite, ritual, and tradition, and overall sense of familial/communal interaction and support. For measurement in early childhood to be faithful to the phenomena it seeks to document—for it to be meaningful—it must take into account how children are affected by the contexts in which they are reared. Each measurement design need not set the impossible task of taking all of this complexity into account at once. However, in order to give the data meaning, even measurements of relatively isolated constructs or aspects of functioning should be interpreted within a larger conceptual framework.

ASSESSMENT GUIDELINES

A critical component of the measurement context concerns how one engages in measurement activities—the manner in which the assessments take place and their differential effects on eliciting meaningful responses from children. Measurement procedures should follow developmentally and ethically sound guidelines regardless of the purpose of the measurement activity. Suggestions of such guidelines, adapted from a comprehensive list designed for individual assessment (Meisels & Provence, 1989), include the following:

1. *Tests, procedures, and processes intended for assessment should be culturally, linguistically, and developmentally sensitive to the child and his/her family.* This is an extremely difficult guideline to observe. Very few measurement procedures have been formally evaluated to determine whether and to what extent they are biased. Nevertheless, there are obvious procedures that should *not* be followed, e.g., assessing young children outside of their primary language, asking children to respond to receptive language tasks concerning experiences that they may never have encountered previously, assuming that all children learn and respond in a singular fashion, or ignoring cultural differences between children that could affect their reaction to the assessment. Sensitivity to these and related issues reflects a commitment to making measurement decisions that are as appropriate as possible, given our existing knowledge.

2. *Requirements for norm-referenced measures of such highly infer-*

ential constructs as intelligence or psychomotor competence should meet stringent professional guidelines for standardization, reliability, validity, and training in administering the assessment. Whenever norm-referenced constructs are studied, it is essential that the measurement procedures be backed by well-formulated and well-documented standardized data, and by dependable information concerning reliability and validity. Such norm-referenced measures as IQ tests, language assessments, or other similar scales, are often used to make decisions about whether to classify a child as disabled or to determine a child's eligibility for services. In such "high stakes" situations, it is essential that the information on which these decisions are based be of extremely high quality, and that the normative sample be similar to the one being assessed.

3. *Evaluations of parent-child interaction should be included in developmental assessments, and should, whenever possible and appropriate, include observations in the home.* Assessments of the child in isolation are potentially misleading. The primary context of the child is the child's family, and measurement designs should not overlook this. Some specialized assessments, e.g., tests of articulation or motor development, can take place without this input. But attempts to explain between-child or between-group differences may depend on the availability of contextual information.

4. *Assessors and assessments should actively solicit information about the child from the family, incorporate parent report data into the assessment, and be sensitive to family needs.* Measurement activities should view the child's family as potential collaborators in the process of obtaining important information for worthwhile decision making. This means that designs should include parent report data whenever possible and appropriate. Also, explanatory information about the assessment should be prepared in the parent's native language, confidentiality should be respected, and informative feedback should be provided to parents whenever possible. It is essential to bear in mind that parents from different cultural traditions may look upon the assessment of their children in radically different ways (see Vincent, Salisbury, Strain, McCormick, & Tessier, 1990). This necessitates that the family's background become part of the interpretation of the child assessment.

5. *Assessments should tap multiple sources of information, thus reflecting the multi-determined nature of development and the cumulative nature of early childhood risk.* The breadth of a particular measurement or assessment is contingent on the goals or purposes of the design in use. As noted earlier, if one is only interested in a narrow aspect or construct of development, multiple sources of information may not appear to be necessary. But since measurement procedures yield only

inferential information, multiple perspectives, like multiple vantage points for viewing a complex phenomenon, will increase accuracy and meaningfulness.

6. *Assessment should focus on those aspects of children's experiences that are central to their development, and should do so, if possible, in a setting that is natural, nonthreatening, and familiar to the child and family.* Measurement procedures that occur outside of the typical boundaries of children's experience may result in highly misleading information. Use of highly specialized equipment, interview protocols, or settings might result in one learning more about a child's response to novelty than about the aspect of the child that is under investigation. Natural activities performed in naturalistic settings have the highest likelihood of resulting in meaningful information, although the task of interpretation is complicated by uncontrolled variables in natural settings.

7. *Measurement activities should be part of an ongoing, dynamic process taking place over time, with multiple components.* One-shot measurements, like one-shot interventions, may make an immediate impression, but may not yield information that is useful in the long term. Nevertheless, some measurement designs are cross-sectional, and not all measurement activities should be judged by their long-term outcomes. Yet, even such a limited activity as preschool developmental screening should have reasonable predictive accuracy for 9 to 12 months, and the explanatory power of a cross-sectional study can be enhanced by examining multiple aspects of functioning, rather than a single, static component.

Overall, the above guidelines, which are part of the clinically sensitive framework of individual assessments, can be a model upon which larger measurement designs are built. Although the purpose for which the measurement is used will influence how relevant each of these guidelines is, the closer a design stays to these guidelines, the more likely it is that it will result in meaningful information. If certain procedures are inappropriate and invalid in measurement activities with individuals, the same prohibitions should apply to other types of designs.

PRACTICAL PROBLEMS OF MEASUREMENT WITH YOUNG CHILDREN

In addition to the design considerations noted above, measurement in early childhood is marked by recurrent practical problems of formulation and administration, or "vicissitudes," as Messick (1983) calls them. Many measurement techniques used with older children are inappropriate for use with children below school age, or even below grade 3. For example, the following methods are extremely unlikely to yield valid information about normative trends in development: paper and pencil questionnaires; lengthy interviews; abstract questions; fatiguing assessment protocols; extremely novel situations or demands; objectively-scored, multiple-choice tests; isolated sources of data. None of these methods are consistent with principles of "developmentally appropriate assessment."

Many factors contribute to measurement error in early childhood assessment. Such "errors" affect measurement activities with both disabled and non-disabled children. In particular, four systematic barriers to effective child assessment can be identified (see Bailey & Wolery, 1989, and Martin, 1986, for more extensive treatment of these issues).

1. *Young children have a restricted ability to comprehend assessment cues.* Assessment cues consist of verbal instructions, verbal stimuli, situational cues, or written instructions and stimuli. Since young children cannot read, the most widely used technologies of behavioral and personality measurement for older children, adolescents, and adults—such as written self-report measures—cannot be administered (Martin, 1986). Similarly, because of their limited vocabulary and conceptual development, meaningful interviews of preschool children cannot be conducted except in the context of highly structured protocols where the way a child responds is just as important as the content of the child's response. Piaget's research highlighted this insight more than 50 years ago.

2. *Young children's verbal and perceptual-motor response capabilities are limited.* Young children's restricted verbal abilities often require the examiner to make inferences about whether a child understands a certain concept or has a specific cognitive skill based on overt motor behaviors, or parent report, rather than on direct response (Bailey, 1989). Preschoolers are able to respond to pictures and to create stories based on visual stimuli, but these responses may be brief, or limited, thus offering relatively little information for interpretation. Developmental changes early in life mean that a child's perceptions at one time may be radically different when the same child is assessed at a later point. Such differences may be further exaggerated by the presence of sensory, motor, or cognitive impairments, or reliance on childrearing practices that inhibit exploration, questioning, competition, and so forth. Response stability in early childhood—especially in infancy—is difficult to achieve.

3. *Some types of questions require complex information-processing skills that young children do not possess.* Martin (1986) points out that the question, "'Do you like going to school (preschool)?' calls for the child to remember positive and negative occurrences, and to give differential

weights to them, depending on the importance of these events, before making a response (p. 217)." Preschoolers are likely to be captured by the "recency phenomenon" of the last important thing that happened, or they may simply report their current state, i.e., how they are feeling that day. Alternatively, different attitudes towards schooling that are propounded by a child's family could result in very different reactions to this question. Observers' interpretations and generalizations about such responses should take into account children's limited abilities to respond to complex requests for information.

4. *Young children may have difficulty understanding the demand characteristics of the measurement situation, and they may not be able to control their behavior to meet these demands.* Infants and toddlers are very likely to be wary or even frightened of unfamiliar adults or poorly explained tasks. They may also respond poorly if rapport has not been established with the examiner. Older children are also strongly influenced by the measurement setting. Studies of 5- and 6-year-olds to whom whole-group, standardized achievement tests were administered show that the students' behavior is anything but standardized. They get out of their chairs, call out answers, try to help one another, act disruptive, or display attentional problems (Wodtke, Harper, Schommer, & Brunelli, 1989). Similarly, Martin (1986) notes that children's assessment behavior can be affected by fatigue, boredom, hunger, illness, or fearfulness because of separation from their parents, or because the assessment situation reminds them of painful occurrences elsewhere, such as visits to the physician's office. As noted, these issues are not unique to early childhood. Siegal (1991) points out that the demand characteristics of many measurement situations put children of a wide range of ages in situations where they perceive that conversational rules have been violated and where "incorrect responses may reflect uncertainty, a misinterpretation of the meaning or purpose of the question, a desire to give attention-seeking answers, or simply a wish to end the conversation" (p. 121). Moreover, the child's behavior may be affected by the ethnicity of the examiner, or simply by the match or rapport between child and examiner. Cultural expectations concerning competition, cooperation, humility, silence, appropriateness of imitating adults, and so forth, all may play a role in establishing this rapport.

All these factors contribute to the instability of early childhood measurement results. However, the conclusion to draw from this discussion is not that measurement activities should be eliminated, but that young children should be assessed carefully, and in ways that are consistent with their developmental capabilities. This means gaining rapport with a child, establishing motivation for the child to participate, using extremely clear and understandable instructions, maintaining the child's attention, and helping the child cope effectively with boredom, distraction, and fatigue (see Messick, 1983, p. 479). Still other strategies that reduce measurement error include the following:

1. Be aware that the measurement environment may cause unusual emotional reactions, such as anxiety or defensiveness, that are atypical of the child, and that impair the child's ability to respond optimally. Thus, it is important to establish as friendly and natural an environment as possible (Martin, 1986, p. 228).
2. Given the problems noted earlier, be certain that the instruments or techniques used to collect data contain or create as few formal measurement errors as possible (e.g., continuous behavior sampling has a much lower error rate than time sampling [Mann, Ten Have, Plunkett, & Meisels, 1991]).
3. Since behavior that is sampled over a period of time will be more accurate and representative than behavior that is sampled once or on infrequent intervals, try to use multiple measurements in a longitudinal design.
4. Observers, raters, and interviewers may unknowingly bias the data they collect. Try to include multiple observers, multiple sources of data, and multiple approaches in collecting data to increase the likelihood of obtaining reliable measurements of young children.

Meaningful measurements begin with meaningful interactions between assessors and children. These interactions are a necessary condition for obtaining useful information for making evaluative decisions about children.

THE SEARCH FOR DEVELOPMENTAL PREDICTORS

Although many measurements take place without the explicit aim of being predictive, predictability is often thought to be fundamental to early childhood measurement. This follows from the teleological nature of growth in early childhood. For example, when we measure visual recognition memory in infancy, maternal-child interactions in the second year of life, language acquisition among 2- to 3-year olds, or virtually anything else in the first 5 years of life, part of the meaning of this measurement is its presumed relationship to some other characteristic that is yet to emerge. As Cicchetti and Wagner (1990) point out, "If constructs were inherently evanescent, then there would be little utility in creating an assessment instrument to sample them" (p. 249).

However, it is well-established canon in developmental research that long-term predictions based on data obtained from measurements in early childhood are tenuous at best. Led by McCall and his colleagues' research (Kopp & McCall, 1982; McCall, 1979, 1981; McCall, Appelbaum, & Hogarty, 1973; McCall, Eichorn, & Hogarty, 1977), instability in individual differences during the first 2 years of life has been demonstrated repeatedly in mental and motor test performance. Age-to-age stability in mental performance rises at about 2 years, increasing rapidly until approximately 5 years of age for normally developing children. It is important to note that high-risk and disabled children show an increase in stability coefficients somewhat earlier (Kopp & McCall, 1982). This is most likely a result of the decreased variance in the performances of these children. Data from a number of sources strongly suggest that "there is no consistency across or within age in a wide variety of tests purported to measure infant mental functioning" (Lewis, 1976, p. 13). Although socioeconomic variables (e.g., parental occupation, maternal education) appear to be reasonably reliable predictors of childhood development, SES is a demographic variable. In and of itself SES tells us nothing about the process of acquiring developmental abilities, knowledge, or skills (Lewis & Fox, 1980).

Except for children who have experienced severe damage to the central nervous system, predictions of developmental outcome based on data collected during the first 2 years of life are generally not very impressive. As expected, the best predictions emerge from studies that incorporate multiple sources of data, such as individual testing and assessment of the home environment, into a multivariate index (see Siegel, 1981), and that sample predictor and outcome variables at points in temporal proximity (Chamberlin, 1977). Moreover, research shows that the most accurate predictions in the first 2 years of life include measures of caregiver-infant interaction in the predictive equation (Bee et al., 1982; Sameroff, 1978; Sigman & Parmelee, 1979). However, even when assessments of maternal responsiveness are combined with measures of infant status, long-term predictions from data collected early in life are still not very stable.

If we cannot make reliable predictions, based on our measurement data, are these measurements still meaningful? In beginning to answer this question, it is useful to consider the wide range of independent variables that are relied upon as a basis for predictions (see Meisels, 1984, for a more complete review). The characteristics of these variables may provide some insight into the perils and the promise of early childhood pre-diction. The range of predictors of development that has been explored includes judgments based on single predictors (e.g., rapid eye move-ments, Apgar scores, or visual recognition memory); multiple predictors (e.g., morbidity or medical complications scales); information obtained from parents, teachers, or other sources (e.g., questionnaires, assess-ments of life stress, and teacher rating scales); or information obtained by observation of the child's behavior (e.g., Q-sorts, time sampling, and other rating scales). When these predictors are studied longitudinally, it is clear that the type of information collected in the first 12–18 months differs substantially from that studied in the next year to year and a half. Infants do not communicate, locomote, or solve problems in the same way that 3-year-olds do. As research with the Brazelton Neonatal Behav-ior Assessment Scale shows, even the behavior of 3-day-old infants dif-fers from that of 1-month-old babies. Recovery from the birth experience, postnatal neurological maturation, and the effect of the infant's caregiver all modify the baby's reflexes, regulatory abilities, and interactive capac-ities (Brazelton, 1982). From this vantage point, it would seem that devel-opmental realities constrain psychometric possibilities. In other words, sensory motor performance alone does not predict well to such domains as language and verbal intelligence. Only in multiple predictor equations is there reasonable continuity between early predictions and later out-comes (Kochanek, Kabacoff, & Lipsitt, 1987).

Research focusing on preschool and kindergarten children follows a relatively similar course, but with greater predictive success. This research uses both single- and multiple-variable predictors. Studies using single-variable predictors usually rely upon a single test or indicator of general developmental ability, perceptual-motor skill, intelligence, or school readiness to obtain a score that is related to an outcome variable. Multiple-variable studies typically employ a combination of reading-readiness tests, standardized intelligence and perceptual tests, and other predictive indices composed of several variables.

Multiple-variable predictive batteries are used principally to predict academic achievement and performance. A wide range of studies has been completed, differing vastly in methodological rigor (see Tramon-tana, Hooper, & Selzer, 1988). Among the major variables that were con-sidered to be the best predictors of first grade performance when kinder-garten children were tested include: ability to attend to auditory and visual stimuli and to order attack skills (Colarusso, Plankenhorn, & Brooks, 1980); duration of attention (Becker, 1976; Feshbach, Adelman, & Fuller, 1974; Forness, Hall, & Guthrie, 1977); performance on tasks of cognitive development (Kaufman & Kaufman, 1972, derived from the work of Piaget and Gesell); level of perceptual development (Morency & Wepman, 1973); and conservation of number (Dimitrovsky & Almy, 1975). Although there is little agreement among these investigations, a general review shows the wealth of possibilities available for use in predictive studies of development and school-related achievement.

However, when the methodology of these studies is analyzed, their findings become more difficult to interpret. Few conclusions about particular predictors can be drawn from the extensive multiple-variable predictor studies that have been conducted. Indeed, several investigators (Feshbach, Adelman, & Fuller, 1977; Meisels, 1989b; Rubin, Balow, Dorle, & Rosen, 1978; Stevenson, Parker, Wilkinson, Hegion, & Fish, 1976) even caution against the use of data from their prediction studies as a basis for diagnostic classification and labeling. Although high preschool and kindergarten scores may be predictors of normal or superior academic performance, poor preschool test performance usually does not provide enough information to construct valid high-risk groupings. Predictions improve with advances in children's chronological age, although the importance of assessing multiple factors and attending to context remains constant, even as children grow older. Moreover, the results of these studies indicate that, to the extent that the criterion measures are related to school performance or school success, predictors based on school-related tasks are significantly more reliable than other types. Stevenson et al. (1976) suggest that "later performance depended not only on accomplishments of the child before entering school, but also upon the child's learning and memory abilities" (p. 398). In other words, insofar as school success depends upon the level of skill acquisition, it depends also upon the ability to acquire skills. These abilities emerge slowly, and sometimes in unexpected patterns, over the entire early childhood period. Unfortunately, our models of prediction are linear and main effect in design, rather than interactive and multivariate and may not fit the shape of human development or cultural difference very well. Moreover, these models rarely view developmental characteristics as organizational constructs or patterns in which it is possible to find continuity in a coherent framework (e.g., attachment) even when such continuity is not apparent in individual traits or abilities (e.g., amount of crying, proximity to the caregiver, specific linguistic features) (see Sroufe, 1979).

Although considerations of prediction are highly appropriate in a discussion of measurement, another equally important function of measurement is to describe, document, or catalogue contemporaneous performance. In other words, predictive validity is one feature of measurement, but so is concurrent validity. Contemporaneous, or concurrent validity may potentially be independent of predictive validity. Although assessments about individual future outcomes may be unstable, much can be learned about a child's present level of functioning through measurement techniques. To the extent that these measurement activities abide by the principles, assumptions, and guidelines presented here, this information is likely to illuminate patterns of growth and development.

McCall (1982) reminds us that development means change, and one should not be surprised if long-term predictions in early childhood are somewhat disappointing. He further notes that the propensity for change in children obviates short-term enrichments and is a bane to prediction. Nevertheless, our inability to predict such individual outcomes as IQ at age 6 from developmental assessments in infancy, or social behavior in preschool from parental assessments of infant temperament, does not mean that meaningful and interpretable results about groups and intergroup differences are impossible. Indeed, predictions about outcomes based on data from groups of children are significantly more accurate than estimates of individual functioning, when samples are large and carefully stratified.

The connection between these comments about prediction and the earlier discussion about maximizing meaning in measurement rests on the importance of viewing the child from multiple perspectives, and seeing the child within a broad context, rather than as an isolated source of information. Whether the purpose of the assessment is to obtain concurrent information or longitudinal data, early childhood measurement relies heavily on fitting specific information obtained from the child and the child's setting into a very broad developmental perspective. We may not be able to predict great developmental distances, but we can usually hint at the next steps in the developmental process. Context plays a role in both the administration and the interpretation of early childhood measurement techniques. Understanding the child within context is key to understanding the child.

Much more remains to be learned about measurement. For example, there may be evolutionary paths between early and later assessments that are nonlinear, that a comprehensive, longitudinal, multivariate design can test. Such a longitudinal design would permit us to examine which variables, sampled in which specific ways, at which particular points in time, distinguish between those children who display various forms of competence and those who do not. In other words, although our individual predictors are not very strong, and are often fairly reductionistic in their emphasis on single variables or isolated measurement techniques, the problem of prediction may lie as much with the analytic design and the plan for implementing the assessments as with the phenomena being measured.

In short, the relationship between early and later assessments must be strengthened and examined at every step, at every link. Predictors must be chosen carefully and their dimensions understood systematically; covariates must be described clearly and their sampling covered comprehensively; and measurements must take place according to the recommendations of best practice, such as those reviewed here, in concert with current research about children's development and the multiplicity of factors that affects their growth. Only after these conditions have been met, will we begin to understand the meaning of early childhood measurement.

ACKNOWLEDGMENT

This chapter is based on a paper commissioned in 1991 by the National Center on Education Statistics, Office of Educational Research and Improvement, U.S. Department of Education. The opinions expressed are those of the author.

REFERENCES

Ainsworth, M. D. S., Blehar, M. C., Waters, E., & Wall, S. (1978). *Patterns of attachment: A psychological study of the strange situation*. Hillsdale, NJ: Erlbaum.

Bailey, D. B. (1989). Assessment and its importance in early intervention. In D. B. Bailey & M. Wolery (Eds.), *Assessing infants and preschoolers with handicaps* (pp. 1–21). New York: Merrill.

Bailey, D. B., & Wolery, M. (Eds.). (1989). *Assessing infants and preschoolers with handicaps*. New York: Merrill.

Balow, B., Rubin, R., & Rosen, M. (1975). Perinatal events as precursors of reading disability. *Reading Research Quarterly, 11,* 36–71.

Becker, L. (1976). Conceptual tempo and the early detection of learning problems. *Journal of Learning Disabilities, 9,* 433–442.

Bee, H. L., Barnard, K. E., Eyres, S. J., Gray, C. A., Hammond, M. A., Spietz, A. L., Snyder, C., & Clark, B. (1982). Prediction of IQ and language skill from perinatal status, child performance, family characteristics, and mother-infant interactions. *Child Development, 53,* 1134–1156.

Bredekamp, S. (Ed.). (1987). *Developmentally appropriate practice in early childhood programs serving children from birth through age eight* (expanded ed.). Washington, DC: National Association for the Education of Young Children.

Brazelton, T. B. (1982). Joint regulation of neonate-parent behavior. In E. Tronick (Ed.), *Social interchange in infancy: Affect, cognition, and communication* (pp. 7–22). Baltimore, MD: University Park Press.

Caldwell, B. M., & Bradley, R. (1970). *Home Observation for Measurement of the Environment (HOME)*. Little Rock, AK: University of Arkansas.

Chamberlin, R. W. (1977). Can we identify a group of children at age 2 who are at high risk for the development of behavior or emotional problems in kindergarten and first grade? *Pediatrics, 59,* 971–981.

Cicchetti, D., & Wagner, S. (1990). Alternative assessment strategies for the evaluation of infants and toddlers: An organizational perspective. In S. J. Meisels & J. P. Shonkoff (Eds.), *Handbook of early childhood intervention* (pp. 246–277). New York: Cambridge University Press.

Colarusso, R., Plankenhorn, A., Brooks, R. (1980). Predicting first-grade achievement through formal testing of 5-year-old high-risk children. *Journal of Special Education, 14,* 355–363.

Dimitrovsky, L., & Almy, M. (1975). Early conservation as a predictor of later reading. *Journal of Psychology, 90,* 11–18.

Dunst, C. J. (Ed.). (1986). Infant and preschool assessment: Child, environmental, and family approaches Special Issue. *Diagnostique, 11,* 3–4.

Emde, R. M. (1981). Searching for perspectives: Systems sensitivity and opportunities in studying the infancy of the organizing child of the universe. In K. Bloom (Ed.), *Prospective issues in infancy research* (pp. 1–14). Hillsdale, NJ: Erlbaum.

Feshbach, S., Adelman, H., & Fuller, W. W. (1974). Early identification of children with high risk of reading failures. *Journal of Learning Disabilities, 7,* 739–644.

Feshbach, S., Adelman, H., & Fuller, W. (1977). Prediction of reading and related academic problems. *Journal of Educational Psychology, 69,* 299–308.

Forness, S., Hall, R., & Guthrie, D. (1977). Eventual school placement of kindergartners observed as high risk in the classroom. *Psychology in the Schools, 14,* 315–317.

Francis, P. L., Self, P. A., & Horowitz, F. D. (1987). The behavioral assessment of the neonate: An overview. In J. D. Osofsky (Ed.), *Handbook of infant development* (2nd ed.) (pp. 723–779). New York: John Wiley and Sons.

Garbarino, J. (1990). The human ecology of early risk. In S. J. Meisels & J. P. Shonkoff (Eds.), *Handbook of early childhood intervention* (pp. 78–96). New York: Cambridge University Press.

Gibbs, E. D., & Teti, D. M. (Eds.). (1989). *Interdisciplinary assessment of infants: A guide for early intervention professionals.* Baltimore, MD: Paul H. Brookes.

Johnson, B. H., McGonigel, J. J., & Kaufmann, R. K. (Eds.). (1989). *Guidelines and recommended practices for the Individualized Family Service Plan.* Chapel Hill, NC: NEC*TAS and ACCH.

Kaufman, A. S., & Kaufman, N. L. (1972). Tests build from Piaget's and Gesell's tasks as predictors of first-grade achievement. *Child Development, 43,* 521–535.

Kochanek, T. T., Kabacoff, R. I., & Lipsitt, L. P. (1987). Early detection of handicapping conditions in infancy and early childhood: Toward a multivariate model. *Journal of Applied Developmental Psychology, 8,* 411–420.

Kopp, C. B., & McCall, R. B. (1982). Predicting later mental performance for normal, at-risk, and handicapped infants. In P. B. Baltes & O. G. Brim (Eds.), *Life-span development and behavior* (Vol. 4) (pp. 33–61). New York: Academic Press.

Korner, A. F., Kraemer, H. C., Reade, E. P., Forrest, T., & Dimiceli, S. (1987). A methodological approach to developing an assessment procedure for testng the neurobehavioral maturity of preterm infants. *Child Development, 58,* 1478–1487.

Krauss, M. W., & Jacobs, F. (1990). Family assessment: Puroposes and techniques. In S. J. Meisels & J. P. Shonkoff (Eds.), Handbook of early childhood intervention (pp. 303–325). New York: Cambridge University Press.

Lewis, M. (1976). What do we mean when we say "Infant Intelligence Scores"? A sociopolitical question. In M. Lewis (Ed.), *Origins of intelligence: Infancy and early childhood* (pp. 1–17). New York: Plenum.

Lewis, M., & Fox, N. (1980). Predicting cognitive development from assessments in infancy. In B. W. Camp (Ed.), *Advances in behavioral pediatrics* (Vol. 1) (pp. 53–68). Greenwich, CT: JAI.

Mann, J., Ten Have, T., Plunkett, J. W., & Meisels, S. J. (1991). Time sampling: A methodological critique. *Child Development, 62,* 227–241.

Martin, R. P. (1986). Assessment of the social and emotional functioning of preschool children. *School Psychology Review, 15,* 216–232.

McCall, R. B. (1979). The development of intellectual functioning in infancy and the prediction of later IQ. In J. Osofsky (Ed.), *Handbook of infant development* (pp. 707–741). New York: John Wiley and Sons.

McCall, R. B. (1981). Early predictors of later IQ: The search continues. *Intelligence, 5,* 141–147.

McCall, R. B. (1982). A hard look at stimulating and predicting development: The cases of bonding and screening. *Pediatrics in Review, 3,* 205–212.

McCall, R. B., Eichorn, D. H., & Hogarty, P. S. (1977). Transitions in early mental development. *Monographs of the society for research in child development, 42* (3, Serial No. 171).

McCall, R. B., Appelbaum, M. I., & Hogarty, P. S. (1973). Developmental changes in mental performance. *Monographs of the society for research child development, 38* (Serial No. 150).

McCarthy, D. (1972). *McCarthy scales of children's abilities.* New York: Psychological Corporation.

McCune, L., Kalmanson, B., Fleck, M. B., Glazewski, B., & Sillari, J. (1990). An interdisciplinary model of infant assessment. In. S. J. Meisels & J. P. Shonkoff (Eds.), *Handbook of early childhood intervention* (pp. 219–245). New York: Cambridge University Press.

Meisels, S. J. (1984). Prediction, prevention and developmental screening in the EPSDT program. In H. W. Stevenson & A. E. Siegel (Eds.), *Child development research and social policy* (pp. 267–317). Chicago: University of Chicago Press.

Meisels, S. J. (1987). Uses and abuses of developmental screening and school readiness testing. *Young Children, 42,* 4–6; 68–73.

Meisels, S. J. (1989a), *Developmental screening in early childhood: A guide* (3rd ed.). Washington, DC: National Association for the Education of Young Children.

Meisels, S. J. (1989b). Can developmental screening tests identify children who are developmentally at-risk? *Pediatrics, 83,* 578–585.

Meisels, S. J., & Provence, S. (1989). *Screening and assessment: Guidelines for identifying young disabled and developmentally vulnerable children and their families*. Washington, DC: National Center for Clinical Infant Programs.

Meisels, S. J., & Wasik, B. A. (1990). Who should be served? Identifying children in need of early intervention. In S. J. Meisels & J. P. Shonkoff (Eds.), *Handbook of early childhood intervention* (pp. 605–632). New York: Cambridge University Press.

Messick, S. (1983). Assessment of children. In W. Kessen (Ed.), *Handbook of child psychology: History, theory, and methods* (Vol. 1) (pp. 477–526). New York: John Wiley and Sons.

Molfese, V. J. (1989). *Perinatal risk and infant development: Assessment and prediction*. New York: Guilford Press.

Morency, A., & Wepman, J. (1973). Early perceptual ability and later school achievement. *Elementary School Journal, 73,* 323–327.

O'Donnell, K. J., & Oehler, J. M. (1989). Neurobehavioral assessment of the newborn infant. In D. B. Bailey & M. Wolery (Eds.), *Assessing infants and preschoolers with handicaps* (pp. 166–201). New York: Merrill.

Rubin, R. A., Balow, B., Dorle, J., & Rosen, M. (1978). Preschool prediction of low achievement in basic school skills. *Journal of Learning Disabilities, 11,* 664–667.

Sameroff, A. J. (1978). Caretaking or reproductive casualty? Determinants in developmental deviancy. In F. D. Horowitz (Ed.), *Early developmental hazards: Predictors and precautions* (pp. 79–102). Boulder, CO: Westview.

Sameroff, A. J., & Fiese, B. H. (1990). Transactional regulation and early intervention. In S. J. Meisels, & J. P. Shonkoff (Eds.), *Handbook of early childhood intervention* (pp. 119–149). New York: Cambridge University Press.

Sameroff, A. J., Seifer, R., Barocas, R., Zax, M., & Greenspan, S. (1987). Intelligence quotient scores of 4-year-old children: Social-emotional risk factors. *Pediatrics, 79,* 343–350.

Siegal, M. (1991). *Knowing children: Experiments in conversation and cognition.* Hillsdale, NJ: Erlbaum.

Siegel, L. S. (1981). Infant tests as predictors of cognitive and language development at two years. *Child Development, 52,* 545–557.

Sigman, M., & Parmelee, A. H. (1979). Longitudinal evaluation of the pre-term infant. In T. M. Field, A. M. Sostek, S. Goldberg, & H. H. Shuman (Eds.), *Infants born at risk* (pp. 193–218). New York: Spectrum.

Sroufe, A. (1979). The coherence of individual development: Early care, attachment, and subsequent developmental issues. *American Psychologist, 34,* 834–841.

Stallman, A. C., & Pearson, P. D. (1990). Formal measures of early literacy. In L. M. Morrow & J. K. Smith (Eds.), *Assessment for instruction in early literacy* (pp. 7–44). Englewood Cliffs, NJ: Prentice Hall.

Stevenson, H., Parker, T., Wilkinson, A., Hegion, A., & Fish, E. (1976). Longitudinal study of individual differences in cognitive development and scholastic achievement. *Journal of Educational Psychology, 68,* 377–400.

Tramontana, M. G., Hooper, S. R., & Selzer, S. C. (1988). Research on the preschool prediction of later academic achievement: A review. *Developmental Review, 8,* 89–146.

Vietze, P. M., & Vaughan, H. G. (Eds.) (1988). *Early identification of infants with developmental disabilities.* Philadelphia: Grune & Stratton.

Vincent, L. J., Salisbury, C. L., Strain, P., McCormick, C., & Tessier, A. (1990). A behavioral-ecological approach to early intervention: Focus on cultural diversity. In S. J. Meisels & J. P. Shonkoff (Eds.), *Handbook of early childhood intervention* (pp. 173–195). New York: Cambridge University Press.

Wachs, T. D., & Sheehan, R. (Eds.) (1988). *Assessment of young developmentally disabled children.* New York: Plenum.

Werner, E. E. (1986). A longitudinal study of perinatal risk. In D. C. Farran & J. D. McKinney (Eds.), *Risk in intellectual and psychosocial development* (pp. 3–28). Orlando, FL: Academic Press.

Wodtke, K. H., Harper, F., Schommer, M., & Brunelli, P. (1989, Fall). How standardized is school testing? An exploratory observational study of standardized group testing in kindergarten. *Educational Evaluation and Policy Analysis, 11,* 223–235.

12

• • • • • •

Teacher Perspectives on the Strengths and Achievements of Young Children
Relationship to Ethnicity, Language, Gender, and Class

MARIANNE N. BLOCH, B. ROBERT TABACHNICK,
AND MIRYAM ESPINOSA-DULANTO

The need for increasingly accurate assessments of young children's strengths and weaknesses as they begin public school has received increased attention in recent years. While many push for new tests to evaluate a child's readiness for school, as well as new objective assessment techniques in school, others criticize standard assessments that suggest young children's readiness or competencies can be reliably or validly pinpointed. These criticisms become particularly sharp when tests and other assessment tools are conceived and interpreted from the perspectives of a majority culture but used to make judgments about children whose cultural knowledge may differ markedly from that of "majority" children, with some of their intellectual strengths being overlooked by the tests or interpreted as response errors.

There are three strands of criticism. The first focuses on the idea that standardized assessment techniques are unreliable or lack validity when used with young children because of their age, test inexperience, anxiety, or inability to perform consistently. These issues are represented in calls for more developmentally appropriate assessment, and for increased attention to improving cultural and language sensitivity in test/assessment construction (e.g., National Association for the Education of Young Children and the National Association of Early Childhood Specialists in State Departments of Education, 1991). The second focuses on the social construction of the concepts of readiness and assessment. From this theoretical position, readiness and assessment cannot be conceived of as "objective" entities represented by scores; instead, these are socially constructed concepts that communities, teachers, and parents participate in creating (e.g., Graue, 1992). Finally, the third critique, which has several strands, suggests that schools lack readiness for children from diverse backgrounds, rather than that these children are not ready for school. In this view, schools, as representatives of dominant, middle-class, Euro-American culture, embody concepts of readiness and children's competence with built in biases that favor children from white middle- and elite-class families (e.g., Erickson, 1987; Heath, 1983; Vogt, Jordan, & Tharp, 1987).

The second and third critiques recognize that assessments of children are not representations of "objective" information about children, but are cultural and political constructions of the competencies children have and/or need for school. These critiques are absent from most calls for reform and they are absent from much practice that affects children. On the other hand, since the mid-1960s, efforts have been made to improve testing in children's primary language and to create tests that are culturally sensitive. Other reform efforts have called for "authentic" forms of assessment such as portfolios of information on children collected by teachers, children, and their parents over time; however, these too are subject to various problems of bias and interpretation (Gomez, Graue, & Bloch, 1991).

This chapter will explore these issues through descriptions of teacher assessments of kindergarten and first grade children in three schools in one midwestern school district we call Lakeside. We examine teacher constructions of children's strengths and weaknesses, with a particular focus on teacher perspectives toward children from diverse cultural and language backgrounds.

The term "perspectives" is used to emphasize that assessments are social constructions based upon selected information available to and used by teachers. Perspectives are "a coordinated set of ideas and actions that a person uses in dealing with some problematic situation." This view of perspectives is derived from Becker, Geer, Hughes, and Strauss (1961). According to this view, perspectives differ from attitudes since they include actions and not merely dispositions to act. Also, unlike values, perspectives are defined in relation to specific situations and do not necessarily represent general beliefs or teaching ideologies. (See the discussion of "teacher perspectives" in Tabachnick & Zeichner, 1986).

What affects teachers' perspectives on assessment, in general, and about children's competencies, as these develop over time? Recent literature suggests that teachers' perspectives are affected in highly complex and interrelated ways by the following factors:

1. Their personal autobiographies of experience and beliefs both as a person and as a professional (e.g., Ladson-Billings, 1990; Zeichner, Tabachnick, & Densmore, 1987);

2. Teacher and school beliefs about how assessment takes place for young children, as these relate to the child's age, developmental "level" or "readiness" for school, and cultural and class background; and normative beliefs and policies promoted at the national, school district, and school levels (Graue, 1992; Shepherd & Smith, 1989; Smith & Shepherd, 1988; Zeichner et al., 1987);

3. Teacher knowledge or lack of knowledge about children's strengths or weaknesses (Delgado-Gaitan & Trueba, 1990; Heath, 1983; Lareau, 1989; Richardson, Casonova, Placier, & Guilfoyle, 1989; Taylor, 1991);

4. Broader social structural factors that relate to teacher constructions of children as "different" based upon ethnic, racial, gender, language, and class "group" identities or perceived membership (Apple, 1979; Tabachnick & Zeichner, 1986).

In the following sections of this chapter, we will use data from our ethnographic study of children in three schools to illustrate the importance of these factors as they have emerged in our analyses to date.

A CASE STUDY OF TEACHER PERSPECTIVES OF CHILDREN IN THREE SCHOOLS

In the fall of 1988, we began a study of 23 children who were just entering into kindergarten in three racially integrated schools in the Lakeside School District, a midwestern school district of about 200,000 population composed primarily of middle-class whites. We interviewed children's teachers and their parents over a 2-year period (from kindergarten through first grade) and observed children at home and in their classrooms. While we continued to follow selected children through their second grade year, this report focuses on teacher perspectives across kindergarten and first grade.

We examined patterns of home and school learning within three different ethnic groups of children for whom available research typically would predict problems. Our focus has been on children from backgrounds that are commonly perceived as "at risk" (Swadener, 1990) based on background characteristics that include socioeconomic class, race, ethnicity, limited English proficiency, and family marital status. The child participants in our study were Hmong (a Southeast Asian refugee group of children whose primary or first language is Hmong), African American, and "Latino" (a group of children who came from, or whose parents came from, several different regional/national origins including Central and South America; the majority have Spanish as a primary or first language.) All but three of the children (one Latino boy, one African-American boy and one African-American girl) were from low-income families based on criteria that included eligibility for free or reduced lunch at school, eligibility for subsidized housing, parent educational background, and occupation.

District Context

Academic rankings of the Lakeside School District on national assessments show that district children typically test above average, often in the top quartile. The vast majority of children in the district attend public schools, and support and pride in the school system is generally high.

In addition to already established programs, the district has responded to national movements for educational reform with many innovations. Recent reform efforts have included pilot "primary education" schools that model their kindergarten to second grade educational plans after the developmentally appropriate curricula proposed by the National Association for the Education of Young Children (e.g., Bredekamp, 1987). The primary education model schools include, for example, more attention to multiage grouping, alternative types of assessment such as portfolios (Gomez et al., 1991), and emphases on concrete and active experiences rather than passive drills or worksheets. Efforts to reform the most common parent involvement practices (e.g., PTO, once or twice a year conferences, Open Houses) are being made across schools (see Bloch & Tabachnick, in press, for greater discussion of these efforts). In response to critiques of standardized assessment for young children, a locally developed kindergarten screener, comprised of a checklist of children's skills with letters, number recognition, and selected concepts, was developed in the early 1980s. The screener is administered by kindergarten teachers, with interpreters for children whose primary language is not English, and is given during the spring prior to children's entry into kindergarten or during the first week of kindergarten. In addition, in 1988, national standardized tests before grade three were abolished. Efforts to modify the wording and categories used in the 3 to 4 times a year report cards sent to parents at the primary levels have been made in all elementary schools; in some, increased parent conferences have also been added to discuss teacher-parent assessments of children's progress. In response to increasing racial, ethnic, and class diversity, the district introduced increased access to English-as-a-second-language (ESL) or bilingual programs, Chapter I, new reading programs such as Reading Recovery, and whole language programs. Also introduced were enhanced multicultural curricular offerings and strategies to include more cooperative group learning and teacher training in multicultural education that focused on cultural differences.

While the majority of children, families, and teaching staff in the district represent the dominant white middle class, the proportion of elementary school children of color, and/or from non-middle-class backgrounds in the Lakeside School district rose from 10% of the population in the early 1980s to 23% of the total elementary school population in 1992.[1]

This demographic shift was primarily caused by migration of African-American families from other cities in the southern and mid-western United States and by an influx of Southeast Asian refugee or immigrant families to the area. African-Americans were estimated in 1992 to be 14% of the elementary school population while Hmong children were estimated to be 5% of the elementary school population. A smaller (3% in 1992) but significant number of Latino families had also moved to the district over the past decade. Largely because of low-cost housing patterns, low-income families of color had congregated in several areas of Lakeside over the 1980s. In 1983, a suit by parents led to a controversial but voluntary city plan to racially integrate schools by "pairing" several schools that had high percentages (approximately 80%) of low-income children of color, with schools that had more than 90% middle-class, Euro-American child enrollment. In the three different pairings that were done, three schools became K–2 grade level schools, while the other three schools took third to fifth grade children. These schools are described in further detail below.

School Context

Our study has been done in three racially integrated schools in the Lakeside school district. Two of the K–2 schools described in this paper, called Greendale and Lakelawn to protect school confidentiality, were part of the "paired" integration plan (see above). Greendale School had 33% of the school population listed as African American and seven of those children were selected as representatives of the group in our sample. In Lakelawn School, approximately half of the minority ethnic population was Asian American, with the largest group of Asian American children being Hmong. Ten children from Hmong ethnic background

and one child from Latino heritage were selected for our study from
Lakelawn School. The third school, a K–5 school we call Oakhill, was not
part of the integration plan, but had 28% children of color. Five of the six
children of Latino ethnic background selected to participate in our study
were from Oakhill School.

GREENDALE SCHOOL. This was one of the K–2 schools involved in the
pairing effort described above. It is in the northern area of the district and
is "linked" with Fillmore Elementary, an eastern area school that had
approximately 80% children of color including the largest percentage of
African-American children in the city. At the time we began our study
with Greendale School, 55% of the school population were listed as
"White," 33% of the children were listed as African American, and 12%
were from Asian American backgrounds. Approximately 45% of the children in the school were eligible to receive free or reduced price hot
lunches or breakfasts.

At Greendale School, only 2 out of a staff of 25 teachers were African
American (first and second grade) and there was one Hmong bilingual
aide/interpreter. The rest of the teaching staff were Euro-American and
female. The two sample kindergarten teachers and one of the two sample first grade teachers had had extensive (10–25 years) experience
teaching at their grade level, and each had been at Greendale School for
at least 5 years at the time of our study; the remaining first grade teacher
with whom we worked was relatively new as a teacher (3 years experience), and was in her 2nd year at this school. Again, each of the teachers had reputations as effective classroom teachers based on principal
and parent reports, and observations we had made prior to beginning
the study confirmed their reputations.

The school principal had initiated many reforms including multiage
grouping, cooperative learning, whole language instruction, a specialized reading recovery program, and increased emphases on multicultural
education. This school was not using portfolio assessment yet. Assessments were done with report cards, and one conference with parents
each year. As with each of the schools, children who were in specialized
programs, such as English as a Second Language (ESL) or Chapter I,
received additional assessments as part of that process.

Five of the seven African-American children we followed in this study
were classified as low socioeconomic status (SES) based on their eligibility
for federal subsidies for free/reduced breakfast and lunch, subsidized
housing, and/or parental occupational/educational background. Two of
the children (one boy, one girl) came from families where both parents
had been educated beyond the high school level, both parents were work-

ing, families were living in nonsubsidized housing, and neither child was eligible for free/reduced meals. Two children (two boys) were in a Chapter I program at Greendale, while none were in ESL.

LAKELAWN SCHOOL. Lakelawn is also a K–2 school, situated in the city's east side. It too was involved in the city's "paired-schools" plan. At the time of integration, approximately 75% of the children attending Lakelawn were low income and/or of minority ethnic and linguistic background. At the time our study began during the 1989–1990 school year, the majority of the city's Hmong population children attended Lakelawn. Children of color represented 38% of the total school population, with approximately half of the minority ethnic population Asian American, primarily Hmong. African-American children are the largest other single minority group in the school and 33% of the school's children were eligible for free or reduced lunch.

We worked with three of the six kindergarten teachers at Lakelawn and four of the eight first grade teachers; one kindergarten teacher with whom we worked was an African-American female, while all the other teachers at the school, except ESL teachers, were European American and female; six of the total of seven kindergarten and first grade teachers were female. Teachers varied in teaching experience; two teachers were in their first year of teaching, while others had taught from 7 to 20 years. The male principal had been principal of the original K–5 school (prior to pairing) for over 20 years and was considered in the district to be a strong leader.

The school had initiated model pilot "primary education" programs, based on Developmentally Appropriate Practice guidelines, and had also initiated the first district pilot program on portfolio assessment. The school chose to offer two conferences with parents per year. The ESL program, which all of our sample children were in, also gave additional assessments on language and reading by ESL teachers during both the kindergarten and first grade years in both Hmong and English.

All of the 10 Hmong children (6 girls, 4 boys) lived in a low-income subsidized housing area called Runnymeade from which they were bused to Lakelawn School. All 10 were considered to be from low-income, lower class families, as they were in subsidized housing and were eligible for free and reduced price meals. While the majority of mothers had attended no or only some primary school and the majority spoke little English, the educational backgrounds of the fathers varied more, with some fathers speaking more English than others, and two attending a local technical college. In addition, others in the home, such as children's older siblings, varied in English use, and language use in the

Hmong homes was an important variable as we tracked children's progress and parent-teacher interaction through their early school years.

OAKHILL SCHOOL. This is the K–5 grade school we included in our study. It was not part of the original pairing plan. Located in a well-to-do neighborhood in the city's northern region, there were about 425 children in the school at the time of our study. More than 70% of the children were European American, while 28% of the children were Latino American, African American, and Asian American. About 66% of the school's children were from middle- to upper middle-class family backgrounds while 33% received free or reduced-price breakfasts and hot lunches.

Five of the six Latino children (one girl, four boys) we studied were in Oakhill School, with the sixth, a boy, a Lakelawn School student (described above). All five of the Latino children from Oakhill were living in subsidized housing and all were eligible for free and reduced lunch. All five were in ESL programs, although only four of the five were limited English speakers. Parents' backgrounds varied; the majority of the children lived in extended families with two or more adults (grandparents, aunts, uncles) and Spanish was the primary language spoken in the children's homes. The majority of families had at least one parent who worked, in a low-wage job, and most had high school education or less. The one Latino boy whom we studied at Lakelawn School had a Mexican-American mother and an Anglo-American father; both parents spoke fluent English and had been educated at the university level. They lived in a single family house and were considered middle class.

The two kindergarten and two first grade teachers from Oakhill School who participated in our project were European-American females. Indeed, with the exception of aides, and the principal, who was male, the remaining members of the staff were European American and female. Sample teachers' teaching experience ranged from 5 to 25 years at their grade levels. The school was considered innovative and effective, and was involved with a variety of reforms, including each of the reform efforts described above, including special after-school parent involvement programs, half-day afternoon kindergartens for low-income children of color, portfolio assessments, and additional conferences with parents.

Methodology

SELECTION OF SCHOOLS, TEACHERS, AND CHILDREN. As suggested above, the three schools we worked with were selected primarily on the basis of varying race, ethnicity, language, and class populations. Principals were approached and once they agreed to allow us to ask teachers to participate, meetings with kindergarten teachers for the first year of our study were arranged. We described the objectives of our study generally to kindergarten teachers in all three schools. Teachers were selected if they volunteered for the study, were recommended as effective by principals, and had three or more children in their classroom from at least one of the ethnic groups we were interested in including in our sample, as our intent was to select no more than three classrooms, from each school, to study intensively. Seven kindergarten teachers across the three schools were selected in this manner. When children moved to first grade, these procedures were repeated, but were dictated by child placement to a much greater extent. Eight first grade teachers were included in the second year of our study.

At the beginning of kindergarten, African-American, Hmong, and Latino children were selected after parents were approached about their child (and the family) participating in the study. Each family who agreed to participate in the study was told that the study would require home as well as school observations of children during at least a 2-year period, interviews with parents and children's teachers, and permission to have access to children's school files, scores, and other data. Each family was promised a small stipend for their time each year. We were unable to reach some parents to obtain permission, despite many attempts. All of the Latino and Hmong families who were approached agreed to participate. The majority of the African-American families also agreed to participate, but several did not, due to time constraints or stated discomfort with observers in their homes.

The 23 kindergarten-age children whose families agreed to participate (6 Latino, 7 African-American, and 10 Hmong children) were observed an average of once per week in classrooms and at least once per month in homes throughout their kindergarten and first grade years (1989/90 and 1990/91), as well as during the summer between these 2 school years. Each observation (home or school) lasted approximately 3 hours. The first two authors, both European Americans, conducted school observations and teacher interviews, while the third author, a Peruvian native, conducted home observations and parent interviews in Spanish with Latino families; two African-American research assistants conducted the majority of the observations and interviews with African-American families; and two European Americans who spoke Hmong and one Hmong research assistant conducted observations and interviews with Hmong children and families over the years of the study. Each teacher was formally interviewed twice per year (January and May or June) regarding a variety of issues, including assessments of the targeted children we were observing as well as assessments of other children in their classes. They were also interviewed regarding parent-teacher communication (see Bloch & Tabachnick, in press). In addition, parents were interviewed periodically with a particular focus on parent-teacher involvement and their perceptions and understanding of school-based communications including report cards, conferences, and newsletters, and about their understanding of children's progress in school.

ANALYSES: ASSESSMENT OF TEACHER PERSPECTIVES ON CHILDREN. We examined teacher beliefs and perspectives about children by looking at ways teachers had talked or written about them. Data analyzed for this paper include screener results, teachers' informal and formal remarks about the need to do referrals or special assessments of children, tape-recorded remarks made during formal twice per year interviews with teachers, informal remarks made about children's progress in school, and ratings and comments in the two to three times per year report cards sent home to parents. In the formal tape-recorded interviews, teachers were asked, "When you think about *child name,* would you consider him/her to be in the top, middle, or lower third of his class in academic areas? in social behavior? in development?" Teachers were asked to describe the way they thought about academic or social development. They were specifically reminded "that teachers think of these in different ways, and have somewhat different priorities for teaching and assessment" before they described what they thought about when they described children as being in the top, middle, or lower third on academics or social behavior. In addition, for the Hmong and Latino children, we specifically asked for a report on children's language skills. Data were analyzed and are presented based upon teachers' ratings of children (the next section), and on the basis of their qualitatively analyzed remarks (the final section of data analysis).

Report cards were developed by each school and were rated somewhat differently (1, 2, or 3 vs. check, check plus, or U, S, S+). The report cards, and other narrative comments that accompanied report cards, or that were in children's files, were analyzed for the substantive direction of assessment (e.g., "child is still having trouble identifying letters") as well as for overall comments. Qualitative analyses of the interview transcripts and records in children's files aimed to develop images of teachers' perspectives of each child's progress.

In our data analyses and in our presentation in this chapter, we were attempting to address the following questions: How did teachers perceive children were doing by the end of first grade? What were the criteria teachers used in making statements about assessments in different areas? In particular, how were they related to the ethnicity, class, gender, and language of children?

Results

KINDERGARTEN SCREENER. In order to examine teachers' perspectives on children's achievement by the end of first grade, we initially examined results on the district-developed kindergarten screener for teacher judgments on skills children had prior to the kindergarten year. While the district screener is not nationally standardized, it represents data teachers collected on children, data they had available to them initially, and data they frequently used to place children in Chapter I or other special service classes (ESL; Special Needs services).

Sample children's scores on the kindergarten screener ranged from 0 missed to 15 missed of the 30 items presented. The average number of items missed by sample Latino children screened at Oakhill School was greater than the average number missed by Hmong children screened at Lakelawn School or the African-American children screened at Greendale School. Although the kindergarten screener was administered in the children's primary language, the timing of the administration was different for the two groups; Hmong children were screened at the end of the first semester in kindergarten under the assumption that there would be greater school and assessment familiarity for children after a short period in school. In contrast, the Latino children were assessed prior to beginning kindergarten; therefore, timing of the assessment may have influenced results. African-American children, who may have had fewer language problems relative to assessment, were also assessed prior to kindergarten entry.

The results of the screener located children for the teachers and indicate that, at least at the beginning of kindergarten, African-American children were on a par with Hmong children, and assessed slightly better than Latino children, given the qualifications made above concerning the timing of testing.

TEACHER PERSPECTIVES AT THE END OF FIRST GRADE: INTERVIEW RATINGS AND REPORT CARD COMMENTS. After examining the kindergarten screener results, we examined classroom teacher perspectives on children as they spoke about them in our interviews, and as they rated and wrote comments about them in children's report cards. Based upon qualitative analyses of reports by kindergarten, first grade, and specialized (e.g., ESL, Chapter I) teachers, we categorized perspectives on individual sample children's academic and social skills by the end of first grade as one of the following:

1. above average by the end of first grade;
2. average academically;
3. low-average (making significant progress toward average); or
4. below average (having a lot of trouble; toward the bottom of class; low reading and math skills, poor work or social behavior).

On this rough basis, according to teacher comments, we determined that two of six Latino children we studied were thought to be average (one boy) or above (one boy). The above average classification was given to the one child in the group whose parents were primarily English speakers, middle class, and had been educated at the university level. Using a similar methodology, we found that two of seven African-American children were also considered to be above average (one girl) or at average grade level (one boy). These two children were from the only two African-American families where parents had one or more years of post-high school or university education. In the Hmong sample, teachers categorized three children (one girl and two boys) as average, and one child (one boy) as above average. While we did not have a formal assessment of parents' English language competence, reports by teachers and our observers on parents' use of English at home and in teacher-parent conferences suggested that the "above average" boy, and the "average" girl had at least one parent at home who spoke considerable English, and that English was used frequently at home with the children.

Three of six Latino children were categorized as being low-average (one girl, two boys) because they were "making good progress but below grade level" in academic areas such as reading. The last child was categorized as below average (one boy). The one girl in the Latino sample, from a family where "Spanglish" was spoken at home, was considered to be doing below average work in reading by her classroom teacher, but closer to average work by her ESL teacher, and was, as others were, placed in the low-average grouping because of this type of mixed description. Three of seven (two girls, one boy) African-American children were considered to be at low-average (making good progress, but still lower than average grade level), and two at below grade level (two boys) by the end of their first grade year.

In the Hmong sample, teacher comments were more explicit about some children being in a "low-average" group. While our interview question asked for a three-category type of rating (above, average, below), they initiated the term "low-average" which, after consideration, we also used for children from other schools. Teachers categorized 4 of 10 Hmong children as low-average (3 girls, 1 boy) and 2 children (2 girls) as below average.

These frequencies are represented in Table 12.1 and suggest that in our small sample, by the end of first grade, there were no obvious differences in teachers' assessments by gender. About 78% of the children were said to be doing "low-average," "average," or "above average" work (18 of 23 children across the three schools). The few children who were doing above average work were children of better educated parents, or in the case of the Hmong, parents who spoke the most English in the home. A majority of the children we studied at all three schools were still reading below first grade level, according to assessments done at the schools, with five children (the "below average group") having significant problems at the end of first grade. According to our referral reports (see below), three of these "below average" children were being assessed for possible special education/special needs classroom placement, although, as we've followed children into second grade, none were so placed during their second grade years.

In the analysis above, we used "low-average" as a *positive* category representing the progress of some children. Examining the data from a different perspective, as the evidence of children's failure to at least reach their class average level, shows a different portrait. If "low-average" is added to the "below average" category, and our terminology for description is somewhat changed, we might say that "only 8/23 children studied were said to be doing average work or greater" or "15/23 children in this sample were below average in their work according to teachers." The minor change in tallying process and language in both quoted passages underlines the social constructions involved in discourse and categoriza-

Table 12.1. Teacher Assessments of Below, Low-Average, Average, or Above Average First Grade Work[1]

School:	Oakhill		Greendale		Lakelawn		
Ethnic Group:	Latino ($n = 6$)		African American ($n = 7$)		Hmong ($n = 10$)		
Gender:	F	M	F	M	F	M	Total
Above Average		1	1			1	3
Average		1		1	1	2	5
Low-Average	1	2	2	1	3	1	10
Below Average		1		2	2		5
Total	1	5	3	4	6	4	23

[1]Based on review of interview/report card data.

tion systems as we label children, or try to draw a static picture of assessment, for decision purposes. By school, we see that the picture appears similar according to this latter classification system.

SPECIAL PLACEMENTS OR REFERRALS. We examined teacher reports of children's placement in ESL and Chapter I classes. All but one of the Latino and Hmong children attended ESL classes despite the fact that one of the Latino children only spoke English; none were also in Chapter I classes because school policy was against doubling the "pull-out" of children. The only Latino child not enrolled in ESL was the "above average child," at Lakelawn School, who entered kindergarten speaking excellent English (English is the parents' first language). Two of the seven African-American children we studied were in Chapter I in the kindergarten and first grade years.

Suggestions for physical checkups because teachers perceived potential problems, or decisions to initiate referral/assessment processes for special educational needs and services were examined. At Greendale School, three of the seven African-American children we studied were referred at some time during their first 2 years at the school. One girl was referred for physical checkups because "she walked and moved so slowly" during her early months in kindergarten; one boy was referred to "Building Team" to check for learning disabilities during first grade because he was judged to be slow, relative to others the teacher had taught, in learning letters and letter sounds, and also was considered a behavioral problem. A second boy was referred for checkups for attention deficit disorder, because according to his teacher, he did not attend to his work for long enough to regularly get it done within assigned time periods. At Lakelawn School, one Hmong girl was being referred for "Building Team" consideration because her teacher worried that her mathematical concept development was low in first grade, compared with other children; the teacher suggested that the child only knew the concept of "twoness," which was deficient at that point of first grade. When asked if the child had been tested in Hmong, the teacher thought it hadn't been done, but would be a good idea. There were no reported referrals for Latino children in our sample at Oakhill School. Thus, by the end of first grade, there had been three (3/7) suggestions for referrals for physical or special needs assessment at Greendale School for African-American children, one (1/10) suggestion for referral for Hmong children at Lakelawn School, and no suggestions for referrals (0/6) at Oakhill School for the Latino children.

DISCUSSION. The brief examination of teacher assessments based on kindergarten screener, other assessments, including portfolio data on a variety of reading/language skills, and other skills and behavior children displayed showed us that:

1. Schools and teachers varied in the ways they talked about and attempted to categorize or label children, and rough categorization systems (above average, average, low-average, below average) did distinguish children to some degree by their ethnicity, language background, class (if educational background of parents is used as the primary indicator), and gender (see the next section for more discussion of this category); the clearest pattern was that children whose parents had some knowledge and use of English at home, as well as those whose parents had somewhat greater education than the others were perceived as doing better than children whose parents had less English or less education;

2. Referrals for special examinations or diagnosis for disabilities or special needs were made by well-intentioned teachers without full knowledge of children's background or skills, and referrals were slightly higher with the African-American children in Greendale School than in the other schools where Hmong and Latino children were being observed;[2]

3. Teacher assessments on children's "level" were very difficult to interpret across the three schools because teachers used different ways of talking about children and criteria for making their summary judgments of "average," "low-average," and "below average."

What Evidence Did Teachers Use to Form Their Perspectives?

While we examined a variety of forms of evidence relating to academic, intellectual, language, and social aspects of children, in this section we focus on the teachers' knowledge of language and its role in the development of their perspectives about children. We then turn more briefly to ways in which teachers expressed their knowledge of children's social and cultural abilities as these categories represent the way teachers spoke of children, and appeared to have been primary influences on the way teachers and others perceived children.

LANGUAGE. Language was an important factor in teachers' assessments of the academic and social development of children in all three groups. While our home observations showed the rich use of language in each of the children's interactions with others at home and in their play and story-telling with siblings, relatives, and peers outside the home, classroom teachers appeared to know little of the language competence of their Latino, Hmong, or African-American children other than the fact that they spoke Spanish, Hmong, or non-standard English at home, and were making progress in learning or perfecting standard English.

For Hmong children, for example, language was an obvious contributor to their level of success in their classrooms. Hmong children were observed to speak in Hmong to one another as they carried out school tasks or played outside at recess. This pattern, as long as there were other Hmong friends in the classroom, continued throughout kindergarten and first grade.

Hmong children continued to use their native language in school and playground much more frequently than we observed with Latino children. Two Hmong children whose parents spoke English at home, spoke English with non-Hmong speakers earlier than the other children; even these two appeared to prefer to speak Hmong with other Hmong children, when it was possible. Perhaps to discourage continued reliance on Hmong, several of the Hmong children's parents made requests that their children be placed in classrooms with no Hmong friends in them. Of the 10 children we observed, three parents made this explicit request so that their children "could learn English faster."

The Hmong children used English haltingly and with noticeably accented speech. They typically sat at the back during large group instruction, often attending to each other rather than the teacher and appeared to understand little of a story or instruction. As we did our interviews with teachers, one of the first characteristics these teachers commented on was the children's use or nonuse of English. Teachers noted that they spoke little English or that they were beginning to speak more and participate more in the language-saturated activities of the kindergarten and first grade classrooms—sharing and telling stories, listening and following directions, reading, writing, and interacting casually in play. Teachers were generally sensitive to the Hmong children's struggles to understand, but at times the teachers were unable to decide if they were confronting misunderstanding or misbehavior. As one teacher noted:

> The three of them have just really come on. People comment on how they have just changed from being very quiet and to themselves. More positive interactions. . . . They are participating more in the group. You know, when you ask them a question and they don't answer, then you wonder if they understand what you are saying.

Neng talks a lot more . . . in English, so you get a better idea of what his thought processes are and what his language actually is. But Re, *she refuses to talk. She has a real stubborn streak in her* and I don't know whether language is a problem for her or she's just afraid to make a mistake, so (she doesn't) say anything. (First grade teacher, 11/90)

At Lakelawn School, ESL teachers and the Hmong bilingual interpreter did many assessments of children's language and reading abilities, and worked closely with children's reading instruction. Because of the frequency of specific assessments on language and reading development, the ESL teachers were able to give detailed comments about children's understanding of language and its relation to the reading and classroom process. Despite this, our transcripts show little communication between these teachers and the classroom teachers; therefore, classroom teachers' knowledge of children's native and English language abilities was incomplete and inevitably affected the accuracy of their own assessments, and in many cases instruction. This was particularly true when assessing little girls, who were much more likely to be quiet in the classroom. Teachers had little knowledge of children's oral language competence in Hmong. Teachers' assessments, based on oral participation in English, easy writing in English, and fairly rapid accumulation of sight words, beginning and end sounds, and vocabulary, were biased against girls who were taught not to participate as actively in discussions with adults and against children whose parents could not or would not speak English at home.

For the Latino children, language may have been masked as a factor influencing comprehension and academic achievement because unlike the Hmong children, the Latino children appeared to speak unaccented English fairly fluently. Although several had almost no English when they entered kindergarten, by the end of the kindergarten year they were never heard to speak Spanish in the classroom. Teachers were aware of each child's language background, but still tended to overlook its details or to interpret children's behavior as though language was not an influencing factor.

Even with his math and that type of stuff, you don't think he's listening but he will give you the right answer once in a while and (I'll think), "It came from you, Pedro?" And we do. We have an image of each child and it's like, "Gee, that sure didn't fit what I thought." (Kindergarten teacher, 3/90)

His drawings are very carefully done and lots and lots of little details. He sees a lot. And the children will say to you that Antonio is a good artist. He's getting better at writing in his journal but he chooses to draw rather than do the writing...and I have to push him to do some writing to go along with the drawings, but he has absolutely gorgeous drawings. He's very talented. (First grade teacher, 2/91)

Art is a language with enormous potential for describing and interpreting experience so that it can be communicated to others. While Antonio's artwork is valued for its own sake, his teacher does not seem to connect his drawing to his interest in communicating to others what he is thinking. Antonio, on the other hand, does not appear to recognize ways that words and phrases can extend and enhance his artistic statements. That Antonio prefers artwork to writing as a way to "speak" through his journal may be because he believes he controls the language of art more completely than he controls writing in English.

Both teachers are very positive about these two children and sensitive to subtleties of their behavior. Why does Pedro appear not to be listening, not paying attention to the teacher's instruction? Why does Antonio use drawing to "write" in his journal? It is not at all clear how to answer. Children whose first language is English are encased in the sounds and rhythms of English from the time they begin to hear. Throughout the first 5 or 6 years of life, they have experienced the English language as a part of being. Words and phrases leave acquired layers of meaning through connections to other words, to words in different forms and contexts (spoken, written, used for different meanings), and to actions and nonverbal images. That thickness of layers is a reservoir of meanings that may be missing or much shallower for children for whom English is not a first language. When Pedro does not seem to be listening (he doesn't react or can't answer a question or follow a direction), he might be inattentive; alternatively, he may simply not understand what is required. When he does respond well, he may understand or guess correctly what he has been asked to do. It is, indeed, unclear if the absence of reservoirs of meaning for English words and sentences has led to behavior that can be explained in terms of struggles to make sense of language or if these are social choices (e.g. inattentiveness) that these children are making.

Success in using language in context and difficulties when elements of language are decontextualized hints, at least, that a fragile understanding of English may be a critical factor in each child's academic achievement.

Teachers use students' ability to decode isolated words as a source of assessment, as in this comment.

> Antonio (is) really soaring this year. He's doing very well. Although AV (the first grade teacher) was discouraged that . . . or maybe not discouraged, but she observed that on some of the tests he has trouble reading words in isolation or he didn't seem to test at the level she thought he was at, but he can read independently very well. (ESL teacher, 6/91)

Mastering English affected children's entire school experience. The following quote from a teacher interview illustrates this.

Interviewer: What does Julio do best?

Teacher: Lots of socializing. . . . He loves to talk . . . he interacts with the other children quite well. Now he's had some difficulties with fights, but I think it's more getting drawn in. I don't think he's the one that initiates the disagreements, or . . . he gets more talked in, "let's go fight this person."

Interviewer: Who does he fight with?

Teacher: Well, with Rafael, and then some other children from his area . . . Jorge . . . I think Julio is a very gentle, sweet boy. I think he enjoys his friends. He enjoys being in the classroom. I think he immensely enjoys school, but I think it's more for the social. . . . I think that's what he's here for right now, and we really have to push him to start working harder.. . . . I see him as kind of being kind of a quiet, meeker personality, and perhaps all the socializing is good for him this year . . . he's learning how to interact. He's doing a lot of talking to solve problems. He's learning a lot of school behaviors. And that's all real important so he can settle down.

Interviewer: School behaviors like?

Teacher: Just learning to follow routines. To be where he's supposed to be. To sit down at his desk when he's supposed to be working. Those are big things at the beginning of the year. They were really tough for him to do. And so I think he's gaining confidence in all that . . . in all those routines so that he feels good about where he's supposed to be and what he's supposed to be doing. But we have to get him to attend more . . . he doesn't tend to ask questions . . . he doesn't tend to ask for help. . . . He'll sit there for a while before he says anything, and you don't realize that he needs you. Where if Rafael wants you, you know it right away. He comes right up. "I don't know how to do this" (First grade teacher 2/91).

The ESL teacher in Oakhill School says in a separate interview that Julio has struggled with language all year, perhaps more than others. He complains in the privacy of ESL that he doesn't understand whole group instruction, or problem solving situations when explained verbally. He's not comfortable talking or asking questions in English. There are very similar issues at Lakelawn School where some of the Hmong children seem to be faulted in the same way, whereas the two Hmong children (one girl and one boy) whose parents speak better English at home and whose parents asked specifically for their children to be in first or second grade classrooms with few other Hmong children are assessed more positively, and appear to be doing better in subjects dominated by English comprehension.

Finally, for the African-American children in our study, language was an invisible factor to teachers in accounting for some of the children's "nonconventional" behavior. When a child was observed to spend only a short time concentrating on trying to complete an assigned task, his behavior was labeled "potential attention deficit" or his inability to understand the directions given were taken to be signs of low ability or even of disability. When a child had difficulty, or hesitated to answer what was, to the teacher, an obvious question, it was frequently interpreted as resistance or inability. There was little expectation that the form of the language used or the context of language use might be so unfamiliar or different that the child would need to be taught the point of the question or the command before the adequacy of a response could be judged. (See, for example, Heath, 1983.)

For children in all three groups language was an important factor influencing teachers' decisions about children's academic and social performance.

Social Behavior

At Oakhill, Lakelawn, and Greendale Schools, we also saw other interesting twists on interpretations of social behavior. At Greendale School, the African-American children were consistently assessed poorly for social difficulties in school and out on the playground. At the Oakhill and Lakelawn schools, by contrast, social difficulties, such as the fighting by several Latino children mentioned in an earlier example, were seen as problematic, but solvable. They were viewed as developmental issues, and also as part of the dynamic nature of friendship relations for boys; at Greendale, fighting on the playground was treated as an offense punishable by a visit to the principal's office. Repeated offenses by Brian, the one "average" ability African-American boy at Greendale, colored his teachers' judgements over both his kindergarten and first grade years; they were discussed at each parent-teacher conference, and took up half the brief time allotted for report card conferences. The same types of repeat offenses by Rafael, an average ability Latino boy at Oakhill were seen as "mischievous" behavior that could be handled. The construction of both the meaning and the consequences of the behavior were different for the two boys. It seems likely that the consequences in the long run for Brian at Greendale School, where he has been seen as a periodic "trouble maker" since kindergarten, will outweigh the fact that he is otherwise doing well in school. Supporting evidence for this is that reference to his "misbehavior" takes up most of the space in his cumulative file while little reference is made about his academic achievements (e.g., science project for which Brian was honored during his first grade year.) Comments on other children, in teacher interviews and report cards, suggest that the African-American children at Greendale are being seen as breakers of school rules for social behavior.

Our argument here is not that there were no incidents at any of these schools, but that both our field notes and our interviews across the first 2 years of the study provide evidence that Greendale School teachers were faulting children for social behavior, especially at an early age. While the philosophy was to stop poor behavior early before it escalates, and to make the "school safe for everyone," the 5- and 6-year-olds' social behavior works decidedly against them within the school context at Greendale compared to the other two schools. As Ladson-Billings (1990) and others have written, a more culturally-relevant curriculum for African-American children would be organized around movement, the pride in voice and telling stories, and would capture the strengths children bring, rather than ignoring them or faulting children for their display.

Within this context, it is surprising to note that teachers in the other two schools said they wanted the Hmong children, particularly girls, and, on occasion, Latino children, to be less passive and more assertive in asking questions; fighting was seen as "merely" mischievous and manageable. On the other hand, African-American girls' "busy-bodiness" or fighting by several of the boys at Greendale, was assessed as neither mischievous, nor easily handled, even by the principal. School cultures differ. Some can accommodate difference: some insist on narrow conformity.

CONCLUSION

The purpose of this paper was to illustrate issues we have encountered in looking at teachers' assessments for these different children. We still do not know whether there are "school" or "teacher cultures" of assessment, based upon our analysis to date, but the existence of both teacher and school cultures is a strong possibility for one interpretation of our data. We do not know how general our findings are, or whether other teachers in the same schools or other teachers in different schools would assess African-American, Latino, or Hmong children the same way, or quite differently.

However, we believe that in the schools in which we have done observations there are issues and problems related to children's assessment that have to do as much with school norms and belief systems as they have to do with children's individual strengths or their family backgrounds. We believe that teacher perspectives and knowledge of children's strengths have as much to do with perspectives and knowledge about their backgrounds as with their in-school abilities, achievements, and characteristics.

The most important of our messages is about the ways in which images color the canvas differently for children on the basis of the types of information teachers have, their backgrounds of experience, and beliefs that they bring to the formation of ideas about children. For example, while the portfolio assessments used by teachers in Oakhill and Lakelawn Schools were important additions to the assessment process, the way the portfolio contents were used, prioritized, and sifted by teachers as they made their judgments about children is most important. We conclude that there's likely to be no "objective" assessment of children; that all assessments are socially constructed on the basis of current and prior knowledge and the history of images that teachers bring to the schooling process.

In this chapter, we try to show the relationship between teacher perspectives on what should be assessed and what teachers, schools, and districts perceive is important; thus assessment is tightly woven into teacher/school curricular philosophy, and what people/systems believe is important. Thus, even if portfolio assessment, whole language, and cognitively based mathematics instruction are acknowledged as important within a district, school, or individual teacher's guidelines, other factors that are more important to the teacher are given greater priority in speaking of children, and in their instruction, and referral, if necessary. Over and over again, we saw teachers sifting through the information they had but paying greater attention to those aspects most important to them. Many times, assessments in reading, acknowledged to be critical, were overwhelmed by assessments of social behavior, that often weighed disproportionately heavily in teachers' and other school staff's ways of talking about children.

We also saw an affective tone in our data, similar to that which Smith and Shepherd (1988) and others point out, which appeared to influence the assessment process and outcomes. In Oakhill and Lakelawn Schools, where Latino and Hmong children were observed, there was a sense of the "we can do it" philosophy that was a catching and optimistic aspect of the atmosphere. While teachers still had trouble understanding children's backgrounds and language to the extent that we might wish, their attempts to see children as "making progress" and "getting better" rather than worse gave us hope for these children. In Greendale School, where African-American children were observed, this sense of expectation, positive affect, and optimism about helping children make progress, was felt only occasionally in our interviews. Any positive affect was less pervasive and indeed, often, replaced by a sense of "there are too many problems," "we can't surmount them." Yet many of the children's "problems" at Greendale school appeared surmountable within the school context; the difficulty seemed due to both teacher and staff perceptions of social problems children had in and out of school that were perceived, on occasion, as overwhelming and therefore clouded the way in which teachers and staff worked toward helping children in their academics. For example, teachers appeared to have given up on the two children (both African-American boys) that were being referred for possible special needs placement by the end of first grade; yet our observations suggested that there were many other options that remained for these children within the school, had the norms of the school supported other approaches. A third African-American boy at Greendale viewed as average in academic ability in teachers' perceptions and our category system, was having, according to his teachers, too much trouble socially. This perception of social difficulties, rather than the average academic work, colored judgments about the child and were disproportionately the subject of discussion with parents.

Finally, the most pervasive theme in our data was that the teachers, though typically very well intentioned, still had too little knowledge of all of their children's backgrounds to understand all of the different ways in which children's competencies could be utilized in the classroom and their learning. There was still a sense of school norms for language and behavior that included little room for the strengths, language, or values of others who were not part of the majority, middle-class European-American culture. In contrast, even with well-intentioned teachers, implicit standards affecting overall judgments were all based on the normative skills the majority culture of children could acquire. Even when teachers wished to speak about children's wonderful progress since they'd entered into school, there was still a pervasive expectation of needing to get children to the "average" or beyond on English language proficiency, reading, writing, arithmetic, and obedient social behavior. This "assimilationist theme" was believed to be for children's benefit; Hmong and Latino parents, to some extent, also pushed for rapid assimilation and language proficiency as their hope for children's success in school; several expressed wishes that their children would not be placed in following grades with their friends in order to facilitate English language learning for their children. The potential cost of this strategy is the loss of cultural or ethnic identity which could have long term effects on children, their families, and the broader multicultural community. Another possibility is resistance to such pressure, which also seems to cost children in the long run (e.g., Erickson, 1987).

Thus, the inability to acknowledge the strength of children's competence in their primary language or knowledge of the strengths children brought to school from their own cultural backgrounds hinders teachers' abilities to construct different, more inclusive, and stronger assessments of children, and to provide optimal instruction for children. Hmong girls were faulted in some ways for being very quiet in class (although in some ways teachers encouraged this quiet behavior), with no recognition of the cultural mandate to remain quiet in large groups or in formal settings. Their abilities in telling elaborate oral stories in Hmong that we observed in their homes were never known to teachers because the structure and expectations and knowledge systems failed to provide opportunities for such behaviors within the school setting. Similarly, a Latina girl and an African-American boy were praised to a small degree for the caretaking and responsibility they showed within the classroom, but these behaviors, taught to children at home, were not part of the general system of assessment for all children, and therefore were marginalized and less important aspects of teachers' assessments of children. Finally, teachers' perceptions of children's English language competence was imprecise, at best. As mentioned earlier, this, across all schools, had important effects on teachers' assessments of children, and most likely on their instruction for these children. In these ways, and others that we illustrated earlier, we have seen teachers' perspectives colored differently for children from different ethnic, language, gender, and class backgrounds.

Interaction must take place and should overlay cultural barriers. In those few cases where an individual has learned from experience to expect that collaboration, mutual interests, and mutual respect *do not exist* but *can be created,* an openness to learning across cultures can lead to greater mutual understanding and more effective communication. In those more frequent cases where personal histories have taught expectations of hostility, rejection, and conflicting interests that are not resolvable, then miscommunication continues and the gap of understanding and separate objectives widens. These personal histories of acceptance or rejection, of reaching out or protecting against contact, are based on layers of experience and individual (child, parent, teacher) and group (family, community, school) understandings. For parents it may be of childhood rejections and failures in school, of insensitive or hostile government officials, with schools being perceived as just another government agency trying to do them harm. For teachers it may have begun with learned distortions of history and learned attitudes of disrespect in childhood, seemingly confirmed by parents who "choose" not to attend school meetings or report card conferences or to fulfill other school-driven expectations.

In summary, we have tried to emphasize that many children were viewed fairly positively by teachers, and that there was a sense of optimism and success for some of the children we were observing as they were pushed toward acquiring the skills their middle-class European-American counterparts were also learning, or had acquired. We have also stressed teachers' good work, despite the image that their perspectives on assessment many times displayed the human frailties of bias, lack of sufficient knowledge, and others.

At the same time, the social constructions of "how children are doing" may and often do affect children throughout their lifetime. These constructions may affect their parents, their friends, and societal judgments about groups of children and people of different ethnic, language, gender, and class groups. In this chapter, we hope to illuminate some ways in which instruction and learning for all of these children can only get better.

ACKNOWLEDGMENTS

This chapter was originally presented at the 1992 American Education Research Association Meetings in San Francisco, California. Support for this project was provided by the Spencer Foundation. We acknowledge the assistance of research assistants and members of school staff and families who participated in the study. In addition, we thank Seehwa Cho, Jay Hammond Crodle, Carolyn Dean, and other assistants who helped us with the study.

NOTES

[1]The demographic statistics are from 1992 school district data, which are not cited specifically here to protect the confidentiality of the district. Sources are available when requested with confidentiality protected.

[2]This point—that labeling for disability or placement occurs without full knowledge of children's capabilities, and too easily for children of nondominant ethnic backgrounds—is not new (e.g., see Mehan, 1986; Taylor, 1991; and Trueba, et al., 1990).

REFERENCES

Apple, M. (1979). *Ideology and curriculum*. Boston: Routledge & Kegan Paul.

Becker, H., Geer, B., Hughes, E., & Strauss, A. (1961). *Boys in white*. Chicago: University of Chicago Press.

Bloch, M. N., & Tabachnick, B. R. (in press). Improving parent involvement as school reform: Rhetoric or reality? In N. Greenman, & K. Borman (Eds.), *Changing schools: Recapturing the past or inventing the future?* Albany, NY: SUNY Press.

Bredekamp, S. (1987). *Developmentally appropriate practice in early childhood programs serving children from birth through age five*. Washington DC: National Association for the Education of Young Children.

Delgado-Gaitan, C., & Trueba, H. (1990). *Crossing cultural borders: Education for inmigrant families in America*. London: Falmer Press.

Erickson, F. (1987). Transformation and school success: The politics and culture of educational achievement. *Anthropology and Education Quarterly, 18* (4), 335–356.

Gomez, M. E., Graue, M. E., & Bloch, M. N. (1991). Reassessing portfolio assessment: Rhetoric and reality. *Language Arts, 68,* 620–628.

Graue, M. E. (1992). *Ready for what: Consructing the meanings of readiness for kindergarten*. Buffalo, NY: SUNY Press.

Heath, S. B. (1983). *Ways with words*. London: Cambridge University Press.

Ladson-Billings, G. (1990). Like lightning in a bottle: Attempting to capture the pedagogical excellence of successful teachers of black students. *The International Journal of Qualitative Studies in Education 3,* 335–344.

Lareau, A. (1989). *Home Advantage*. Philadelphia: Falmer Press.

Mehan, H. (1986). *Handicapping the handicapped: Decision-making in students' educational careers*. Stanford, CA: Stanford University Press.

National Association for the Education of Young Children and National Association of Early Childhood Specialists in State Departments of Education. (1991). Guidelines for appropriate curriculum content and assessment in programs serving children ages three to eight. *Young Children,* 21–38.

Richardson, V., Casonova, U., Placier, P., & Guilfoyle, K. (1989). *School children at risk*. Philadelphia: Falmer Press.

Shepherd, L., & Smith, M. L. (1989). *Flunking grades: Research and policies on retention*. Philadelphia: Falmer Press.

Sleeter, C. and Grant, C. (1988). *Making choices for multicultural education: Five approaches to race, class, and gender*. Columbus, OH: Merrill.

Smith, M. L., & Shepherd, L. (1988). Kindergarten readiness and retention: A qualitative study of teachers' beliefs and practices. *American Educational Research Journal, 25* (3), 307–333.

Swadener, B. B. (1990). Children "at risk:" Etiology, critique and alternative paradigms. *Educational Foundations 4* (4), 17–39.

Tabachnick, B. R., & Zeichner, K. (1986). Teacher beliefs and classroom behaviors: Some teacher responses to inconsistency. In Ben–Peretz, M., Bromme, R., Halkes, R. (Eds.), *Advances of research on teacher thinking*. Berwyn, PA and Lisse, West Germany: Swets/North America and Swets and Zeitlinger.

Taylor, D. (1991). *Learning denied*. Portsmouth, NH: Heinemann Educational Books.

Trueba, H. T., Jacobs, L., and Kirton, E. (1990). *Cultural conflict and adaptation: The case of Hmong children in American society*. New York: Falmer Press.

Vogt, L., Jordan, C., & Tharp, R. (1987). Explaining school failure, producing school success: Two cases. *Anthropology and Education Quarterly 18*, 276–286.

Zeichner, K., Tabachnick, B. R., & Densmore, K. (1987). Individual, institutional, and cultural influences on the development of teachers' craft knowledge. In J. Calderhead (Ed.), *Exploring teachers' thinking*. London: Cassell.

13

• • • • • •

Language and Diversity in Early Childhood

Whose Voices Are Appropriate?

CELIA GENISHI, ANNE HAAS DYSON, AND REBEKAH FASSLER

The sounds of young children talking in schools and centers have always reflected the cultural and linguistic diversity of the United States, and this diversity is increasing. Listen, for example, to these two young students:

Child 1: F-H-I-S.
Child 2: No, T-H-I-S.
Child 1: Oh. T-H-I-S. T-H-I-S. Is same?
Child 2: Is same.
           (Fassler, in progress)

Here a Russian child is helping a Haitian child match words on a work-sheet. Their first languages, Russian and Haitian Creole, are just two of the nine languages these children and the teacher hear in their kindergarten classroom. It is quite different from a setting in which all speak standard English, as in the classroom of this pair of playful conversationalists:

Kevin: I'm not a boy. I'm a bully.
Dawnn: I'm not a girl. I'm a girly.
        (Wang, 1989, p. 5)

Or this one, a K–1 classroom populated by children who speak different dialects or varieties of English:

Anthony: And did you see those big ol', the big huge, the huge ol' fish? [The children have just returned from a trip to the aquarium.]

James: Yes.
Anthony: Gol. Hecka big.
Jesse: That was hecka, really, really big. That could eat us.

In this classroom, the phrase "hecka" was used almost exclusively by children, like Anthony and James, who spoke black vernacular English. But Jesse, a standard English speaker, seemed to be working to gain control over that word, just as Anthony, who used "hecka" with ease, worked to gain control over "huge."

These three examples of young children talking in school settings not only demonstrate how much each child knows about language, they also raise questions about how she or he came to know so much and how adults can create a curriculum that is appropriate for every child. When classrooms differ from each other and when children within them represent a variety of cultures, the issue of developmentally appropriate curriculum becomes a special challenge (as discussed by Williams in chapter 8). In this chapter we address aspects of that challenge, including recent research on developmentally appropriate practice, processes of language acquisition, and classroom interactions that support the oral and written language growth of children of different cultures.

THE FRAMEWORK OF
DEVELOPMENTALLY APPROPRIATE PRACTICE

The much-cited document, *Developmentally Appropriate Practice in Early Childhood Programs Serving Children from Birth through Age 8* (Bredekamp, 1987) was written in response to needs within the field of early childhood care and education. These needs were (1) quantitative, to aid the rapidly *increasing number of practitioners* with varied backgrounds and training who may lack information about "good" practice, and (2) qualitative, to offer general guidelines about *what kinds of practices* would benefit young children. Those practices contrast with highly structured or academic ones, once found mainly in skills-oriented elementary classrooms.

In our view the document describes "developmentally appropriate practice" (DAP) as *holistic* (providing for all areas of children's development: physical, emotional, social, and cognitive); *individual-focused* (curriculum grows out of teacher observation and informal assessment of each child); and *developmental-interactionist* (learning is an interactive process that takes into account the child's need to act upon the environment in a wide variety of contexts). Thus recommended practices do not include the teaching of skills through highly structured activities or using means of assessment that rely primarily on standardized testing. Recommendations also briefly refer to cultural differences and the need for non-stereotyping materials and activities.

Since the publication of the DAP guidelines, many observers have focused their attention on cultural differences among children and families, and some educators have articulated contrasting perspectives. Walsh (1989), for example, recommends that we view early childhood practices within a context broader than the classroom and a theoretical perspective that extends beyond individual development. Further, we should consider how practices fit into the history of the field and into the goals of particular communities.

Other researchers have not taken issue with the DAP guidelines directly, but their studies suggest alternative approaches to making decisions about early childhood practice. Graue's study (1992) of social interpretations of readiness for kindergarten is illustrative. Her ethnographic study shows through interviews with parents and teachers and observations in the participating schools that notions of readiness are *socially constructed*. Individual communities have their own views, that stem from their particular social and cultural history and values. The definitions or understandings of *appropriateness* that many parents and practitioners embrace, then, may have little to do with professional guidelines.

O'Loughlin (1992) offers a thorough critique in which he discusses the biases underlying DAP. He argues that many call Piagetian theory "constructivist," that is, each individual has a predisposition and ability to construe reality and construct knowledge and meaning for herself or himself; but O'Loughlin believes that in fact Piagetian theory is narrow because it values only rational (western) thinking. The author recommends a reconsideration of the term appropriate (for *whom* is DAP appropriate?), a questioning of the developmental/Piagetian theory on which it is based, and a challenge to the view of the teacher that DAP implies (as one who accepts prescriptions from an authoritative organization). Thus from a critical perspective, O'Loughlin articulates what he views as the bias toward white middle-class values in DAP.

LANGUAGE DEVELOPMENT FROM MULTIPLE PERSPECTIVES

Much of what we know about how children develop a first language is grounded in the perspective that O'Loughlin judges as too narrow, that of the middle class. In this sense the "classic" research on child language acquisition may be viewed as both pioneering and restricted. In the 1960s and early 1970s, for example, researchers such as Lois Bloom (1970), Roger Brown (1973), Wick Miller and Susan Ervin-Tripp (1964), and Katherine Nelson (1973) studied relatively small numbers (between 1 and 18 children in a single study) of middle-class subjects.

Some of these researchers' general conclusions about how children acquire language seem to be universal: For example, from the beginning children talk about actors and actions. They use language first about objects and people that are prominent in their worlds, and much of that language refers to their *own actions*. In addition, as children begin to develop *syntax,* or the grammatical rules that enable them to combine words in phrases or sentences, they develop a number of *grammars*. These are related to, but not identical to, adults' rules. Thus, English-speaking children might use words like "foots" or "hided" as they figure out for themselves how language works.

In the 1970s and 1980s, as researchers began to study infant language development, they found that even before words, infants learn intonational patterns—the melody of speech—as they also use gestures and facial expression to communicate, to participate in a "dance" with caregivers as they later fuse actions, melodies, and words (Bruner, 1983; Stern, 1977). At the same time, children learn the social rules about how words and sentences are used within the contexts of their families and communities.

Taking into account more varied contexts, researchers shifted their attention from English learners to members of other cultures (Ferguson & Slobin, 1973; Schieffelin & Ochs, 1986) and from the acquisition of linguistic *forms* or syntax to *functions* or uses of language. The kind of language a child acquires depends on how language functions in the social contexts of the child's family or community (Cazden, John, & Hymes, 1972; Heath, 1983; Labov, 1969), and ways of using language vary from context to context. Sociolinguists, as these researchers are called, found that from the beginning children learn not only rules for creating the sounds, words, and sentences of their language, but also social rules for communicating. Together the social and linguistic rules make up their communicative competence.

In the early years, then, between birth and about age 5, first-language learners acquire the fundamentals of a whole system of rules and meanings, rules about forming sentences, as well as conversations (see Dyson & Genishi, 1993; Genishi, 1988, 1992). To broaden their scope to include non-white, non-middle-class, or non-English-speaking perspectives, researchers and educators now need to take a sociolinguistic approach, that incorporates multiple perspectives, to see how language is acquired in different communities and in varied situations within communities and particular social contexts. A variety of school settings are presented next as we discuss aspects of language variation within the contexts of early childhood classrooms and the curricula enacted in them.

COMMUNITY-BASED SETTINGS: A BILINGUAL EXAMPLE

The multiple perspectives from which we view language development are reflected in the wide range of educational settings offered to families with young children. One example is the "alternative" model, that often originates from a need or desire within a particular community and may be a "community-based" or "magnet" center or school. A program for maintenance of bilingualism is an exemplar of this setting, and one such program is described next.

Maintaining Two Languages

A program we will call the "Center" was established in the 1970s in response to activist parents who wished to establish or maintain their children's abilities to use Spanish and English and, of equal importance, to transmit knowledge of and respect for their Mexican-American, or Chicano, heritage (Genishi, 1978). The Center, part of an urban public school system, took the form of a combined day care center and kindergarten (other grades were added in later years). The program had the look of many early childhood programs: a teacher and an aide, free-choice activities within the kindergarten classroom, some whole-class activities, some focus on learning letters and numbers, free play in and out of doors, and free-choice activities in the day care setting.

The *sound* of the Center, though, was not typical. For example, this is part of a class discussion conducted in Spanish about not interrupting when someone is speaking:

> Teacher: Una cosa que tenemos que aprender es cuando esá hablando otra person, tiene que esperar.
> [One thing that we have to learn is that when another person is talking, you have to wait.]
> Arturo: Como dice mi papá, que esperan, que tienen que esperar cuando están hablando la, la gente grande.
> [As my dad says, you have to, you have to wait when the, the grown-ups are talking.]
> Teacher: ¡Cierto! [Right!]
>
> (Genishi, 1976, p. 121)

Teachers, children, parents, and the Center administrator used Spanish and English, although a few children spoke little English and a few, little Spanish. Further, the content of whole-class lessons often focused on the community's culture; the history of pre-Columbian Mexico or the significance of the ongoing farmworkers' strike in California were occasional topics when Celia Genishi (1981) was observing in the kindergarten classroom. With little emphasis on teaching either Spanish or English formally, adults followed their own unstated rule of using Spanish with the children whenever possible.

The children in this setting, especially the four that Genishi studied in depth, appeared to speak the language that their listener knew best. Thus their primary goal was to communicate, to get their messages across. Teachers seemed to support this goal since they were never heard to tell children to speak one language or another.

Arturo illustrated his ability to alternate between languages, or *code switch,* as he played with toy astronauts:

> Arturo: Carlos, I'm going to (unclear) this thing.
> Carlos: Where's the astronaut? Where's the astronaut?
> Arturo: (speaking now to Jorge) Carlos me lo dió. [Carlos gave it to me.]
> Jorge: No, éste no es tuyo. [No, this isn't yours.]
> Arturo: ¡Yo lo hallé! [But I found it!]
>
> (Genishi, 1981, p. 140)

This brief conflict over who was entitled to the astronaut shows that Arturo, who most often spoke English easily, switched to Spanish when he spoke to Jorge, a child who spoke Spanish most of the time.

Similarly, in a tattling episode Arturo used Spanish with his teacher to talk about Miguel, a Spanish monolingual:

> Arturo: (speaking to Miguel) Mire, qué hicistes. [Look what you did.]
> (speaking now to teacher) Liz!
> Teacher: ¿Qué?
> Arturo: Lookit, qué hizo Miguel. [what Miguel did]
> El rayó mi papel con la tinta. [He put lines on my paper with ink.]
> Ves, Liz? [See, Liz?] Liz, ven aquí. [Liz, Come here.]
>
> (Genishi, 1981, pp. 147–148)

It seemed most important to Arturo that Miguel understand his tattling although the teacher remained less than responsive.

Through their use of language, then, the children in this bilingual setting easily accommodated to the frequent alternation between Spanish and English. The four children who were the focus of the study showed that their bilingualism was a resource across the varied settings of the Center, as well as with their families.

The overall goals of the Center were clearly both educational and political. Community and Center explicitly supported the use of more than one language and the cultural and historical views of a specific group. We see, then, why this was an alternative program; its goals are probably not those of the majority of parents or of taxpayers. Moreover, whether public schools should be the site for the maintenance of bilingualism is a point of conflict.

Considering Societal Contexts: Enduring Issues

The issues related to bilingual education that were discussed in the 1970s are still controversial in the 1990s. Many citizens do not support the maintenance of languages other than English and instead believe that children need to "become American." To clarify some aspects of this controversy, researchers as well as experts in bilingual education and second-language acquisition have taken looks at children whose lives include languages other than English.

In particular, Lily Wong-Fillmore (1976, 1991) has studied a variety of settings and language groups that vary in the ways they use language but are similar in the strength of parental and community concern with their children's learning and language education. Like the parents who helped found the Center, Wong-Fillmore believes that bilingualism is indeed a resource and that *losing* one's home language is as much a problem as acquiring English as a second language. Since language is an integral part of a family's culture, lacking a common language may create tensions within families and between generations.

Many who have lost their first/home languages are sympathetic to that position. Yet there are continuing questions about the effectiveness of bilingual education. A study by Ramirez, Yuen, and Ramey (1991, cited in Cazden, 1992), for example, shows that children in long-term bilingual programs perform about the same academically as those in other programs. Specifically, "late-exit" bilingual programs that attempt to maintain two languages throughout the elementary years are not statistically more effective than "early-exit" programs in which two languages are used through the second grade or English immersion ("English-only") programs. The descriptive (nonstatistical) data, though, seem to favor the late-exit bilingual classrooms.

Pease-Alvarez, Garcia, and Espinosa (1991) explore factors related to effective bilingual programs from the perspective of a kindergarten and a first-grade teacher, both bilingual in Spanish and English. The study highlights the importance of factors that are also discussed by Ramirez et al. (1991): the background and qualifications of teachers as well as parental involvement. Both teachers in the report by Pease-Alvarez et al. (1991) stated that their eagerness to learn about innovations (such as holistic approaches to instruction), their knowledge of the community, and the inclusion of family members in the classroom and curriculum contribute to whatever success they enjoy.

BRIDGING THE GAP:
WHEN THERE IS NO COMMON FIRST LANGUAGE

Listen in on a conversation involving speakers of Russian, Albanian, Vietnamese, and Punjabi in a setting quite different from the Center and other bilingual classrooms:

Rachel: We're friend.
Heddy: I your friend.
Thao: Me your friend Saritha.
Saritha: She likes you. She likes me.

These kindergartners are learning English as a second language, but their primary goal here seems to be to negotiate who is whose friend as they simultaneously handle their Play-Doh. Like first-language and bilingual learners, the girls demonstrate that social relationships are inseparable from the language-learning process.

Their classroom is one Rebekah Fassler has been observing for a period of 7 months during 2 academic years. Mrs. Barker, the teacher in this self-contained English as a Second Language (ESL) kindergarten, has been trained in both early childhood education and ESL, although her native language is English and she shares none of the children's home languages. The two observed classes in an urban public school have been composed of between 31 and 34 students, representing between seven and nine language backgrounds.

Since many children tend to be influenced more by peer contact than by talk with adults in second-language (L2) learning situations (Piper, 1993), the lack of native English-speaking children in this classroom has contributed to making this a less than ideal situation for language learning. However, as Rachel and her friends illustrated, the children, with their novice English and no other common language, have found ways to communicate about many things and for many purposes.

Finding Common Ground: Activity and Interaction in a Language-Rich Classroom

In this classroom, Mrs. Barker created an atmosphere in which talk was allowed to flourish over a wide range of activities. We describe a sampling of them here. During the first month of school in one area of the room, a seesaw was the site of oral communication as children negotiated turns and squealed "stop!" or "you have to push up there!" Opportunities for social interaction characterized by verbal communication were not limited to designated "play times."

The first table activities that were assigned as tasks for all members of the group were not academic, but art activities. During these activities, the teacher quickly established routines that fostered children's personal initiative: Children were encouraged to leave their seats to get their own materials and to approach the teacher to ask what to do next, to get verbal feedback on their work, and to obtain permission to "play." Early in the year Mrs. Barker explicitly referred to art time as "your time to talk."

As the teacher introduced academic activities, such as individual homework assignments involving writing letters and numbers and, later, copying the Class News from the blackboard, these activities were carried out in small groups with or near the teacher, while other children chattered freely over art work and manipulative toys. There was no clear demarcation (such as talking/no talking) between nonacademic tasks and academic tasks, and there were no explicit rules about speaking only English or not speaking other languages.

Further, the teacher did not forbid interaction or oral expression among children where it seemed to emerge naturally. Thus, she allowed partners on line to transform waiting for the bathroom into a social opportunity. On one such occasion, Penny (a Chinese speaker) fingered the long braids of her partner Irina (a Russian speaker), who then clapped Penny's hands. They and Joanna, Penny's twin, became involved in teaching and learning clapping patterns; and Irina interacted in part by kissing Penny on the cheek and hugging Joanna, who hugged her back. The fact that Irina had been speaking only Russian to everyone for the first 3 weeks of school made this nonverbal exchange a poignant one.

Materials often provided a common focus for communication. In early October, the teacher tried to guess Irina's meaning as Irina, talking earnestly in Russian, led her to her table and pointed to her crayons. Mrs. Barker said that she could use any color and selected an orange crayon for her. When Irina turned this down, Mrs. Barker on a hunch took her to look at a larger selection of crayons. Irina brightened as she chose a red crayon. The teacher commented, "Oh you want red!"

Phrases from Mrs. Barker's regulatory language also formed the core of conversation as they circulated among the children as, for example, when they argued over who loosened Vasti's name label from the table. As Saritha (Punjabi speaker) swept the floor nearby, Vasti (Spanish speaker) urged her to call the teacher over to see the damage and fix the blame on one of her table mates. When Saritha called the teacher over, Mrs. Barker said that "we can fix it" and "Don't make trouble, Saritha." Saritha immediately repeated to Vasti, Rachel, and Magda: "Don't make trouble, OK?" With the label fixed, Vasti proclaimed: "Now my name beautiful!" Rachel (Russian speaker) warned: "And no more, teacher say. No more. I forgot. No more trouble."

At group times, the teacher "listened hard" to children's verbal contributions as it took children's persistence plus Mrs. Barker's to figure out what was meant. On a morning when Mrs. Barker solicited children's suggestions for a list of "P" words that she was writing on a large chart, the children flooded her with P words from pickles to pigs, pumpkins, picnics, and potatoes. The teacher was at first mystified with the Chinese twins' offering of "P for pie-pie." With the recent Chinese New Year celebration still in mind, Mrs. Barker asked, "Is it something to eat?" The girls said no, and when they reminded her that "we didn't do pie-pie," Mrs. Barker asked Joanna to draw it so she could see what it was. As Joanna drew, her sister Penny began to sing "Pie-pie the sailorman." The mystery was cleared up, and Popeye was added to the list.

Constructing Shared Meaning: Strategies for Communication

Wong-Fillmore (1976, 1991) has found that successful negotiation of shared meaning in interactions involving second-language learners requires a mutual desire to be understood and to communicate. In our brief glimpse into an ESL kindergarten classroom, this mutual desire was visible in a wide variety of situations. Some of the situations, such as enjoying the ups and downs of the seesaw, by their nature required children of diverse language backgrounds to use English to accomplish a common goal. The opportunity to communicate for authentic purposes, considered essential for L2 learning (Seliger, 1983; Urzua, 1989), was present in many of the other situations described because the children were allowed to transform into social events such occasions as standing in line, doing art activities side by side, reading picture books, and working with letters.

Trying out a new language involves risk taking (Wong-Fillmore, 1991), and L2 learners make their own individual choices about whether, when, and with whom to talk (Genishi, 1989; Urzua, 1989). Even a child's formulaic repetition of the words of the song "Open, shut them"

with two friends may require more courage than chiming in anony-
mously amid 30 other children's voices. Encouraging children to move
around the classroom, allowing peer talk to be a component of most
activities, and varying children's seatmates for different activities widens
their choices of communicative partners.

Two factors that promote L2 acquisition, techniques for negotiating
shared meanings and a range of opportunities to interact for authentic
communicative purposes, were abundant in Mrs. Barker's classroom.
Moreover, it was evident from these classroom scenes that there is more
to communication than talk; nonverbal behavior, sensitive listening, and
a good deal of watching, all play crucial roles. These three elements
enhanced children's knowledge of the second language as well as the
teacher's ability to expand it.

In sum, although all children in this class had been designated "limited English proficient," they brought with them varying degrees of communicative competence that they applied as they used both their native
language and English. Mrs. Barker supported their enjoyment of social
interaction and in the process broadened their options as social beings
within a classroom community, speakers of English, children "learning to
be students," and emerging readers and writers.

VARIETIES OF ORAL AND WRITTEN ENGLISH: AN URBAN PRIMARY SCHOOL

The school children attending the urban K–3 school observed by Anne
Haas Dyson (in press) also reflected the differences in social and cultural
backgrounds found in city schools. The school served both an African-
American community of low-income and working-class households and
an ethnically diverse but primarily European-American community of
working- to middle-income households. For 2 years, she observed in this
school, guided by six "key" children, kindergartners through third
graders, all African American, who allowed her access to their peers and
neighborhood friends. Both the K–1 classroom observed the first year of
the study and the third grade observed in the second year were taught
by the same skilled teacher, Louise.

Exploring and Expanding Discourse Options

Unlike the children in the bilingual Center and Mrs. Barker's kindergarten, most of the children in this school spoke only English, but they
spoke diverse varieties of English. Listen, for example, to Berto, who is

Mexican American, and Jameel and Monique, who are African American. All three are English speakers, but they use features of English grammar (word choice, syntax, pronunciation rules) that are rooted in their socio-cultural heritages.

Jameel: [God's] bigger than everything.
Berto: No he isn't. He ain't bigger than everything.
Monique: (to Berto) You don't know.
Jameel: (to Berto) Uh huh.
Berto: No he ain't.
Jameel: Jesus his son.
Monique: He really Son. Uh huh. He's the Son. He is.
(Dyson, in press)

Attitudes toward varieties of English reflect the history of power rela-tionships in our society. Those varieties that are associated with the work-ing class and with ethnic and racial minorites are considered "nonstan-dard" or less prestigious, but they are fully developed language systems. Moreover, when children have opportunities to interact with others from different social and cultural backgrounds, they may use those forms as powerful options that help them accomplish their ends. "He ain't," Berto seems to know, is more definitive than "He isn't." "He really Son . . . He is," Monique asserts, using the *to be* verb for emphasis, a verb that, in black vernacular English, is optional in certain syntactic structures.

Children control not only different grammatical options but, also, dif-ferent stylistic options in language use, and these differences too reflect children's sociocultural heritages. For example, in telling lively stories with her friend Eugenie, Monique exploited the performative or artistic aspects of language, including its expressive sounds, its melodic intona-tions, and its potential for dramatic dialogue; such performative aspects of language use are rooted in oral traditions (Smitherman, 1986). In this conversation, Eugenie and Monique have been discussing how someone might get on your nerves and cause you to worry and become angry.

Eugenie: I'm talking about, it's this girl. Her name is Jennifer. She asks
    about *every*thing. . . . And she—and she—and she *wor::*ies me a lot.
    And she make me *an::*gry! (The colon indicates elongated sound)
Monique: 'Cause you couldn't—I know her. She supposed to be in a
    bungalow [a small building for preschool classrooms]. She goes
    blah, blah, blah. I say to [a child's name], "Let's stay by ourselves
    and don't let her bring that butt in here."
Eugenie: Oh: Wo::ah:!
Monique: Wo:ah!

In contrast, with her teacher, Monique's talk was invariably soft-spo-
ken, relatively standard in its grammar, and, often, straightforward, as she
used complex clauses, phrases, and carefully chosen vocabulary to make
her points. For example, during a class discussion of careers, Monique
explained why people say police *officers* instead of police *women:*
"Because they don't have to say man or woman they can just call their-
selves police officer. That's the best way to say it, without having to talk
about whether they're a boy or a girl or a woman or a man."

In her ethnographic project, Dyson aimed to illustrate that young
children may exploit discourse options when they learn to write, just as
they do when they speak. Young children's "written" texts are often mul-
timedia affairs, interweavings of pictures, written words, and spoken
ones. But those texts too draw on diverse cultural and language
resources. The children she observed used varied kinds of oral and written texts to accomplish a range of social goals.

For example, a dominant kind of social work in children's as well as
adults' worlds is *to establish social cohesion.* To do so with their peers,
the children often drew on material from popular culture—stories about
superheroes, verses by rap stars, or scenes from horror movies. Such
material was apt to elicit an "Oh yeah, I saw that too" from a child
addressee, or a "Me too, I like that too." Third grader Ayesha, for
instance, wrote a list of rap stars seen on the Grammy Awards show.
During rug time sharing, her piece was enthusiastically received: "M.C.
Hammer, *yes!* Bobby Brown, *yes!*"

On the other hand, all of the observed children also composed *to
engage in artful performances,* through which they hoped to gain others'
attention and respect. In doing so, they often drew on their oral folk
resources (i.e., the features of verbal art), and they also tended to explicitly manipulate their texts. For example, they tried to make words rhyme,
phrases rhythmic, dialogue fast-paced, and images funny. The aim was
not a confirming "me too" but a pleased and, maybe, surprised "Oh!" or
even laughter.

Jameel was an especially dramatic performer. To accompany drawn
and dramatized adventures, he wrote dialogue and rhythmic chants, just
as did some of his favorite children's authors (like Dr. Seuss). One early
text was about "shape space aliens," like Circle Man, who landed on a
small world only to be attacked and eaten by a great giant. Jameel
recorded Circle Man's fate (He [the giant] ut [ate] circle) and then wrote
the lament of the remaining aliens:

ho nos [Who knows]
so ho nos [So who knows]

He recited the verse in a suspenseful voice and then wrote a chant:

circle man circle man circle man

Jameel looked forward to performing his stories and showing his pictures to an appreciative audience during sharing time. During the year, he wrote pop songs and jokes, as well as more prose-like stories.

Jameel seldom wrote simply to present others with necessary information, but, like other observed children, he did so orally when given opportunities *to teach or explain information*. Jameel was careful and relatively explicit in his speech—although he often used humor and metaphoric language as explanatory tools. Like all the children, Jameel was most apt to adopt aspects of Louise's language (for example, special vocabulary words or phrases) when he adopted her guiding role. In the following excerpt, he teaches Dyson about birds:

We got lots of bird books. Would you like to read one of 'em? . . .
  [Jameel gets a bird alphabet book; he skips the pages Louise read
  that morning because "these are the things you already know about
  because you was here."]
This bird is very interesting. It eats little kinds of beans. . . . Let's see.
  This one is a dentist.
  [The dentist metaphor is Jameel's, not Louise's.]
This is a crocodile bird that cleans out the little stuff stuck up in his
  teeth.
  [This assertion is accurate.]
The crocodiles will never eat him. They will never eat their dentist.
  Now this, is a duck. It's a member of the duck family.

The observed children, with their diverse social roles and language resources, only sampled here, did not fit neatly into the social order Louise originally had expected. For example, Louise had imagined that each composing period would begin with ten minutes of "quiet writing time," but the children consistently talked. Moreover, Louise had anticipated children coming to the daily sharing time on the rug to communicate to a peer audience, who would offer comments and suggestions. But the desire to communicate per se was not the children's dominant goal. Further, the children objected to an advice-giving audience, a role, after all, that differs substantively from that of editor or formal critic in our common culture (for elaboration of this point, see Dyson, 1992, in press).

Like the children in the Center and in the multilingual kindergarten, Louise's children transformed their daily activities into varied kinds of peer social events. These events provided rich opportunities for the children to make use of and expand their ways of using language. Louise, in turn, made interactive space for their social goals and language resources, even as she modeled new ways with words.

Rethinking Issues of Discourse Variation in Early Childhood

Issues of English language varieties have been enduring and often divisive ones in early childhood education, whether the concern is linguistic features (word choice, syntax, pronunciation) or discourse strategies (e.g., ways of telling stories). Some educators argue for pluralism—for acknowledging and accepting language variations in the classroom—while others suggest such tolerance is misguided liberalism, denying some children access to the prestigious standard discourse forms.

To move beyond such dichomoties, we emphasize that language in use is inherently diverse—changing with situation, role, and activity—and humans are remarkably flexible language users: given a reason (and opportunities for practice), we are code-switchers, style collectors, and players with speech (Gallas, 1992; Garvey, 1990; Gilyard, 1991; Labov, 1969). Taking a long view, the overriding goal for language education throughout the preschool and school years should not be the mastery of any one genre or dialect but the capacity to negotiate among contexts, to be socially and politically astute in discourse use.

Children's sensitivity to social context—the ease with which they adapt their language to interactional goals they understand—allows us as educators to reconsider a common assumption about children's written language. The end goal of school literacy programs is often assumed to be children's control of a "decontextualized" style of language use (Olson, 1984), that is, language in which ideas are made explicit in tightly constructed prose, rather than implicitly understood by familiar conversational partners.

But language always exists within a kind of social relationship; for example, Jameel, Monique, and their peers produced relatively "decontextualized" language when they were teaching someone, not when they were entertaining others with oral or written stories. Thus, to assess and foster certain kinds of discourse styles and genres, educators may need to deliberately plan appropriate social contexts.

Experts in children's writing have encouraged teachers to arrange social situations in which children receive "responses" to their texts from "authentic" audiences of peers (e.g., Graves, 1983). But, as Louise's children illustrated, we must consider how children themselves interpret such situations. A teacher's occasion for a "whole group writing" conference (a time when individual children get feedback about their texts) might be a child's show time stage or an occasion for social cohesion. Children's expectations for the social roles of audience members, peer helpers, and teachers can be explicitly discussed and planned for with primary-grade children. In such ways we as educators help children begin to reflect on—and gain more deliberate control over—the complex social and language worlds in which they live.

MAKING SPACE FOR APPROPRIATENESS: DEVELOPMENTAL AND CULTURAL

In the literature of early childhood and language education, assumptions about the developmental paths of language learning have been narrowly defined for too long. If our aim is flexible, sophisticated language users, who are encouraged to grow and learn in developmentally appropriate settings, we begin by seeing learners from multiple perspectives. We work to view children's knowledge of diverse languages, dialects, and discourse patterns as a developmental "plus," not a developmental deficiency. Their vast knowledge becomes a deficiency only in classrooms, schools, or institutions that hold to a single model of language development. Thus our understandings of development cannot be rooted only in images of English-speaking children that are well "read-to" at home and accustomed to the lesson-like question-answer sequences of middle-class discourse. And we cannot assume that there are specific curricula that "match" specific ethnic and linguistic groups, for example a single ideal program for Spanish speakers or one for African-American children.

Research that looks carefully at what children do and say shows that classroom cultures are realized in particular ways: shaped by children's own ways of interpeting and responding to school situations and activities. In the classrooms we have just sampled, children can learn in diverse ways from each other and from adults who offer many opportunities for learning collaboratively to be speakers, friends, students, writers, and readers. A classroom culture is collaboratively created that is inclusive, spacious enough to incorporate what children construct together—the dynamic social order of their classroom—and what they bring with them from the cultures of home and community. As they grow as communicators, children continually draw on their knowledge of language and the world, their delight in the rhythm and rhyme of the languages and dialects they already know and those they are trying to learn, their fascination with popular media, and their abiding interest in each other.

REFERENCES

Bloom, L. (1970). *Language development: Form and function in emerging grammars*. Cambridge, MA: MIT Press.

Bredekamp, S. (Ed.). (1987). *Developmentally appropriate practice in early childhood programs serving children from birth through age 8* (rev. ed.). Washington, DC: National Association for the Education of Young Children.

Brown, R. (1973). *A first language: The early stages*. Cambridge, MA: Harvard University Press.

Bruner, J. S. (1983). *Child's talk*. New York: Norton.

Cazden, C. B. (1992). *Language minority education in the United States: Implications of the Ramirez Report*. Educational Practice Report: 3. Santa Cruz, CA: University of California, National Center for Research on Cultural Diversity and Second Language Learning.

Cazden, C. B., John, V. P., & Hymes, D. (Eds.). (1972). *Functions of language in the classroom*. New York: Teachers College Press.

Dyson, A. H. (in press). *Social worlds of children learning to write in an urban primary school*. New York: Teachers College Press.

Dyson, A. H. (1992). The case of the singing scientist: A performance perspective on the "stages" of school literacy. *Written Communication, 9,* 3–47.

Dyson, A. H., & Genishi, C. (1993). Visions of children as language users: Research on language and language education in early childhood. In B. Spodek (Ed.), *Handbook of research on young children* (pp. 123–136). New York: Macmillan.

Fassler, R. (in progress). *The growth of the use of English in a self-contained multi-language English as a second language kindergarten*. Dissertation in progress, Teachers College, Columbia University, New York.

Ferguson, C. A., & Slobin, D. I. (Eds.). (1973). *Studies of child language development*. New York: Holt, Rinehart & Winston.

Gallas, K. (1992). When the children take the chair: A study of sharing time in a primary classroom. *Language Arts, 69,* 172–182.

Garvey, C. (1990). *Play* (enlarged ed.). Cambridge, MA: Harvard University Press.

Genishi, C. (1976). *Rules for code-switching in young Spanish-English speakers: An exploratory study of language socialization*. Unpublished doctoral dissertation, University of California, Berkeley.

Genishi, C. (1978). Language use in a kindergarten program for maintenance of bilingualism. In H. LaFontaine, B. Persky, and L. Golubchick (Eds.), *Bilingual education* (pp. 185–190). Wayne, NJ: Avery Publishing.

Genishi, C. (1981). Code-switching in Chicano 6-year-olds. In R. Duran (Ed.), *Latino language and communicative behavior* (pp. 133–152). Norwood, NJ: Ablex.

Genishi, C. (1988). Research in Review: Children's language: Learning words from experience. *Young Children, 44* (1), 16–23.

Genishi, C. (1989). Observing the second language learner: An example of teachers' learning. *Language Arts, 66,* 509–515.

Genishi, C. (1992). Developing the foundation: Oral language and communicative competence. In C. Seefeldt (Ed.), *The early childhood curriculum: A review of current research* (rev. ed.) (pp. 85–117). New York: Teachers College Press.

Gilyard, K. (1991). *Voices of the self: A study of language competence*. Detroit: Wayne State University Press.

Graue, M. E. (1992). Social interpretations of readiness for kindergarten. *Early Childhood Research Quarterly, 7,* 225–244.

Graves, D. H. (1983). *Writing: Teachers and children at work*. Portsmouth, NH: Heinemann.

Heath, S. B. (1983). *Ways with words: Language, life, and work in communities and classrooms*. New York: Cambridge University Press.

Labov, W. (1969). The logic of nonstandard English. In J. E. Alatis (Ed.), *Report of the twentieth annual roundtable meeting on linguistics and language study* (pp. 1–44). Washington, DC: Georgetown University Press.

Miller, W., & Ervin, S. M. (1964). The development of grammar in child language. In U. Bellugi & R. Brown (Eds.), The acquisition of language. *Monographs of the Society for Research in Child Development, 29,* 9–34 (1, Serial No. 92).

Nelson, K. (1973). Structure and strategy in learning to talk. *Monographs of the Society for Research in Child Development, 38* (1–2, Serial No. 149).

O'Loughlin, M. (1992, September). *Appropriate for whom? A critique of the culture and class bias underlying developmentally appropriate practice in early childhood education*. Paper presented at the Conference on Reconceptualizing Early Childhood Education: Research, Theory, and Practice, Chicago.

Olson, D. (1984). "See! Jumping!": Some oral antecedents of literacy. In H. Goelman, A. Oberg, & F. Smith (Eds.), *Awakening to literacy*. Portsmouth, NH: Heinemann.

Pease-Alvarez, L., Garcia, E. E., & Espinosa, P. (1991). Effective instruction for language minority students: An early childhood case study. *Early Childhood Research Quarterly, 6,* 347–361.

Piper, T. (1993). *Language for all our children*. New York: Macmillan.

Ramirez, J. D., Yuen, S. D., & Ramey, D. R. (1991). *Longitudinal study of structured English immersion strategy, early-exit and late-exit transitional bilingual education programs for language-minority chidren*. Final report to the U. S. Department of Education. Executive Summary and Vols. 1 and 2. San Mateo, CA: Aguirre International.

Schieffelin, B. B., & Ochs, E. (Eds.) (1986). *Language socialization across cultures*. New York: Cambridge University Press.

Seliger, H. W. (1983). Learner interaction in the classroom and its effect on language acquisition. In H. W. Seliger & M. H. Long (Eds.), *Classroom oriented research in second language acquisition* (pp. 246–267). Rowley, MA; Newbury House.

Smitherman, G. (1986). *Talkin' and testifyin': The language of black America*. Detroit: Wayne State University Press.

Stern, D. (1977). *The first relationship: Infant and mother*. Cambridge. MA: Harvard University Press.

Urzua, C. (1989). I grow for a living. In P. Rigg & V.G. Allen (Eds.), *When they don't all speak English* (pp. 246–267). Rowley MA: Newbury House.

Walsh, D. (1989). Changes in kindergarten: Why here? Why now? *Early Child-hood Research Quarterly, 4,* 377–392.

Wang, M. H. (1989). *Playful language.* Unpublished term paper, Ohio State University, Columbus.

Wong-Fillmore, L. (1976). *The second time around: Cognitive and social strategies in second language acquisition* (Parts 1 and 2). Unpublished doctoral dissertation. Stanford University, Stanford, CA.

Wong-Fillmore, L. (1991). Language and cultural issues in early education. In S. L. Kagan (Ed.), *The care and education of America's young children: Obstacles and opportunities* (Part I) (pp. 30–49), the 90th Yearbook of the National Society for the Study of Education. Chicago: National Society for the Study of Education.

Index

•••••••

269

About the Authors
• • • • • •

Jane B. Atwater: *Associate Scientist, Juniper Gardens Children's Project, University of Kansas.* For the past 10 years, I have conducted research in a variety of early childhood programs for typically developing children and children with disabilities. These opportunities have enriched and challenged my understanding of effective teaching, facilitative child care environments, and factors that promote successful inclusion. One of my greatest influences has been the experience of working at the Juniper Gardens Children's Project—a project that has been based in a diverse inner-city community for 30 years and which works cooperatively with members of the community to foster the development and education of young children. My own work at Juniper Gardens has focused on the development of strategies to facilitate the inclusion of children with disabilities in educational settings and on the identification of risks and protective factors in early caregiving environments.

Helen Bair: *Visiting Lecturer in Special Education, College of Education, University of Illinois.* My undergraduate studies in anthropology at the University of California at Berkeley left me with a profound appreciation for the diversity of the human condition, and for the essentially social nature of human adaptation. My emerging belief that each individual's potential for satisfying adaptation is nurtured by supportive yet challenging interactions with other persons was solidified by years of work with young children and families whose life experiences ranged from poverty and endless struggle to affluence with bountiful supports and opportunities. Across this range of children and families, there always emerged some whose relationships seemed marked by a kind of attunement which I could sense but could not describe. Graduate studies at the University of Illinois, in Early Childhood Education and in Special Education, led me to an intellectual base that could account for and support my observations and intuitive theories. Research and theories regarding the essentially reciprocal nature of human development, and regarding parental scaffolding in particular, provided the means for systematically describing my previous hunches. These theories have brought me full circle to an increased understanding of the uniqueness and dignity of individuals across a broad range of contexts and niches. By directing my future work toward understanding and developing applications of scaffolded instruction, I hope to be able to support individuals in their diverse adaptations to their social worlds.

Terry R. Berkeley: See *Barbara L. Ludlow*

285

Marianne N. Bloch: *Professor of Early Childhood Education, Departments of Curriculum and Instruction & Child and Family Studies, University of Wisconsin-Madison.* I received my Ph.D. at Stanford University working with Robert Hess and Pauline Sears, who encouraged my interest in cultural and class influences on early child development and education. While at Stanford, I worked on projects related to parent education, family influences on education, and issues related to minority children's education. After graduate school, I went to West Africa where I worked in a rural Senegalese village on the relationship between women's work, child care, and child development. Over the years I have been to West Africa, especially Senegal, for numerous education, child development, and gender-related projects. I had the opportunity to work with Beatrice Whiting, Robert LeVine, and Rebecca New from 1978–1980 during a postdoctoral fellowship at Harvard's Laboratory for Comparative Human Development before coming to Wisconsin to teach. These various experiences along with my different projects at Wisconsin have continued my focus on home-school relationships and the education and development of young children from various cultural and class backgrounds. Over the years, I have turned more toward anthropological explanations and research approaches to examine the relationships between culture, development, and education. The project described in the chapter in this volume involved a longitudinal, ethnographic study of children from three U.S. ethnic and linguistic minority communities as they made a transition into public schools.

Barbara T. Bowman: *Vice President for Academic Programs, Erikson Institute.* My interest in cultural differences is long-standing, growing in large measure because of my early experiences. As an African American child attending largely white schools, I became adept at an early age in moving back and forth between two social systems. It was obvious to me when I was quite young that the lives and social organization of my family, friends, and community members were quite different from those of my school friends. As I grew I was less able to adjust to the problems of the prejudice and discrimination I met along the way, and brought into adulthood numerous "hurts" that remained an unresolved core of pain.

As an adult, I have traveled extensively in Africa and in the middle and far east. Living with people from other cultures extended my interest in cultural difference and heightened my sensitivity. I lived for 6 years in a small town in southern Iran, teaching in the University and working in a hospital. This gave me a close-up opportunity to see how cultural differences affect human service practice and how principles of development can be used across groups to inform practice. I continue to follow these interests as I teach at Erikson Institute and work in public schools serving different cultural communities.

Judith J. Carta: *Associate Scientist, Juniper Gardens Children's Project, University of Kansas.* A number of factors have influenced my thinking about developmentally appropriate practice and its role in shaping the educational programs of young children with disabilities. First, because I received my master's training from a program with an emphasis in typical early development and curriculum, and my doctoral training from a program that focused on early childhood special education, I have had to integrate these two approaches in developing my personal philosophy toward educating young children with disabilities. Second, the goal of my line of early intervention research at the Juniper Gardens Children's Project has been to develop strategies that optimize the development of young children who are at-risk or who have disabilities. This work has focused on procedures that are not only effective but that teachers and caregivers in natural environments find usable and acceptable. Finally, as a parent of a child with a disability I realize that what really counts is that children with special needs receive every opportunity to learn the skills they need to be full participants in their communities today and tomorrow.

Anne Haas Dyson: *Professor of Education, School of Education, University of California-Berkeley.* My professional interests are rooted in part in my own early childhood experiences. I grew up in a small rural village, far from the urban settings in which I have conducted all of my research. And yet, like many of the children I have studied, I grew up in a single-parent, low-income family. A family without a father was out of step with the social rhythms of village life, which revolved heavily around activities planned by the Lions Club and the Legionnaires—that is, around the activities of men. In primary school, not only was a father assumed but so was a certain degree of economic privilege, such as a car, a telephone, book club money, and summer camp. On the other hand, the village had a two-room library, where I spent every Saturday of my childhood from age 6 to 17. Books were free. Vera Schwartz, the village librarian (and choir leader), was friendly, and reading was a way to imagine oneself outside the town's square mile. The experience of being different, I think, accounts for my comfort as a teacher with children defined as "different" and for the years I spent as an inner-city teacher. My Saturdays in the library no doubt fueled my preoccupation with literacy: As a researcher and university professor, I have tried to develop ways of thinking about literacy learning, and, more broadly, early schooling that are inclusive of children from diverse social and cultural backgrounds.

Miryam Espinosa-Dulanto: *Master's candidate, Department of Educational Policy Studies, University of Wisconsin-Madison.* I am a Peruvian teacher currently finishing graduate work in the United States. For 12 years, I

worked in Peru's shantytowns as a school teacher and as a grass roots devel-
oper in the areas of adult education, community organization and women's
and children's rights. Since then, I have developed an interest in minority education and students' learning processes, and in how to work out curricula for
multicultural settings. My graduate work is oriented by a cross-cultural and
comparative perspective based on experiences and theoretical frameworks
that I have been developing in my country, and at the University of Wisconsin-Madison. My terms of reference are my own experience in Peru, my work
as a graduate research assistant with Marianne Bloch and Robert Tabachnick
on a Spencer Foundation project investigating home-school-university communication, and collaboration in Latino-, Asian-, and African-American communities. My involvement with the project presented here has alerted me further to the complexities of working with populations that are diverse and
multilayered and leery of external review. My fluency in Spanish enabled me
to understand and discuss many cultural nuances that illuminated similarities
and differences between the Latino and mainstream western culture.

Rebekah Fassler: *Doctoral candidate, Department of Curriculum and
Teaching, Teachers College, Columbia University.* While I was growing up in
Montreal, Canada, the landscape of my life reflected three different cultures:
English Canadian, French Canadian, and Jewish. Many of my neighborhood
girl-friends looked forward to their debut, when they would go to England
to be presented to the queen. In my househould, the royalty we identified
with were the biblical kings David and Solomon. The French Conservatory
of Music in a French neighborhood downtown was the site of my weekly
flute class, where I would first sit in on the lessons of two French-speaking
students before my own. My school French had not prepared me to understand any of the conversation in that room. Despite my love for music, I
found it difficult to learn well in an environment where the lack of a common language made me feel like an outsider. Perhaps it was my awareness
of the interface of multiple cultures in my own life that led me to study of
cultural anthropology, before preparing for my later work as a preschool
teacher. This multicultural interest again surfaced when in the course of the
last 14 years of supervising preservice teachers in urban schools, I noticed
more and more teachers trying to come to grips with the challenges posed
by the diversity of languages and cultures represented among their students.

Celia Genishi: *Associate Professor, Department of Curriculum and Teaching, Teachers College, Columbia University.* It is difficult to sort out which
life experiences have contributed most to my interests in language and cultural diversity. In the spirit of early education and development, I would
return to my earliest experiences. I was born in an internment camp for

Japanese Americans during World War II, and Japanese was my first language. But I grew up as part of a working-class family in a New Jersey town with very few families of color. Instead of maintaining Japanese, I eventually became bilingual in Spanish and English. A feeling of "difference" probably led me to empathize with and take an interest in those who were outside the mainstream. My teaching experiences in eighth through twelfth grades and later in preschool were within the mainstream in New York City and Berkeley, in schools where about 25% of the children were children of color; but those who spoke or acted in other than mainstream ways were the most memorable. My academic training (in Spanish and then in early childhood education), research, and other experiences have incorporated my interest in people that are bilingual and often nonmainstream and multicultural. Mine is a multicultural and very "American" story.

Sally Lubeck: *Assistant Professor of Education, School of Education, University of Michigan.* Academics are socialized to provide a litany of accomplishments, credentials, and affiliations in biographical sketches, yet these things frequently say little about who we are and what we do. My own revisionist social history would include the influence of my mother, who never finished high school, and my grandmother, a remarkable woman who never finished grammar school but who, once retired, frequently read 7–10 books a week. My early interest in culture was sparked during trips with her to the second-hand bookstores that she frequented. While she searched for the increasingly rare book she had yet to read, I became an avid reader of musty issues of *National Geographic*.

My grandmother became a single parent when her husband was hit by a trolley in the 1920s. With three young children to support she worked long hours, first in a laundry and then in the upholstery department of a large department store. My aunt's memories of the Depression recount the stories she told her children at night to stave off hunger, stories told and remembered in the light flickering through the stove's eisenglass.

I come from a long line of children at risk, but I was born in a time when opportunities for women were expanding. I was the first person in my family to attend college, the first to marry outside my faith, and the first to be divorced, a single parent in turn. For me, postmodernism has been a curious thing—neither "post" nor "modern." I grew up with stories—and lives—that ran counter to the dominant ideology. The stories are still being told.

Barbara L. Ludlow: *Associate Professor of Special Education, Department of Education, West Virginia University.* **Terry R. Berkeley:** *Associate Professor of Education, Department of Administration and Supervision, Gallaudet*

University. We have known each other as friends and colleagues for many years and have collaborated extensively in a variety of professional activities, including research, publishing, conference presentation, committee work for professional organizations, guest lecturers in each other's classes, and, most recently, international personnel preparation. Our work as researchers, jointly and individually, has taken place in rural, urban, and suburban locales, in early intervention and preschool programs, in hospitals, in schools, in regional centers, in the courts, at institutions, with local and state governments, with the national government, with legislatures and the Congress, and with advocacy groups. Together, our work has revolved mostly around urging special educators to rethink the developmental model and its embodiment in developmentally appropriate practice. We also share a long-standing interest in exploring ethical issues and professional decision-making in education and human services.

Through our observations and participation in each other's work, we have explored the inconsistencies in our own thinking in terms of conceptual and practical issues. And, we have found that it is crucial to strive to an ideal in what we do. This ideal, we hope, is reflected in our work. From that and from our view that children deserve the best from each of us, we have come to believe that challenging sacred cows will allow us to give our best to children, especially infants and young children with disabilities and their families.

Jeanette A. McCollum: Professor of Special Education, College of Education, University of Illinois. My beliefs about early childhood education stem, in large part, from my own experience with children, and particularly two children, one with autism and the other with deaf-blindness. By making me look at myself as a facilitator of another person's interactions with the environment, both children dramatically heightened my awareness of the complex interactions among the individual, the interpersonal context, and the object world. Once having become aware of this with children who were beyond the norm, I became able to apply it to all children. Emerging literature on scaffolding put a name to what I was experiencing. The link to parent-child interaction represented a natural progression in thinking, as I began to realize that my own interactions with these particular children were very like those of other adults in their environments, but very different from my own interactions with other children; I began to wonder why. For me, writing for this volume represented an opportunity to think about this, and to bring my past and emerging knowledge to bear on what had long been an evolving idea. It is my hope that whatever insights I have derived from my own unique set of experiences will assist others along the path of understanding children and the teaching/learning process.

Scott R. McConnell: *Associate Professor of Education and Director, Institute on Community Integration, University of Minnesota.* My commitment to effective early intervention services draws heavily on my earliest experiences working with children, including elementary students who were at risk for school problems because they were poor or because they had mild disabilities. From these earliest experiences, I learned that truly effective intervention was the best, and most respectful, service I could provide. By teaching new skills to these children, they were able to conquer new challenges, experience new successes, and enjoy a new image of their own competence. This simple notion of effectively teaching important skills that increase a learner's independence has stayed with me in my work with preschoolers and their families, my research on social interaction, and even my work with university students and inservice professionals.

Bruce L. Mallory: *Associate Professor of Education, Department of Education, University of New Hampshire.* The experiences that have most shaped the ideas I expressed in this book include my work as a teacher in inner-city schools in the early 1970s; VISTA volunteer in a small milltown where I worked in early childhood and adult basic education programs; director of Head Start programs in central New Hampshire; and legislative staffer for the New Hampshire House Education Committee. While completing the doctoral degree in special education and community psychology at George Peabody College, I had the opportunity to work as part of a dynamic, progressive interdisciplinary team, led by Nicholas Hobbs, at the Center for the Study of Families and Children in the Vanderbilt Institute for Public Policy Studies. Field work in the southern Appalachian Mountains allowed me to continue to focus on families living in rural communities. Since my appointment at the University of New Hampshire in 1979, I have coordinated the graduate program in Early Childhood Special Needs and more recently chaired the Department of Education. Throughout this time, I have tried to understand the conditions that lead to endemic poverty, disenfranchisement, and educational inequities, particularly when these are associated with childhood disability. My teaching, research, writing, and community work have been profoundly informed by children and families whose voices are too often ignored. Working within the discipline of early childhood special education, I hope to give back to these children and families, albeit indirectly, as much as they have given to me.

Samuel J. Meisels: *Professor and Research Scientist, Center for Human Growth and Development & School of Education, University of Michigan.* The chapter I wrote for this book encapsulates many of my beliefs about assessment. Fundamental to these beliefs is a commitment to fairness in working with and evaluating children. My interest in young children was sparked when I became a student teacher in a private preschool in Cambridge, Massachusetts in 1968. At that time I was primarily interested in epistemology, and wanted to see for myself what Piaget had been talking about. That experience changed the course of my studies and my career and I spent the next 3 years as a teacher of preschool, kindergarten, and first grade in private and public schools in the Boston area. I gave up epistemology ("knowing about") for curriculum development and intervention ("knowing how"). By 1972, just before I finished my doctorate at Harvard Graduate School of Education, I took a position in the Department of Child Study at Tufts University where for the next 5 years, beginning in 1973, I served as Director of the Eliot-Pearson Children's School. Following this, I spent a year at the Developmental Evaluation Clinic at Boston Children's Hospital, and in 1980 I moved to the University of Michigan. My research has focused on long-term consequences of high-risk birth, early intervention policy, developmental screening of young children, and performance assessment for children from age 3 to grade 3. Throughout this my central concerns remain focused on how adults can improve the life chances of all children. Early intervention is one means of accomplishing this, as are fair and meaningful assessments of children that are designed to enhance and contribute to children's overall growth. It is only by blending commitment with knowledge that we will be able to eliminate the unnecessary barriers that prevent children from reaching their potential.

Rebecca S. New: *Associate Professor of Education, Department of Education, University of New Hampshire.* My experiences as a parent, teacher, teacher educator, and researcher have combined to support both my interest and my stance regarding developmentally appropriate practice in early education. My first classroom teaching experiences in a rural Florida school took place in the context of early integration efforts amid the pernicious remains of the South's racial history. Subsequent graduate level work—first under the tutelage of Ira Gordan at the University of Florida and ultimately with anthropologists Robert A. LeVine and Beatrice Whiting at Harvard's Laboratory of Human Development—heightened my interest in cultural values as reflected in parental child-rearing goals and practices. My understanding of the interdependent relationship between adult ideologies of child care and development and the sociocultural context in which young children live was—and continues to be—expanded as a result of my ongoing work with families in a small town in central Italy, and my collaboration with educators in Reggio Emilia. These experiences have provided a crucial vantage point from which to consider the intersection of developmentally appropriate practices and cultural diversity.

Several years ago I enthusiastically participated in the early stages of articulating DAP guidelines as a means of advocating for my son's needs within an academically oriented first grade. Now, I find myself urging teachers to thoughtfully consider the guidelines' merits even as they actively seek to better understand the needs, capabilities, and goals represented by the diverse children within their classrooms. These efforts and experiences inform my growing appreciation of the dialectical and practical dilemmas that arise in the process of fostering diversity while promoting the principle of inclusion.

Carol Brunson Phillips: *Executive Director, Council for Early Childhood Professional Recogntion.* My interest in cultural influences on development stems from curiosity about my own personal development as an African American. A native of Chicago, I pursued coursework about children and families during study for a B.A. degree in Psychology from the University of Wisconsin, a Masters in Early Childhood Education from Erikson Institute, and a Ph.D. in Education from Claremont Graduate School.

Throughout my career in early childhood education, my interest in the topic has grown through work teaching 4-year-olds in urban communities and human development to college students. I have developed courses and published articles on multicultural education, racism and human development, and culture and cognition. My work in Washington, D.C. involves extensive collaboration with the Head Start Bureau and with national early childhood associations to ensure the success of the Child Development Associate (CDA) National Credentialing Program. In that role, my interest in culture and young children continues to shape my views in the national policy arena regarding programs serving diverse children and families. I also serve on national panels and advisory groups working to develop innovative approaches to respecting and appreciating cultural differences in our changing nation and world.

Douglas R. Powell: *Professor and Head, Department of Child Development and Family Studies, Purdue University.* My approach to the roles of parents in early childhood programs stems from my early research on parent-staff relationships in urban child care programs; experiences as director of a community-based parent-child support program in a low income neighborhood; and reflections on my involvements as a father in early childhood programs. My professional and community work for 10 years in inner-city Detroit was especially influential in shaping my understandings of race, class, and the dominant ideology of the United States. Currently, my scholarly efforts are focused on teaching and research, and on facilitating contributions to the field's knowledge base as editor of the Early Childhood Research Quarterly.

Ilene S. Schwartz: *Assistant Professor of Special Education, College of Education, University of Washington.* My first experience with inclusion (although at that time it was called mainstreaming) was in the early 1980s when I worked with a Head Start program in Massachusetts to include a young boy with autism. We all learned a lot that year, but the lesson that has stayed with me the most was the need to provide additional support for the child to facilitate his success within the context of the Head Start classroom. That lesson has helped to shape my professional philosophy and activities, and was reinforced during my graduate studies at the University of Kansas and my work at Juniper Gardens Children's Project. Since my appointment at the University of Washington in 1991, I have served as the faculty advisor for an inclusive preschool program. This experience of observing the changes in both children with and without disabilities in the classroom has strengthened my commitment to blending the best practices of early childhood education and early childhood special education in my teaching, writing, and research to develop and disseminate practices that integrate systematic and explicit instruction within the context and activities of a preschool classroom.

Frances M. Stott: *Dean of Graduate Studies, Erikson Institute.* The personal and professional experiences that have most shaped my views about development and diversity began when, as a first grade child born of Greek immigrants, I taught my unschooled mother how to read. I acquired a deep and abiding belief in the power of literacy and education. My subsequent schooling and work experiences helped frame and reframe my ideas about the profound influence of context. My master's thesis at the University of Chicago, based on my work with severely disturbed children in the milieu of a psychiatric hospital, investigated the social competence of these very disturbed children. While completing my doctoral degree at Northwestern and working with Dr. Diana Slaughter-Defoe on a study of exploration and play in black toddlers, I learned many powerful lessons about the influence of culture on development. Since my appointment at Erikson Institute in 1979, I have taught human and cognitive development to a diverse and exciting group of graduate students and, as a result, I more fully understand that while formal knowledge of theory is necessary, it is not sufficient. Students need practical guidance and supervision in order to bridge theory and practice—and to work effectively with people who inevitably act in ways that are not adequately addressed by current theories. Finally, I am indebted to the students, children, and families with whom I work for helping me stretch and transform my thinking and practice to embrace new and sometimes uncomfortable perspectives.

B. Robert Tabachnick: *Professor of Curriculum and Instruction & Educational Policy Studies, Associate Dean, School of Education, University of Wisconsin-Madison.* My motivation for exploring the issues and questions raised in our research comes from my experience as a teacher educator. The driving question has been how to prepare teachers to begin teaching and to continue their teaching as a creative search for understanding the way children interact with social contexts in which they live and learn. Teacher education students often expect to respond to children as "universalized" individuals and they overlook the cultural knowledge that the children, and they as teachers, bring into the classroom. If they are to become competent in teaching to the diversity of most contemporary classrooms, teachers need to learn how to discover who their pupils are and what their pupils' out-of-school communities are like. My contribution to the research reported in our chapter builds on my background and experience of varied peoples in African and Southeast Asian countries, as well as my work as a teacher and researcher in urban classrooms and urban communities in the United States.

Leslie R. Williams: *Professor of Education and Chairperson, Department of Curriculum and Teaching, Teachers College, Columbia University.* My deep interest in Native-American systems of thought stems from both close family ties and professional experience. My father's family retained some of its distant Mohawk traditions, not its outward culture but its world views, and my grandfather's second wife, from the pueblo of Isleta near Albuquerque, deeply influenced my understanding of the intellectual and spiritual life of the Tewa speaking people of the southwestern United States. Immediately following college, I accepted an assignment as a VISTA Volunteer in the Alaskan interior where I worked to help institute one of the first full-day Head Start programs in the Denaina (Athapaskan) village of Nondalton; and in the following years, I worked as the Assistant Coordinator of Head Start Training and Technical Assistance first for the Indian Community Action Project, and then for the Dakota Committee Coordinating Early Childhood Education, serving Head Start programs on nine Native American reservations in North Dakota, South Dakota, and Nebraska. There I had extended contact with Lakota (Sioux), Chippewa, Mandan, Hidatsa, and Arikara people who further expanded my understanding of value systems held in common by many Native-American groups. The ideas expressed in chapter 8 were "field tested" in a presentation I did in October, 1992, for the American Indian Head Start Institute sponsored by Three Feathers Associates in Breezy Point, Minnesota. The past 20 years of my work as a teacher educator have centered on multicultural early childhood education, spurred on, in part, by the reservoirs of my early work experience and the culturally rich setting of New York itself. As the Chairperson of the Department of Curriculum and Teaching and one of the faculty members in the specialization in early childhood education, I have had the opportunity to continue to examine and explore value systems through work with experienced early childhood teachers and a variety of curriculum development projects.